CELEBRATION

CELEBRATION

THE AUTOBIOGRAPHY OF
GRAHAM DAVID SMITH

MAINSTREAM
PUBLISHING

EDINBURGH AND LONDON

First published in 1996 by
MAINSTREAM PUBLISHING COMPANY (EDINBURGH) LTD
7 Albany Street
Edinburgh EH1 3UG

ISBN 1 85158 843 4

The poem on page 179, 'How it was in Italy' by Barry Cole, is repro-
duced from *The Visitors* (Methuen, 1970) by permission of the author

A catalogue record for this book is available from the British Library

Typeset in 11 on 13pt Garamond
Printed and bound in Great Britain by Butler & Tanner Ltd

For my friend and brother,
Peter Jack Smith

To the memory of
John Kenneth Elliker, 1942–87

Loved, idealized voices
of those who have died, or of those
lost for us like the dead.

Sometimes they speak to us in dreams;
sometimes deep in thought the mind hears them.

And, with their sound, for a moment return
sounds from our life's first poetry —
like distant music fading away at night.

From *The Collected Poems of C.P. Cavafy,*
translated by Edmund Keeley and Philip Sherrard
(Princeton University Press, Princeton, New Jersey, USA)

Contents

Acknowledgements

FIRSTLY TO SYBIL BANSAL FOR HER PATIENCE AND INDUSTRY. For the many rewrites she demanded of me and for her erudition and her knowledge of the English language. A dear friend who freely gave of her time and love.

My thanks also to Ruth Babb who undertook the Herculean job of deciphering my erratic scrawl into legible type. Her patience and enthusiasm were unbounded.

And to Judy Diamond and Barry Cole for their incisive editing and guidance, and last but certainly not least to Joe Cahn who helped me with great sympathy through the seemingly impossible task of beginning.

Janet Deuters generously allowed me to plunder her photo collection; for this, her continuing friendship and generous spirit, I am deeply grateful.

Prologue

IT'S A STRANGE, STRANGE DAY FOR SAN DIEGO. WARM AND sunny, then suddenly a cold strong wind, thunder, a brief shower – and muggy again; the grey days of May and June, sea mists dampening the spirit, a pause between spring and summer.

I have to go shopping; there is nothing to eat in the house. Walking to the bus-stop I pass an old Mexican a block from where I live. He's sitting just by the sidewalk, at a concrete table in the barbecue area of an ugly, new and already shabby apartment house. He is totally engrossed in de-needling young cacti, and a mound of spines is on the table beside him. As I pass he looks up. I smile and nod. For a moment he looks surprised: a neat, reasonably dressed gringo being friendly. Then he beams back at me, an almost toothless smile, and offers me a pea-green slice. He speaks no English and I, after all these years hovering by the border, have virtually no Spanish.

The taste is deliciously liquid, a little like chewing pea-pods. He grins as I say, '*Bueno.* Good. *Gracias, señor.*' Still smiling, he nods and goes on working, totally absorbed.

My dad. He could be my dad, I realise.

He's just like him, except for the smile. I can't remember my dad smiling much. Well, he had a broken heart. It broke when my mother died. My amazing, hard-working, proud, independent dad. We understood each other completely, although there were times we didn't speak the same language. He hit me only once. Not hard. And boy, did I deserve it. Just the once, and not hard at all.

My dad. My dad, who never hugged me, and never told me he loved me. He did tell me he was proud of me, though. Many times. Ruffled my hair and said, 'You did very well, son. I'm proud of you.'

'And stop crying,' he said, rubbing my broken leg vigorously. 'Come on, son, stop crying. You've only twisted your ankle.' More massage. 'See, it's not even swelling. It's not too bad. It'll be better soon.'

But he had to carry me home. He was strong. And my leg did swell, days later. Swell and turn black and yellow and green. In a semi-coma, I told the people at St George's Hospital, 'No thank you.' I didn't want any anaesthetic. 'Thank you.'

I remembered years before how I fought the ether drops on the mask covering my face. 'No thank you.' Not the awful smell and the retching giddy sickness as I came to. A dining-room table seems a funny place to have your tonsils removed, especially your own dining-room table, in your own dining-room. But that's where Dr Macpherson operated on me. That's where he took out my tonsils.

Mary, my sister-in-law, and my dad held me down early one morning as I tried to talk my way out of this horror. What on earth were they doing to me? Just repeating 'Don't be silly, it won't hurt,' as they slapped boiling hot kaolin poultices on my chest and back. That didn't work any more. I was not fooled by that any longer. Clawing at the mask on my face, I went out fighting.

'We're going to have to re-break your leg. Are you sure you don't want any anaesthetic?' Bloody stupid question to ask a delirious ten-year-old boy.

'No thank you. Anything but that.'

I didn't cry this time. I was a brave boy as they took hold of my leg and snapped it. I was very brave. I just screamed and fainted. Boy, though, it was worth it, for when I came round in the hospital bed Dad was there. He held my hand, tears in his eyes, as he apologised again and again. 'I'm sorry, boy. I'm sorry. Sorry.' He kept repeating it. 'I'll make it up to you, son.'

'It's okay, Daddy,' was all I could manage. I'd been taken to the hospital in an ambulance. Pretty serious, in those days. Dad was in shock. He'd been outside the room and had obviously heard me scream. The doctors told him what had happened. He just sat holding my hand, looking at me.

And I had just been given everything I had ever wanted. My dad loved me. He held my hand, leaning forward, tears in his eyes. Just holding my hand. He didn't need to say 'I love you'. It didn't need saying. It covered me, encompassed me; flowing up through his hands, it filled and surrounded my whole being. Thanks, Dad. I love you too. Always. Hold my hand. I really need it. Don't you ever let me go.

So you see, John dear, I couldn't tell you this and all the other things, too. You never had a family. Never knew your mother or your father. Never had anyone to call you son, or say he was proud of you. To tell you this would be like rubbing salt into your open wounds; and John, they were open. Open and raw.

When you died I realised I had told you little of my life, nothing about my childhood, little about the events that shaped and moulded me. So while writing this for me, I'm also writing for you, Sunshine, and I'm calling it a celebration, for I do celebrate my life, life itself, just being alive, the extraordinary, wonderful bloody jumble of it all. And in the best celebrations there is laughter mixed with tears, remembering the joy and the sadness. So here it is, my life, a celebration, for you, for me, for us all.

Author's Note

 MY DESCRIPTION OF MANY OF THE EVENTS IN THIS BOOK may differ significantly from the version of the same times and events presented by Eric Hebborn in *Drawn to Trouble* (Mainstream Publishing, 1991). For this I make no apology and offer no explanation other than the vagaries of memory and the different experiences of individuals caught up in the same events.

In a couple of instances I've changed the names of various people to protect their privacy. I felt this was necessary and offer no apologies.

Part 1

Childhood

 I WAS BORN IN THE EARLY HOURS OF 21 DECEMBER 1937. My mother was expecting a Betty, she'd already named me. Yes, a Betty. She'd had two boys and that was enough and now she wanted a Betty. Well, I suppose she got one, sort of.

I was born in the London Hospital, Whitechapel Road – the one where the Elephant Man was hidden away. According to my father, it was a difficult birth. My mother had had several babies between my brother Peter and me, and all had died.

Anyway, I was taken home to 42 Knight's Road, Silvertown, east London. It's funny how one remembers things, how selective one's memory is; I left number 42 when I was no more than two or three years old, but I remember the address. The house is no longer there: the Second World War blitz wiped out miles and miles of dockland, 42 Knight's Road included, soon after our departure.

Silvertown: what a misnomer! We lived in the shadow of John Knight's, the soap factory where Dad worked as a stoker. Stinkville, not Silvertown, would have been a more appropriate name.

My first memory is like a scene by Von Stroheim: early morning, from my bedroom window, huge mounds, white and moving, writhing. Then, as the sun came up – it does that, occasionally, in England – the white absorbed slowly into the mounds, which were dirty and greyish brown. Fascinating, though the smell was appalling. When I was older and asked Dad about it, he told me it was maggots feeding on the mountains of bones used in the making of Knight's Castile Soap.

I remember trying to pull a little girl by her long golden ringlets through the trellis work that separated our gardens. And I remember I would not let go, had to have my hands prised open. What had happened? I have no idea.

A glimpse of my mother, tiny, slim and elegant, on the grass in a park or recreation ground. Lying in bed next to her. In the huge, pull-out leather settee in the front room, I was falling asleep, touching and playing

15

with my penis. 'Don't do that,' she said. 'It's dirty.'

This is the only thing I remember my mother saying to me. It comes suddenly out of the dark, making me jump and sending shockwaves throughout my life.

'Don't do that. It's dirty.'

Kaolin plasters – boiling hot – slapped on my chest and back. I had bronchitis. A long dark hallway with a half-open door at the end sends a shaft of light into the gloom; a silhouette calls to me. Railroad tracks to cross at one end of Knight's Road. At the other end is the factory, vast, dirty and smoking. German expressionist film at its best.

Dad had moved us from Silvertown when I was two or three years old, moved us into a tree-lined suburb with large houses and gardens. He was very proud of bringing the Smith family out of the slums – and rightly so; he worked hard to do it. Bloody hard. We lived on the corner of Longwood Gardens and Glenthorne Gardens. Across the road was a small row of shops; on the other side was a 'roadhouse', that is, a pub with accommodation – not quite a hotel. Next to the shops was a flourishing farm. Beyond the farm were more very neat villas. It was all a very urban/rural mix; there were few cars around and the bus route was a mile away.

The Second World War. We kids – our gang in Barkingside, Ilford – had a great time during the war. I think lots of kids in England did.

There was a community spirit. Some people say it was the best of times. What they mean, I think, was that everyone was pulling together, that we were all united – well, most of us – to get Hitler. The small things, the everyday nuisances, the grumbles, weren't so important in comparison. I think that's what they mean.

Leaving the house, running into the garden and rushing down the steps in the middle of the night, into an Anderson shelter. It was always inches deep in water. Explosions, flashes, sirens wailing, searchlights crossing the sky, picking out planes and barrage balloons (they had 'ears' on them – great grey, floating, limbless, trunkless elephants). The heavy drone of bombers – or worse: the sudden silence when a doodle-bug (German V1 or V2 rockets) engine cut off and we waited, holding our breath, for the explosion. Would it be us? I was lucky we didn't live in an area that suffered heavy raids. Although there was an airfield two miles away, we were fortunate to have moved away from Silvertown and the docks.

The shelter consisted of pieces of corrugated iron, bent into an upside-down U shape. It was perched over a cement base, dug several feet into the ground with no drainage and a bunk slat on either side. Then a rockery or rock garden was built over it: ice plants, rockroses, London Pride, wallflowers and so on. I'm not sure if this was camouflage or decoration. We just sat, with wet feet, in the Anderson, which shook every now and then and sort of trembled. Well, the ground did, like the faint aftershock of an earthquake. *Boom!* Of course this didn't happen every night.

'Must be the next street,' or 'That's our road. Definitely.'

Sitting quietly, wedged in tight, me on someone's lap, until the all-clear siren sounded.

It was peculiar, though, that no one ever seemed to remember the water. In the mad rush to leave the house and run down the garden in pyjamas, dressing-gowns, slippers and a blanket or two, the water was always forgotten. They remembered umbrellas if it was raining. Yet it seemed hardly worth while opening umbrellas before they had to be closed again, the shelter was so close to the back door. We were in too much of a rush to stop and put on our wellington boots. Anyway, we hit a pond every time we went down those steps and it was always a surprise. 'Where did that come from? I don't remember that being there.'

Before the outbreak of war, Barkingside had been tiptoeing genteelly into the countryside, the countryside in which Dad and I used to take two- and three-hour walks together. There was Tom's Wood loony bin – the mental hospital built as a replica of the Houses of Parliment, with a Big Ben clocktower which could be seen for miles. Well before we reached Tom's Wood, we had to walk through half a mile of broken roads and pavements, no houses, everything weedy, overgrown and neglected. That petered out into fields and woods, half-built housing estates left in limbo by the war: Evelyn Waugh describes the scene brilliantly in the beginning of *Brideshead Revisited*. The difference was that our lunatic asylum was surrounded by a weathered and broken wooden fence instead of cast-iron railings. On our forays we kids didn't 'watch the madmen on clement days, sauntering and skipping'. No, led by the older, rougher boys, we threw stones and shouted: 'Loonies! Loonies! Loony, loony, loonies!' I wasn't supposed to play with those boys, who lived several streets away and went to Gearies School, an ugly Victorian pile. I'd been told they weren't 'our' sort of people. They picked their noses and spat; rough boys who did 'bad' things.

Although it was exciting, I didn't feel good about it at heart. At six or seven years old, throwing stones at adults and calling them names was sort of intoxicating, but even at that age I felt that somehow it wasn't right. The inmates looked so bewildered and vulnerable, totally without defence. I felt there was something nasty about it and, after several outings, stopped stoning the loonies. Instead, I would wander off up the hill, usually by myself, to paddle in the village pond.

Then I was evacuated. Because of the fears of gassing and the Blitz there was a huge exodus of children from London. Trainloads of us were sent out of harm's way into the countryside. It was okay because Mum was still around, so I felt safe and enjoyed the adventure. A terrific train journey; it took hours, all the way across England to Wales. I was about four or five and was having the time of my life.

I went to a Welsh family on Barry Island, just south of Cardiff. To a back-to-back, no front garden, door opening on to the street, row after row of tiny houses – a replica, almost, of Silvertown. I think that 42 Knight's Road did have a front garden, a small one, and it certainly had a back garden. I have a photograph of a plump, smiling me, carrying a black cat down our garden path to prove it. But all these Welsh houses had nothing more then a minute concrete-covered yard, with an outside lavatory.

I arrived in my little linen sailor suit, blue and white with short trousers buttoned to the shirt. A sailor suit with a proper English sailor's flap collar at the back. I had two of them, one dark blue, one light blue, Oxford and Cambridge University colours. White socks, nicely polished sandals – a very properly turned-out middle-class boy, who 'spoke beautifully'. I did, though where I got this middle-class accent, I have no idea.

I don't think any of the children there ever had any new clothes bought for them. They lived in hand-me-downs, so I stood out like a beacon. That and the Welsh accent: 'Just listen to him. Don't he talk nice?'

On my first day I had stepped into the street – literally – over a well-scrubbed front step. I used to sit on that step in the sun and feel its smoothness with my hands. It was one of the great summers.

Just stepping into the street I had my first fight. First ever. And I won it. How, I don't know, but I won a girlfriend, because we got 'married' on the steps of the chapel at the end of the road, and the other kids threw torn-up newspaper over us as we kissed.

As we were returning home for the wedding breakfast, going up the street hand in hand, a boy – I'm not sure if it was the same one I'd had the fight with – stopped in front of me and broke a bottle over my head. I can't recall passing out or collapsing. It didn't seem to faze me. What shocked me were the screaming women rushing out from their houses as I walked up the street, blood pouring down my face, all over my nice sailor suit. I stared down at blood on my front, blood on my hands, blood spattering onto the pavement. I still have the scars. All that sympathy. All that fussing. A wonderful day. It was great.

Our gang made trips into the tree-covered valleys behind the town, once lugging back a sack of unripe hazelnuts. We caught crabs, the huge Dungeness crabs, on the rocks, by the barbed-wire-fenced beach, and took them home to be cooked.

An American truck broke down somewhere near our street, and it was stripped in minutes. It was carrying food, exotic stuff, unlike anything I had ever seen before. The armed American soldiers, keeping the adults at bay, were helpless when we kids were passed over the heads of the crowd and scrambled aboard. I was given half a crown for four oranges, a fortune in those days. Oranges, bananas, tins of ham and Armour Star sausages. I loved those sausages. Luxury beyond belief.

At night in my tiny bedroom, there were three of us, two boys and a girl, in the one bed. Giggling, looking down through the window at the boy next door in his ground-floor bedroom. He was lying naked on his bed, looking at books and doing something weird with his willy. We had no idea what he was doing, but it made us giggle. The girl naturally wanted to see ours, and we hers. She didn't have one. Oh! Lots more giggling. Without warning the light was turned on. Ooops! After that the curtains were drawn and our bedroom door was left open.

The boy next door must have been about fifteen or sixteen and he seemed to carry me on his bare shoulders all the time. He taught me to arm-wrestle and let me win. He saved my life, too. When I climbed way out on the rocks, climbing and jumping from one rock to the other to see how far I could go, never noticing the tide coming back in, he swam, waded and climbed out to me and carried me to safety on his back. He was totally unlike Frank, my eldest brother, but very like Peter. And I worshipped the boy next door as I did my brother Peter.

Then suddenly I was back home and Mum was really ill and the summer was over. More memories of kaolin poultices, chicken-pox, measles, mumps. Lying in a cot with the family's huge faces staring down at me. Around this time, I became aware that Mum needed help. She would suddenly, loudly, defiantly start singing hymns. The ones with a good strong beat, the ones I still sing to myself. 'Onward Christian Soldiers', 'Jerusalem' and 'Did Those Feet in Ancient Times'. Baptist songs, too: 'Yes, Jesus Loves Me', 'Jesus Wants Me for a Sunbeam'.

I am drinking at the fountainhead
I am eating of the living bread
And he who drinketh, Jesus said,
Shall never, never thirst again.
What, never *thirst again?*
No, never *thirst again*
What, never *thirst again?*
No, never *thirst again*
And he who drinketh, Jesus said,
Shall never, never *thirst again.*

My mother spent a great deal of time in bed. When singing didn't do it, when singing just couldn't cover it, she would cry out, an awful, moaning wail of complete, utter pain. Dr Macpherson came round often with morphine injections, and I tried so hard to save her.

I was fighting to save my mum, fighting to keep her with me. Making her cups of tea. Getting her medicine. Lighting fires – setting fire to the hearth-rug and chimney. Frank kept telling me how stupid I was, that I was doing everything wrong. And Mum lying there, getting thinner, weaker, as though she was dissolving into the big leather pull-out settee in the front room.

'Get up, Mum, get up. I'll be a good boy, I promise. Please get up! I won't touch it again.'

The only time I recall seeing my parents together, Mum had got out of bed and Dad was trying to get her to go back. She was screaming, crying out. Dad was saying, 'I can manage, I can manage.' They were both struggling. I think she was delirious. Both were shouting, shouting and struggling. I watched, frozen, from the doorway, then rushed at Dad, hitting his legs, crying.

Sometimes Mum would be in hospital for weeks. I don't remember visiting her – I don't think I was allowed. I do recall a beautiful hospital garden near Brentwood, Essex, filled with flowers and small blue butter-flies, where I was left with a glass of orange juice and a thick slice of fruitcake.

Then, one morning: 'Mum's not having breakfast with us today.' Dad and I were in the dining-room. I have no recollection of what I said or what I felt, sitting at the table with Dad that morning.

How old was I? Six? I realised I had failed to keep her going; failed to get her out of bed; failed to keep her out of the hospital; failed to stop the pain. I didn't know what I was doing wrong, but I certainly wasn't doing anything right.

Something very strange happened. That day or the next, I was outside the house bouncing a ball. I think it must have been the same day, because our neighbours were standing on the pavement or in their gardens. People used to come out of their houses to talk, to whisper over low garden fences when tragedy struck. The women in aprons and headscarves, talking quietly, arms folded across their breasts. I was bouncing my ball. I used to do it for hours. I heard a woman say, 'Poor little soul! He doesn't know what's going on.'

And I remember quite clearly saying to myself: 'Oh yes I do. I know exactly what's going on.'

Then nothing. Dad forbade my going into our front room but I went in just the same. There was Mummy in her coffin, in her wedding dress and veil. I went out quietly. Nothing. I can't remember how I felt or what I did.

I was sent away to the country, to a summer home for slum kids – deprived inner-city kids. I picked my nose until it bled and bled. If there's enough blood, I thought, they'll send me home. That first night I picked at my nose until it was raw. I picked and picked until I had a big red stain on the pillow, and the blood just ran freely. I didn't know what else to do. The other children were sliding up and down the room with one foot in their enamel potties. For some reason, seeing them put their feet in their potties disgusted me, made me feel I was really a long way from home. Finally someone noticed me, got me another pillow, told me to stop crying, turned out the lights, and that was that. They didn't send me home.

I picked fights, too – very unlike me. I deliberately went up to other boys and shoved them or hit them. I was a lousy fighter and usually lost. I just wanted to go home. I thought that if I created enough trouble they'd send me home. They didn't. I acted up all the time I was there. I was rude, aggressive, throwing my food on the floor, arguing. Very unlike the well-brought-up child that I was. In fact, after that summer I was never the same again.

We were taken on an outing to see a Charlie Chan movie. In it, a man at a party steps into a lift, presses a button and the floor gives way, sending him screaming, in a flurry of balloons and streamers, down the shaft to his death. I was carried shrieking out of the cinema and taken back alone. And even later, when I eventually returned home, I used to jump from the doorway of our lavatory on to the seat and, with the door open, do what needed to be done. Then, still crouching, I would pull the chain and leap back onto the landing. I knew our house was only two storeys high. I knew the lavatory wasn't a lift. I knew that when I pulled the chain the floor wouldn't give way, sending me screaming to my death. I knew all this, but reality had absolutely nothing to do with what I was feeling.

I had another girlfriend at the summer home. I sang to her in a concert given at the home:

> *When I wore a tulip,*
> *A big yellow tulip*
> *And you wore a big red rose,*
> *When you caressed me*
> *'Twas then heaven blessed me.*
> *What a blessing no one knows.*

And I had my first sexual experience there, though not with her. A much older boy took me under his wing, as they say. We fed ponies and brushed

21

them, collected eggs together. Like the boy in Wales, he carried me on his shoulders. Then, out in the fields, behind the big old house, he put his hand over my mouth and raped me.

I remember his penis. It seemed very big and hard and smelly, sticking out from his trousers. He told me to rub it and suck it, which I didn't want to do, but I did because he was my friend, and I needed a friend. I don't remember him pulling my trousers down, but the wooden box or rabbit hutch I was leaning over felt rough on my naked belly.

I don't remember the pain either as he thrust into me. I know I cried out, for his hand covered my mouth, and he told me to shut up. He must have used lubrication, because I do remember lying across the wood, looking out through the tall grass at the farm gate and a big old dead tree, and feeling his penis slide in and out quite easily as his body banged against me. When it was over, I felt very angry because he wiped himself on my shirt.

'Don't you tell anyone,' he said. 'If you do they'll send you to prison.'

Then I realised I had done something wrong and it was my fault. I wasn't sure what I had done but I knew it was something to do with my penis being dirty.

He made a habit of coming late at night, whispering, waking me up and taking me into a dark room where he used me orally and anally. I was lost and away from home, six years old, and I didn't want to go to prison. I remember sobbing and him telling me not to be a crybaby. Towards the end of my stay, another boy – his mate – joined in, and they took turns with me in the little dark room, egging each other on.

I felt so guilty, so ashamed; I knew what was happening was my fault. I had let my mother die. This was happening to me because I played with my penis. Because I had let my mother die. I would probably go to prison and never see my dad again.

Then one day out of the blue, with no warning, my dad arrived. My little suitcase was packed and I was home again. Safe with my dad. As we walked to the bus-stop I held his hand very tightly.

Mary was there when I returned from the summer home. Mary was my brother Frank's wife. She looked after me and Mum wasn't mentioned at all.

But I had Dad. We slept together in the same bed, the nights he was at home. When he wasn't, I had the big double bed – feather mattress, feather pillows, feather bolsters and a feather eiderdown – all to myself. Dad and I slept back to back; no touching, no cuddles, no kiss goodnight.

Digging in the garden with my dad. These were happy times. He gave me a large plot for myself. No interference, just advice and support. I could plant what I wanted, but I had to weed it. Flowers, I grew flowers. *Les Fleurs du Mal*, Wilde, Baudelaire, Genet – I don't get it. Don't get the connection between flowers and corruption. Like Colette and her mother Sido, I like planting and growing for the practical pleasure of enjoyment. I used to pick flowers and fill our house with them; when I ran out of vases, I'd use glass pickling-jars.

Flowers for their colour and their scent, particularly their scent. A house in summer, filled with flowers that spill into the garden. All the windows and doors open on a balmy summer's evening. Our house, our garden growing dark, still and quiet, filled with the smell of flowers. The tiny French mignonette – hardly a flower at all, just a wisp of dusty blue – can fill a garden on a warm summer evening with the most glorious perfume. I had a row of Mrs Simpson's pinks – just stunted little white carnations, really, but I couldn't breathe in enough of their beauty. Nasturtiums also had a lovely individual scent. Sucking the sweetness from the long, curled, art nouveau tail.

Dad grew dahlias, huge ones. I wasn't fond of them; they had no scent. Besides, they had earwigs in them, and earwigs get into your ears, and lay eggs, and eat your brains. My brother Frank told me that. 'A bit sissy, isn't it, growing flowers?' he also said. I would never have known the word 'sissy' at that age if it hadn't been for Frank. So I grew flowers, the smell of the geranium leaves hinting at the glorious odour of the greenhouse.

We didn't have a greenhouse, but when Dad retired he worked as a gardener for Dr Macpherson, and of course I helped. Helped or hindered. I went with him. I love greenhouses, small, garden greenhouses, wood-framed with a stove at one end. They have a warm, comforting smell, a damp smell of earth, of geranium leaves and tomato plants. Messing about, repotting in good earthenware pots, mixing soft, dark, rich-smelling earth.

Dad grew dahlias and sweetpeas and vegetables, fresh garden vegetables, with a flavour so strong.

I had a lot of friends, mainly girls, in our gang. Lots of Brendas. 'Little sissy, playing with girls.' According to Frank I was a sissy and skinny with tin ribs; a crybaby with big ears and a huge nose. He'd tickle me until I was sick or cried or both. Poke me, tease me, pinch me. Life was miserable with Frank around.

It was around then that I developed a habit of wandering. I suppose there was no anchor at home for me when Dad was at work. Mary couldn't be there all the time. She had a little girl, Kathleen, my first niece. Frank and Peter went off to war; Mary wanted to be with her parents on the other side of London, Spa Hill, near what had been Crystal Palace. Sometimes I went with her. Sometimes I didn't. Often no one was at home, and I just wandered, wanting to be by myself.

More scattered and unlinked memories. Scattered, random memories written down before they are lost. Walking to school with Brenda and the air-raid sirens going, being pulled into a house, shoved under tables by women we had never seen before. A feeling of outrage.

'Get under that table quick. You never know when they're going to start.'

But we kids felt totally invulnerable.

One day I was standing in the garden with Dad. There was no warning sound, but we looked up and there was a doodlebug, a flying bomb, its engine timed to cut off over London, cruising down towards us. Huge and silent overhead, it seemed to fill the sky. Then it turned and went over the shops. Dad grabbed me and we ran for the house. The explosion shook the ground, literally blew out the windows at the front of the house. Kathleen, asleep in her pram in the front room, was covered in broken glass, but had not one cut.

The bomb had hit the farm. It was great for us kids; we had a new playground. Bombed houses were terrific playgrounds, and now we had a whole farm. Months later, there were bits of animal still to be found: hooves, pigs' feet and, in a bush, hidden by tall grass, a shattered dog's skull.

'Don't you go playing over at that farm, now. Do you hear me?'

'Yes, Daddy.'

Hah! You must be joking. Not play over there? It's the best place in the world to play. The best place anywhere.

The doodlebug had torn off the front part of the farmhouse, and we raced all over it. I was in the roofless attic, looking down, watching a boy run along the top of the wall below me and then jump. He disappeared. Just like that, disappeared into the ground. Vanished. He had jumped through an overgrown, uncovered drain hole. He was found several miles away, dead. I became wary of heights, and have been ever since.

All our parents got together and we were told: 'Never let me catch you playing over there again. Understand?'

'Yes, Daddy.'

I mean, come on. It's the best. But . . .

'Yes, Daddy, of course I won't.'

Well, not till I'm caught again and again.

Tag or 'he'. A chasing game. One kid is 'he' and chases the others until he touches one. Then that kid is 'he' and on and on – a never-ending game. Another chasing game, I can't remember what it was called: one team is given a two-hundred-count start and races off, stopping every five or ten yards to mark the ground with an arrow. We covered miles, running through the streets, parks and alleyways of Ilford and Barkingside, collecting piles of shrapnel and greasy wax-papered rolls of silver ribbons that were dropped to confuse the radar. Our gang looted bombed houses and took collections of china, lamp-stands, cushions and curtains to our camp, which was hidden under brambles at the far end of the farm. Here we had tea parties, played families, spies and, of course, Cowboys and Indians.

Watching searchlights pick out barrage balloons and enemy planes. Seeing one on fire hurtling down towards Fairlop and the American air-force base. Black American soldiers running past on a training exercise. I had never seen a black man, never seen such tall, healthy, beautiful men before.

My golliwog – my favourite doll – which I loved more than my teddy bear, the one that I shaved with Dad's razor. I never connected the golliwog with actual people. It was just a bizarre and wonderful companion. Then there was the golliwog on Robertson's marmalade jars. I used to soak the labels off and cut out this exotic figure.

Picnics with Mary and Kathleen, especially at Crystal Palace. Soft, damp tomato sandwiches – homegrown tomatoes, of course – brown Hovis bread, with Heinz salad cream. Nothing tasted better. Crystal Palace had been a huge, vast greenhouse, built in 1851 for what was still called the Great Exhibition. It had been moved from Hyde Park, central London, to the top of a hill in south London. Dad said it was burnt down on purpose. How does a glass and cast-iron building burn down accidentally? Burnt down on purpose because it was too good a landmark for German bombers, more like. But my brother Peter disagrees. He remembers watching the blaze in 1936 with Dad, Mum and Frank, from across the River Thames in Knight's Road, long before the war started.

Mary held the broken and loose planks of the fence to one side as I pushed the pram through. Pulling those planks apart was like a curtain going up onto Wonderland. The big flat space where the Crystal Palace had been was like an open stage or runway for dreams. And cascading down the hill, flowing out from this space, was terrace after ornamental terrace with wide, shallow steps linking them, curving in a baroque manner. There were heavy classical balustrades, and planted along the balustrades, gazing out over Sydenham and Surrey, staring out with blind cement eyes over the painted, flaking dinosaurs around and in the lake below, were larger-than-life statues. There seemed to be hundreds of them: Indian Indians, American Indians, cowboys, Chinese, Malays, our Empire and Dominions, in cast cement, gazing bleakly into a future soon to end.

Mary and I had the use of that vast stage. We sang together 'Jerusalem,

Jerusalem, lift up your gates and sing' and other baptist hymns. Nothing profane for Mary. And I wandered about and acted out scenes from films. I was very dramatic.

A bomb fell on the Gaumont Palace cinema, built in the Egyptian style. Art deco with real fountains and real water. It was wiped out on a Friday night, a full house. No one survived. We climbed into it once, a huge black hollowed-out shell, and were chased by the police.

Mrs White next door never ate fish. 'Filthy things. Filthy. They eat dead bodies on the ocean floor.' Her husband was the commander of a submarine. Left in her bedroom, I powdered her black cat white. Or as white as I could.

I buried all of Brenda's dolls. I kidnapped them all and buried them and wouldn't tell anyone where the mass grave was. Not for a long time, anyway. The threats of punishment eventually became too intense, and the dolls were disinterred.

I saw a man and a woman in the ruined farmhouse, against the wall. They weren't fighting, although the man was banging against the woman very hard. She had her eyes closed and you could see his white bum. Then they finished doing whatever strange thing they were doing. I watched the man shake his thing, have a pee, pull up his trousers, then walk off with the woman.

The red, sore circle round my legs, just below the knee, made by the constant rubbing of the tops of my wellington boots. Wet hand-knitted woollen mittens with tape connecting them, going up one sleeve and down the another. 'Well, you won't lose them again.'

Shaving my leg and arm fluff with Dad's cut-throat razor and blunting it. 'Don't ever touch my razor again.'

'No, Daddy, I won't ever again.'

But I did. I had seen a Roy Rogers film in which Dale Evans sat by a camp-fire on the prairie with smooth, gleaming legs. I thought they looked wonderful and decided to shave the blond fuzz covering my limbs. All that happened was that it grew longer.

Dad's King George and Queen Mary Coronation shaving mug and badger-hair shaving brush.

A girl from our street wore a beret over her shaved head. Nits; head lice. I had to have my hair combed every day after school with a lice comb over a sheet of newspaper. I didn't have them. Phew! I didn't want a shaved head. The disgrace.

Total, blinding fogs. Great for playing 'knock down Ginger' – knocking on people's doors and running away. Long ice slides. Sliding until the breath burnt my throat and lungs.

Going to sleep under a tabletop made of cast-iron sheets enclosed with wire, a sort of indoor shelter. Trying to keep awake, listening to the grown-ups talking, their feet visible under the hem of a tablecloth.

Parkhill School was a modern concrete and glass building. One wall of each classroom was just sliding glass doors. Acres of green lawn. It was closed down for fear of bomb blasts. All the children had to go to Gearies, an ugly old pile. I refused. Well, I did go to Gearies actually, for about half an hour one morning. Then I wanted to go to the toilet and couldn't find it. Couldn't find my way back to my classroom either, so I went home and refused to go back. I just wouldn't go. After a week, a bus came along, and with four or five other recalcitrant comrades, I was driven off to a small wooden hut overlooking a railway bridge, and that was my school for several months.

I used to go up behind the school bullies, give them an almighty punch, then run. I was a good runner, and eventually ran for my county, Essex. I did this routine again and again: 'Can't catch me!', and they couldn't. But they waited for me the next day. I just didn't get it. Didn't get that there is always a tomorrow.

We went on holiday to Bournemouth on the south coast. Dad insisted that we (my sister-in-law Mary, Kathleen in her push-chair, and me) go down the winding cliff path to the beach, ignoring all the 'Forbidden', 'No Entry' and 'Danger: Shooting Range' signs. I could read by then. He lifted up the chain that blocked the path and led us down. What we were going to do when we got there, I don't know. We couldn't get to the sea. There was barbed wire and stuff all along the sand, and mines.

Suddenly gunfire broke out all around us. Real firing, real bullets. On our hands and knees or crouching, bent over, we got back to the top of the cliffs. Dragging Kathleen along in her push-chair, behind the low stone walls, we crawled to safety. Mary was furious. What had Dad been thinking?

Dad would read to me by the fire under a standard lamp, in the blackout. He taught me to read. I was fascinated by the big butterfly tattoo on his left hand. Toasting bread, slices stuck on a brass toasting fork, the heat of the fire burning my hands.

Dad's stories. He was born in 1884 and died in 1969. His childhood was spent in Malta where he swam naked in the harbour. One morning, the shark bell sounded a warning and he spent the whole day on a buoy, watching the sharks circle, waiting to be rescued. His mother, in layers of Victorian petticoats, burned to death at a family picnic.

Dad was left-handed, which in Malta, in those far-off days, was considered a sign of the evil eye. (I don't think it was tolerated in England either.) He had his left hand tied behind his back and was beaten if he was caught using it. I am left-handed, which caused a good deal of comment when I was a child, but Dad made sure no one interfered.

He was one of twelve sons. Christened Zachariah (all his brothers had Old Testament names), he changed his name to Richard Frank. His father was a publican. Dad hadn't liked him, and left home when still a boy. He had joined the navy, where he got the tattoo of a butterfly. He told me stories about rowing at night in a lifeboat, picking up survivors. Rowing through heavy seas, through minefields, pushing the huge, spiked, spherical mines away, clearing a path for the ship.

His brother, my uncle Bob (what his original biblical name had been, I don't know), had joined the army in the Great War and Dad deserted from the navy to be with him. As desertion of any kind was a treasonable offence, he changed his surname from Ellis to Smith in a bid to evade the authorities.

When I first met Uncle Bob, I was about six years old and he was a huge jovial giant with a moustache, the opposite of my father. 'Kick my leg, Graham. If you can make it hurt, I'll give you five bob.' Five bob was a fortune for a kid in those days – not that I needed an incentive. I kicked with all my six-year-old strength, while Uncle Bob laughed.

Then he pulled up his trouser-leg. He had a false leg, lobster-pink in colour, with a funny knee joint. Uncle Bob had been shot in the thigh and had lain for several days in a water-filled pothole in no-man's-land, eating snails. 'Snails,' my dad told me. Yuck! When he was rescued, the leg was gangrenous and had to be amputated. I really liked Uncle Bob. He always seemed to be drinking and I was usually told to go and play outside when he started telling stories. He tended to swear a lot and his stories were rude. I got the five bob.

On VE-Day there was a street party outside our house. Chairs and tables were placed in the middle of the road, the tables covered in white tablecloths, all different shapes and sizes. Every household brought something to eat: cakes, meat, fish-paste sandwiches, lemonade. We sang and danced the conga, round and round the tables, up and down the roadway, like scenes from a Fellini film (the Barkingside version of *Amarcord*). A party going on in the middle of the street; far off, up and down Longwood Gardens, we could see other parties. I suppose there was one in just about every street in the country. Everyone eating and drinking and singing and dancing. Having a good time and letting the old stiff upper-lip soften a bit.

For VJ-Day we had a party in school and another one in the street. On the radio I heard a woman singing, 'I'm going to get lit up when the lights go on in London', and I bet she did.

The front garden of my childhood home, on the corner of Glenthorne and Longwood in Barkingside, the last house in a small row, had four over-trimmed May trees, two at the front, two at the side. I once brought a bunch of May blossom into the house but it was immediately thrown out. Dad considered it very bad luck to pick May flowers and bring them inside.

There were several clumps of poppies, large, startling red ones, with crepe petals, purplish black inside, powdery and exotic. They had furry stems and leaves, the type of poppy Mucha used so frequently in his work. Mum's favourite rose-bush had dark crimson blooms and a heavy rich scent. The garden path – we had the only broken garden gate on the block – was lined in the early spring with rows of hyacinths, the small blue grape and the large ornamental. Snowdrops and lily of the valley hid under the hedge. Later there were snapdragons or 'bunny rabbits', wallflowers, stocks, carnations and lupins. The gate at the side of the house opened onto a pathway and there was Dad's hand-built shed, the rabbit hutches, and a small oblong plot of earth for potatoes, cabbages, leeks and Brussels sprouts, which, because they got little sun, never did well. I had a large chunk of garden to myself; it was overgrown and over-planted but well weeded. Dad and I had special weeding days. But he never interfered with what I wanted to grow, so plants grew on top of one another, cramped and pushed together with a child's eagerness to try everything at once.

We had a tiny patch of lawn – Dad didn't approve of lawns – with two Cox's orange pippin apple trees. Only one produced fruit, and never more than two each season. Two huge, delicious apples, the best, one for me and one for Dad. (Except the time a Welsh actor I'd met picked one and ate it. Just walked up to the tree without a by-your-leave, a please or thank you, picked it and ate it. Dad and I were too shocked to say or do anything.)

When I was still only about six or seven, I used to go off by myself and wander, as I have said. One of my stops, one of my destinations, was the village blacksmith. Barkingside still had one, and a village green with a pond. The smithy was straight out of a painting. A huge chestnut tree grew beside it. Yes, 'Under the spreading chestnut tree / a village smithy stood', and there it was. I used to sit for hours watching the smith shoe horses. He let me hand pump the fire and gave me sips from his mug of dark, sweet, strong tea. It was a very old and quite magical building, filled with bits of antiquated farm machinery hanging on the walls and from the rafters.

By it, next to the police station, was a public lavatory, just whitewashed walls and a gutter for urine, very utilitarian. I wandered in there one day. I must have been very quiet, probably wearing my Bata sandals, for the two men didn't see me at first. The younger one was bending over, sucking on the older man, whom I knew. I remember walking the back way, the long way, to the alley behind his house. He was holding my hand. His garage had been turned into a workshop. They were both very gentle. Whether it was that first day that they took photographs, or later, I don't know, but I was always being photographed, with either one or two other men or boys. Older boys. I never saw one my age. Time was always taken to relax me, lots of time and patience with their mouths and fingers. I was never truly physically hurt.

It was something that wasn't happening to me, either. A little naked child, one man at his mouth, the other between his legs, thrusting in and out. All the oral stuff they did 'down there' was pleasurable. So was going home with a bag of sweets and a couple of bob – two shillings. I must have mentioned that I didn't want to go to prison, for that became a reiterated threat: 'Don't tell anyone or you'll go to prison.'

So again I knew I was doing wrong. It was happening because I was bad. It was my fault, and so I put it in a compartment, a separate place, not to be thought or spoken about. I didn't want to go to prison, to be taken away from my dad, so I couldn't tell anyone. I went back again and again, even though they kept telling me, 'You don't want your daddy to know what you've been up to. He won't want you.'

Of course this didn't make sense, taken with the 'don't tell' bit, but back I went, until it became routine. This went on for about four years, and by then I came to enjoy it. Or learned to enjoy it, or just enjoyed it, although it was still a separate thing, totally separate from my everyday school and home life. I came to enjoy the smell of a man and the strange feeling of part of a man's body inside me, moving inside me, and the taste of semen, and the feel of a mouth on my hairless genitals. And, of course, the affection. Don't ever forget the affection, being cuddled and held and being told what a good boy I was, being told I was 'taking it like a man'. I remember the praise I got when I managed to straddle a man lying on his back and bounce up and down on his erect penis. It was weird, bouncing up and down, me naked, him with just his trousers round his knees, the other man just kissing and fondling me.

And Dad had no idea, no idea at all. Why should he? I never came home bleeding or crying. I had recurring stomach-aches, but what little boy doesn't? Green apples, green plums – scrumping, was it called? Raiding orchards: our gang raided orchards before the fruit was ripe. Sweets and candies, too. I had Dad's coupons as well as my own and I was always eating sweets, so tummy-aches were considered quite normal and my own fault.

It was around this time I started 'losing' Dad. It happened far too often to be coincidence. We would arrange to meet, to go shopping in downtown Ilford, or, mostly, to go to the pictures on his way back from work. He'd explain exactly which bus-stop I had to wait at and at what time, and I would choose the wrong bus-stop – rarely, if ever, the wrong time – just the wrong bus-stop, and wait. I'd wait for hours, thinking he was dead – like Mum, but in an accident – or perhaps he was fed up with looking after me and had just left or had found out about the garage and no longer wanted me. Eventually I'd work myself up into hysterics. I'd wait, howling, terrified to go home in case he wasn't there, and that was too terrible to think about.

The idea that I might have lost my father, or could lose him, was constantly in my thoughts, forever present.

More memories, captured before they drift off and away. Slippers, I wore slippers as a child. Shuffling and sliding on the polished wooden floors of our hall. Fur on the inside, fur on the outside. Rabbit-fur slippers, made by my dad. From unravelled sweaters he made rugs, too, rag and wool ones, and he helped me draw out the designs for them.

Rabbit-skin slippers. I had a pet rabbit, a huge white rabbit with pink eyes. Poppy was the mother of many offspring that became casseroles, pies and slippers. She, though, was inviolable, or so I thought. Poppy was my only pet. I'd let her out from her hutch and off she'd go, burrowing under fences, escaping. From upstairs windows we could see her, five or six gardens away, enjoying her short-lived freedom. I would be sent off to claim her. Poppy was very large and resented her capture. Carrying her home was always a struggle.

After one prolonged escape, Dad made me hold her by her back legs. Standing there on our little patch of lawn, between the two apple trees, he made me hold her back legs as she writhed and squirmed, while he broke her neck with an axe handle.

Dad was a Victorian, a man brought up to see animals as produce, productive. Poppy was nearing the end of her productivity. Besides, we had rationing and the rabbits supplemented a tiny meat allowance.

Pronounced dead, her back legs tied together, she was taken away from me and hung by a nail next to the kitchen door. A metal meat skewer was forced up her nose into her head, to bleed her, and she was left overnight. I cried myself to sleep. In the morning, she was still alive, feebly struggling upside down, the skewer still in her head. Dad was shocked, but still she became a casserole, which I could not eat.

I loved the Pathé-Gaumont newsreels. But when the war ended there were newsreels of death camps: the graves, the huge piles of bodies, the skeletal survivors. I had the most terrible nightmares. I would wake up screaming and sobbing. My nightmares about them stopped only a few years ago. Being alone at night was no longer fun. The empty house seemed full of dead, threatening shadows. My dreams were of being trapped, of running but getting nowhere, of being chased while the ground under my feet crumbled away. I dreamed of wire fences that rolled around me and hooked onto my clothes as I tried to climb. Behind the closed doors of the landing men waited, listening. Shadow men waiting until my back was turned to grab me, and to take me to a place of no return.

I populated the area under the bed with large animals friendly only to me. In the hallway we had a huge mezzotint of lions, *Monarchs of All They Survey*. Mentally I pulled them out of their frame at night. They were my constant companions, one on each side of me, with a German Shepherd guarding my rear. A few years earlier a German Shepherd had jumped up at me, knocking me into a stack of rubbish bins outside a local hardware store. This incident didn't generate a dislike or fear of dogs, rather the opposite. Besides, I needed a good rear guard.

Complicated patterns on the back of my hand and inside my wrist, made with the milk from dandelion stems. It turns brown as it dries. Sticking coloured transfers all over our hands, faces, legs and arms. They've made a comeback recently as temporary tattoos.

Picking daisies and making long, involved daisy chains for Mary and Kathleen. Dandelion flowers, elderberry flowers and berries gathered on these outings were made into wine. So were parsnips. Peter tells me how, in the early years of their marriage, my mother, exasperated by Dad's frequent drinking sessions with her father, old man Medlicott, packed a suitcase and left it on the front doorstep. When a very drunk Dad returned she let him in the house, but told him that if it happened again, she would throw him out.

Mary and her family were Baptist/Methodist teetotallers, making faces and noises of disapproval whenever Dad uncorked one of his homemade vintages. They were delicious, but sometimes dangerous, exploding behind the sitting-room couch. At one Christmas lunch, Dad started to uncork a bottle of dark-red elderberry wine when the cork shot out with a loud pop. Trying to stem the flood that ensued, he put his thumb over the top of the bottle, nearly but not quite sealing it, leaving an opening through which a forceful jet sprayed out. Instead of turning away to his left, he turned toward the table, spraying the righteous full in their faces. I got sprayed too, and was threatened with bed. I couldn't stop giggling, bursts of choked laughter every time I looked up. There seemed to be red wine stains everywhere. Could Dad have done it on purpose? I've always hoped so.

I recall the story of a paternal great-grandfather in Newcastle, famous for his drinking and fighting, keeping the police at bay by whirling his wooden peg-leg by its leather straps around his head.

Our milk was delivered daily in glass bottles by a milkman with a big white horse and a wonderful open wooden cart. Occasionally I was allowed to help, to ride in the cart and carry full bottles up garden paths to the front door steps and empty bottles back to the cart. I never dropped one.

A less enjoyable task: with galvanised iron bucket and coal shovel, I was sent to collect horse manure for the tomatoes.

Most of the front gardens of Longwood had low, curved brick walls. In the early evenings of autumn and winter, as people returned from work, I would tie black sewing thread to a tree, then stretch it across the pavement to a couple of empty tins or a milk bottle perched on one of those low walls. Then I'd hide, watching with glee for the angry reaction of the victims, jumping as they were caught. I would bait several traps together, then stop for several yards (giving passers-by a false sense of security) before beginning again. Sometimes in frustration they'd walk in the road, some-times cross to the other side, which I had also mined. I was never caught.

One day I watched in horror as a boy inserted a straw into a frog's rectum and inflated it. I threw myself at him, hitting him, trying to save the creature. Too late. Frustration and tears. I was called a sissy and, with my arms held down, had the carcass rubbed into my face.

I weaved in and out of friendships at school, never forming any close, lasting bonds. I had little in common with my classmates other than our wild chasing games. Unlike most families, we had many books. *Through the Dark Continent* packed with wood-engravings of battles with slavers, death on the river and exotic hairstyles of the indigenous peoples encountered by the American journalist Stanley on his expedition through tropical Africa in search of Livingstone, the Scottish missionary and Victorian hero.

Les Miserables, a big English translation, the title of which I pronounced for years as it was spelled. Two sets of encyclopedias. One, the *Wonderland of Knowledge*, had the continuing adventures of Tansy and Bubble, two virtually naked little androgynous sprites. This started my lifelong interest in Greek and Roman myths and history. And the illustrations, taken from Old Master paintings and classical sculpture, were crowded with muscular naked men, divine forms that delighted me and filled my childhood fantasies.

Famous Murders of the Last Fifty Years included Jack the Ripper and many gory descriptions. *The Wind in the Willows* and *Just So Stories* and *The Water Babies*. Volumes of short stories and poetry, 'The Highwayman', 'Hiawatha', 'The Listener', 'The Jackdaw of Rheims', and another de la Mare, mostly forgotten, except for a demand and a refusal:

'Give me your green glass beads, goblin. Give them me! Give them me!'

'No.'

Probably badly remembered. I don't want to find the original in case, on re-reading, the mystery and power of the encounter between a goblin and nymph in a marsh loses its potency. For no clear reason I can think of, the evocation of unrequited desire in this poem thrills me even today.

None of the other children shared my avid absorption of books. There were comics: *Beano*, *Tiny Tots*, *Tiger Tim*, *Radio Fun* and *Film Fun*, and later the *Eagle*, that we swapped, but my friends never read books or took an interest in those I was reading.

Although parents often invited me to tea, because I spoke well and my manners were good, I rarely took friends back home. Dad seemed to be much older than other fathers, with an accent that was different and strange, and which caused unfavourable comment. 'Doesn't your gardener look old?' Remarks like that brought floods of shame to my face. My friends thought Dad was the gardener.

I remember once asking him why he had a funny accent. 'Well, son, we're all different. That's life. Some of us talk one way, others another way.'

I suppose he did look old. Peter, returning from India after the war, said, 'Dad's aged.' He wasn't young, and watching my mother die in pain, slowly over the years, had aged him more. Grief can do that.

Our house was filled with old-fashioned furniture, not 'nice' three-piece suites with matching sideboard, or anything like that. Going under the arched brick porch and entering the hallway just by the front door, there was a large hat- and coat-stand on the left, and a large, woodworm-infested sea chest (one of my mother's brothers had been the captain of a merchant ship), a faded Persian carpet and the mezzotint of lions. The front room – the sitting-room – was dominated by an upright piano, which was itself overwhelmed by a triptych of cut-glass mirrors in ornate frames, and was usually dusty. Under the windows was a fine old gate-leg table with two serpentine chairs, claw-footed, on either side. Then my glass-fronted bookcase (it was always *mine*), painted at one time with bitumen which, spreading as it does, had cracked and opened the covering of dark brown varnish. A bulbous-legged pull-out oak dining table. The dark brown leather settee bed in which Mum died. On either side of a beige-tiled fireplace, two armchairs covered in a 'jazz' art deco maquette fabric, with a round, low, three-legged farmhouse table made of oak planks between them.

The dining-room was much the same, with a radiogram almost as big as a sideboard, tall and fat, with lots of white buttons and dials to push and twirl, producing squeals and rasps of static and strange foreign voices. Our furniture was old and mismatched, nothing like what other people had in their houses. But as a child, by myself, I loved the feel and quality of it. It came naturally to me. But my classmates commented on how odd and old it looked. Why couldn't we have furniture like everyone else? Why couldn't my wonderful Dad be like their fathers?

Reading wasn't the only thing that set me apart from the other children; there was also my art. The first drawing I remember producing was in the toilet, on stiff, antiseptic-smelling Izal lavatory paper. Two mice, two little pencilled mice cuddling together, preserved for years in my mother's bible. Later, when drawing paper was in short supply, I cut out and drew on all the plain fly-leaves from the books in my bookcase.

At school, I would pull my short pants up and draw naked women on my thighs with a dip-in steel pen. We had dip-in pens and inkwells in our solid oak and cast-iron desks. Discovery led to humiliation. I was made to stand on top of the desk, holding up my shorts and exposing the nudes. 'What a silly boy Graham is, just look at him.' And I was sent to Mr Emmett to be caned.

No other child shared my obsession with drawing and reading. Only later, at thirteen, was there any interest. Puberty sparked a demand for my naked ladies – and, from one prefect at school, naked men, which I'd never drawn before.

I was a compulsive giggler. The more I was threatened, the more I giggled. I even had my mouth taped over. I pretended I saw things, saw things coming through the walls of the classroom. I would groan and cry out in mock horror, falling to the floor in spasms of laughter. Off to Mr Emmett again. If he'd hit me before on the same day, he just said, 'Oh, go away, boy.'

For a school play I was Puck in a children's version of *A Midsummer Night's Dream*, in a very short vest, peaked cap and slippers made from silver oilcloth. Another time, In a musical about toy animals on a pedlar's tray, I was a monkey in a fur-fabric suit: 'With a hop and a kick, I'm a monkey up a stick, and my merit you can't deny.' Heavily made-up, wigged, with a pointed hat in another musical, I was a wizard, a wicked wizard: 'You may well turn white/at the awful sight/of me, me/I can dry up wells/I can work real spells./You'll see, see, see.' The story is lost to me.

The wizard's long robe and heavy make-up, including my hands and long false fingernails, meant I couldn't go to the lavatory by myself. But that was okay, I had a volunteer to help me, a student teacher, a young man. He took me into a cubicle and lifted up the heavy black wizard's robe. As I held it, he pulled down my underpants. He asked me if he could touch my penis, my willy. No one had ever asked me before, ever – it was taken for granted. Of course I said yes. He squatted beside me, stroking my body. I did feel a little embarrassed. He wiped my bottom, asking if he could, then stood me on the lavatory basin, kissing and licking it. Another teacher called out to hurry up, so we left.

Several days later, he asked me to stay after school to help pin up some railway posters on the classroom walls. Then, on the crossbars of his bicycle, he took me to his room, a small tidy room in an old house in Rushden Gardens, not far from my home. He undressed me. He told me that he loved me, that I was his precious boy. 'You are my little boy, aren't you?'

'Yes,' I replied.

'Do you love me?' he'd ask.

'Yes.'

He'd often hurt me, unlike the men at the garage, but afterwards he'd kiss and lick me from my feet to my face. 'I love you. You're my precious lovely boy.'

I loved him, too. It wasn't a crush. I loved him and gave my eight-year-old self to him without reservation or guilt. He could do what he wished with me, and he did. When he was moved to another school I cried in his arms. I cried because he was leaving and I couldn't bear it, and I cried because his last love-making had been brutal. He had hurt me badly, and I was bleeding. He said he would write to me. He wrote down my address, but I never received a letter from him. I never told him about the garage, or told the men there about him. He made no threats, always telling me how much he loved me, how much I meant to him. His 'precious, lovely boy'.

School lunches, called school dinners. Proper meals with lumpy mashed potatoes, overcooked vegetables, wonderful meat pies and puddings, roast beef, roast pork with gravy that moved about on the plate. Delicious sweet steamed puddings, tarts with custard, 'spotted dick', jam roll – my favourites. I always went back for second helpings. I was always hungry. Left on my own at home, meals were often nonexistent. Fried bread or toast and Marmite or 'frizzits', a kind of pancake mix which, when poured into a hot, fat-filled frying pan, expanded into a giant salty, greasy crisp. Lemonade powder, a yellow mix of sugar and ascorbic acid that split my tongue. Food parcels from America and Canada, spam and Armour Star sausages.

Valentine's Park, once a private estate, a hall or mansion with extensive grounds, had been taken over by the local council and turned into a public park, as were so many similar estates in England. At one end were ornamental ponds with ducks, moorhens and swans. Dad told me to be careful of the swans, not to annoy them as they could break your arm with their wings. So I backed off when they ran, hissing, wings outstretched, towards me. At the other end was a boating lake, connected to the ponds by ornamental channels alive with sticklebacks and minnows. Great fishing areas. All we needed was a net and a large glass jar with a string handle.

Valentine's Park swimming-pool. Wrapped in a damp towel, sitting on the steps of the pool, listening to my teeth chattering uncontrollably, watching the goosepimples on my bluish skin. I loved it. I spent much of the long summer holidays there. Standing on the water slide – it was forbidden – and speeding down into the water a the deep end. Holding my nose and jumping off the top board long before I could swim. Performing desperate doggy-paddles to the pool's edge.

Paddling through the mud at Southend. Hobbling painfully over flint pebbles on the beach at Brighton. Brighton Rock swimming-pool on a grey, stormy day. My dad watching from the almost-deserted promenade, while below, in a high wind, the waves were breaking over the sea wall and me. I jumped in and out of the pool. I had it to myself. The bliss of dry clothes and hot food, the only way to stop the chattering teeth and convulsive shivering of too long spent in cold water.

More food, seaside food. Fish and chips. Moist flakes of cod, skate in crisp delicious batter. Chips in newspaper soggy with grease and vinegar. Meat pies. Pie mash and liquor – the white parsley sauce made with the liquid from stewed eels – in eel-and-pie shops. Sausage, onions and mash with mushy peas, bread and butter with strong, sweet tea at cafés on the seafront. Musty-smelling tea-shops and occasional high-tea at a posh hotel. Candy floss, and sticks of peppermint rock with the name of the town running legibly all the way through. How do they do that? Watching it being pulled and rolled out by hand, cut up and wrapped in grease-proof waxed paper. The first time I tasted melon, sprinkled with ginger and powdered sugar, at the smart restaurant in the London Zoo, Regent's Park Zoo. Dad showed me how to eat it, with a knife and fork, cutting it away from the rind in small chunks.

The snake-pit near the entrance at the zoo was filled with deadly snakes. Set below ground level, with no rail or guard to stop you falling in, it terrified me. The museum of stuffed animals was a dark and smelly place under Brighton Pier. Complete orchestras of frogs with miniature instruments, puppies and kittens having tea together, dressed like dolls. Glass eyes and tiny little teeth. Dramatic tableaux. Horrible.

37

One evening in the garage, I had been photographed with two much older boys on the blanket-covered workbench. The session went on and on. When it was through, the man taking the photographs took over from the boys as I knelt with my bottom in the air. Nothing unusual or different had gone on, yet I started to cry. Although I tried, I couldn't stop. The man continued having sex with me, ignoring my sobs. When he finished, he seemed rather cross. Then, as my crying escalated, he became concerned. The two boys left and he wrapped me in a blanket and cuddled me. I felt warm and secure and fell asleep. Later the man helped me dress and gave me a pound note, more than I had ever been given before. As I left to go home, he said: 'Now be a good boy. We don't want your father to know what we get up to, do we?'

The house was empty when I returned. Dad was working a night shift. Our bed was cold, and I began crying again. I cried myself to sleep. I can't remember – or don't want to remember – exactly what I was thinking. I know I felt alone, and I wanted my dad. I wanted that man in the garage to cuddle me, to go on cuddling me forever. I just wanted someone to hold me and cuddle me and never stop.

A few days later, I was back in the garage, unasked and on my own initiative. I didn't cry again.

In Barkingside High Street, the further end towards Fairlop, the aerodrome and the ABC Cinema, there was a bookshop. A tiny, narrow store, it was the only one I remember in the area. Buying books was an unindulged luxury. To supplement the ones in my bookcase I borrowed books from the public library. But I had seen Enid Blyton's *The Castle of Adventure* in the shop window and coveted it. The very title, combining the romance of a castle and the magic of adventure, called out to me. Adventure and a castle: what more could a boy want? I dragged my reluctant Dad there. The book was still in the window. I begged him to buy it. It was very expensive, seven shillings and sixpence. 'Please, Dad, I do want it.'

Instead of telling me to get it from the library, he said, 'All right, if you really want it, we'll go in and buy it. It will be your birthday present.'

Overjoyed, I jumped up and kissed him. He pulled away.

'Don't do that. It's silly,' he said.

And around this time I had a dream; most dreams I forget but this dream, though, has never faded. It took place in Persia or somewhere like that. I dreamed that I was identical twin brothers. The first-born was king and ruled. The other was a prince. Although they were connected by a powerful love for each other, the younger brother decided to leave the palace, removing himself from any rivalry or competition, to live far away in the provinces. The king managed badly without his brother's stabilising presence. The younger twin, realising that the kingdom was being destroyed, sadly brought together an army and entered the city. Confronting each other in the royal palace, the brothers fought with swords. The elder brother allowed himself to be forced backward onto the staircase of a tall, white ivory tower, something like a minaret. Higher and higher on the spiralling steps, they fought until they reached the open platform at the top. There the king, who was stronger and loved his brother so deeply, knowing that one or the other must die, stepped off the platform and fell to his death on the courtyard below.

I woke with an intense feeling of loss and yearning. I longed for something – what, I didn't know – with an aching pain in my chest.

When I was nine, I used to play doctors and nurses with two girls, one of whom was slightly older than me. I was always the patient, and of course my genitals and rectum were always being examined, prodded and bandaged, examinations which produced erections, little hairless, pink, nine-year-old erections. These fascinated the girls. I had learned to be quite passive in the garage, and since my doctor and nurse made no demands on me, other than to be an ideal patient and lie still, it was very pleasant and we used to giggle a lot. The bandaging of my penis felt wonderful, especially when it was tight. With all this attention, I was aware of how much pleasure my genitals gave me. It seemed all right for others to touch them, but my mother's stricture (*'Don't do that. It's dirty'*) permeated and overwhelmed my being.

When alone I often tied myself up with string, very tightly. Starting with my foreskin, I bound the loose flesh round and round, pushing my penis back into my body, so that my erections wouldn't show. Sometimes, in my frustration to quell them, I would tie myself so tightly the skin ruptured and bled, and I would leave it like this for hours before I untied it.

At night when Dad was working, I would bind my foreskin tightly. I would also bind my ankles together, bending my knees up toward my chest, and would attach my foreskin to the cord around my ankles, then I would go to sleep. Waking up hours later in pain, holding a torch in my mouth, I desperately attacked the many knots I had made, lying back, biting my lips as the blood recirculated.

I tied my foreskin to doorhandles, taps on the bath, pulled back between my legs and tied to a cord around my waist – sometimes I went to school like this. I never actually bound my penis, just the skin covering

39

it. I knew I mustn't play with it, and I didn't. Others could, but not me.

A boy in my class began following me around. He lived close to Parkhill School but would often walk back to collect Brenda and me early in the morning. He hung around my home at weekends, and followed me on my wanderings. We played Cowboys and Indians together. In our fights, he was very passive and would let me win. He asked me to tie him up, to twist his arm, to show him my willy. Unlike me, he knew what he wanted and needed. He manipulated me into fulfilling those needs. I wasn't a cruel child or a bully, but this boy, this child, brought out a brutal, dark, bullying force in me, a force, an anger that perhaps is hidden in many of us. For a time, just with him, it flourished.

On my command, he would kneel before me. Unbuttoning my flies, he would take my penis in his mouth and suck it. Sometimes (and he asked me to) I would urinate in his mouth or on his naked belly and genitals, his shirt pulled up and his trousers and underpants down. I would punch him and hit him and drag him, unprotesting, through the bushes, across the grass. Finally, throwing myself on top of him, we'd lie panting together, too young to climax.

I gave him a black eye once, a swollen, blue-purple shiner. He and his clothes were often covered with dust and mud and bits of the countryside. Did his family, his mother, ever notice or complain? If they did, he never told me.

I was standing one day with him kneeling before me, my penis in his mouth, in the woods near the lunatic asylum, when some boys from Gearies School surprised us. We were both taken captive. We didn't know the word 'queer', but we did know 'sissy'. Our trousers were pulled down, and we were stretched out by our ankles and wrists. The Gearies boys took turns stomping on our naked buttocks. This led to kicking, outrage to arousal – their arousal, not mine. In tears, I sucked two of the boys to climax. After this, more name-calling and more kicking, we fled. The boy and I never spoke to each other again. That is, he never spoke to me. He avoided me. I felt the attack and violation were my fault. I became angry and jealous when I saw him later, tagging behind the Gearies boys.

I joined a boys' gang for a while. No girls at all. Although we took turns as either Cowboys or Indians, I found myself being tied up and 'tortured', no matter what role I played. I soon tired of this and went back to the Brendas. With them I played 'proper' games, childhood games.

I was ten the summer, the glorious summer, I broke my leg. A total loss at organised games like cricket and football, I found I was a star on the track, winning races for Parkhill School. I could run and jump and leap. I felt at times I was flying – which is how my leg got broken. Returning home with Dad from the pictures one evening, I ran through a game of cricket, leapt over the stumps, slipped and fell on top of them. The heavy plaster cast, from my foot to my thigh, made me itch horribly. I couldn't go swimming, but with a crutch I got around easily. When eventually the cast was ripped off, how I regretted shaving my legs. The wet plaster had stuck to the long hairs. I made a recovery, and my athletic career continued into high school.

A wonderful and terrible winter followed: blinding, heavy snowstorms and floods. Not one house I knew had central heating. We ran the gauntlet from the living-room fireplace to the kitchen stove. Freezing bedrooms. Ice formed on the inside of the windows, hallways and landings. Misery.

But the garage was actually hot. It was a home away from home. Heated with two oil stoves, it became a warm haven of sweaty, dark secrets, Ovaltine, biscuits, cuddles and praise. I would go there as often as I could, in spite of threats, in spite of feeling guilty, I kept being drawn back, even to the extent of missing my favourite children's hour programmes. Then I stopped going. Just stopped. I can't remember why. I can't recall any reason. I often thought about it, but I never went back.

One day a woman arrived: youngish, cheerful, plump, with a perky hat of net and flowers angled to one side of her head. Olive Ruth Strawson Barker, soon to be Smith. Strawson was her maiden name, Barker the name of her ex-husband. She was divorced. Absolutely scandalous, shocking and wicked. A divorced woman, a fallen woman, a pariah, an untouchable in those days.

'Would you like me to come and live with you?' she asked. Why not, I thought. The more the merrier. I didn't conceive for one moment that her coming to live with us meant her marrying my dad and turning me out of his – *our* – bed, the bed Dad and I had shared since Mum died.

High School Years

DAD WAS SIXTY-FOUR YEARS OLD AND I WAS BECOMING WHAT was termed 'a bit of a handful'. I would often miss school and walk around London all day. If I had enough money, and it was warm enough, I'd sleep in the ruins of bombed-out buildings at night. Several times I was returned home by the police, our neighbours an attentive and eager audience watching from their gardens.

A turning-point came when I was picked up by a Welsh actor. A tall, dark-haired young man who worked at the BBC, he had just completed a small role in *The Last Days of Dolwyn*, a film starring Dame Edith Evans. The story was about the drowning of a Welsh village to make a reservoir. He found me in Soho and, as an introduction, bought me an ice-cream from an ice-cream cart. ('You get cholera from those things,' my dad had told me – in fact, I remember a public-safety film warning us about it – so I was living dangerously.) Then the actor took me to see Linda Darnell and Cornell Wilde in *Forever Amber*.

The afternoon showing was sparsely attended and in the back row of the circle, under the cover of his coat, the actor partly undressed me. Holding me in front of him with one hand, his tongue forced halfway down my throat, he came over my bare chest and stomach. He then buttoned himself up and watched the film, leaving me to dry myself and dress. I had come to accept this abrupt turning off of attention, and after the years spent in the garage I knew what to do and didn't have to be coaxed.

After the film we walked to the white art deco simplicity of Broadcasting House in Upper Regent's Street, the home of the BBC, where we had tea in the canteen and I was given a short tour of the building. In one of the lavatories, with my short trousers pulled down and my shirt and jacket over my head, he draped me over a hand basin and attempted to penetrate me. A door opened suddenly (I think the place had double doors) and the actor disappeared into a cubicle leaving me hanging there as some men came in.

Many years later, my partner John told me about a man he encountered in a Woolworth's store when he was about thirteen years old. He had been meeting the man secretly for sex for many months yet when John said hello to him the man walked past as though John didn't exist. John still felt the outrage and hurt when he told me this story and as I write this I feel the same anger for him and for myself.

I didn't show my feelings; I'd learned to keep them hidden. In a blush of embarrassment I dressed and waited outside for the actor. After walking about some more we ate in a café and he took me back to his lodgings. There, in his bedroom, he finished what he started in the BBC lavatory. It hurt and I was making a lot of noise. His landlady came in. It was fairly late by now and, waiting by the door as I dressed, she took me to her bedroom on the ground floor. She phoned Mrs White, our next-door neighbour (we didn't have a phone) and said I was staying with her and that she would send me back in the morning. I slept on a couch next to her bed and early in the morning, after giving me breakfast, she put me on a train.

Dad was waiting for me when I arrived home. 'What happened?' he asked me. 'Did anyone do anything to you?' He was concerned and upset, but not angry. I assured him I was all right, that I had got lost, that it was late and the actor took me home. This seemed to satisfy him. There was no way I would tell him the truth. I was still haunted by the threat of going to prison and being taken away from him. Several days later I phoned the actor and he came to see me.

Dad took an instant dislike to the Welshman and his affected, mannered behaviour and was furious when the actor picked and ate one of our two precious apples.

In my bedroom, skimming through my drawings, he pulled out his cock and pushed my head down on it. Dad interrupted us but didn't see anything and shortly afterwards the man left. Dad told me not to contact him again and to stop wandering off. There was an edge to his voice that made me obey him.

Olive's first visit lasted only a few weeks. I enjoyed her company. Vulgar, lively and funny, and with an energy I found attractive, she was totally unlike the other adults in my life. When she left that day, I was sorry to see her go.

Olive was some thirty years younger than my father. Her still youthful energy, his loneliness and the need for someone to take care of us, especially of me, persuaded him to marry her. I have no recollection of their wedding; I don't think I was there. The wedding breakfast took place in our front room. The leather sofa bed in which my mother died had been sold and a smaller couch was in its place. I remember sitting far down the two tables, put together to seat all the guests (mainly Olive's family), far away from my father. I still wasn't certain what exactly was going to happen. Dad had given me no warning. He hadn't explained anything to me. One night we were together and the next I was on my own in Peter's old room, listening to the bedsprings creaking in what had been my bed, my bedroom.

Within the first few weeks after their marriage a conflict developed that continued more or less constantly throughout the ensuing years. It was an ugly conflict of hostility, quarrels and bitter, angry confrontations that left us, the three of us, shaking, exhausted and miserable. According to Dad, Olive was dirty, the house was dirty and the food was awful. 'She's like something the cat brought up,' was his summation of her and the house-keeping. My home had been a refuge of sorts and Dad a reassuring figure always there for me. Now it became a battleground and I was in the middle.

Desperate to escape or stop the never-ending disputes, I twice attempted to hang myself in the airing cupboard in the bathroom. If I had been determined to end it all I know I would have succeeded. It was a child's drama, a they'll-be-sorry-when-they-find-me, a notice-me call. My suicide bids went unnoticed, though, by either Dad or Olive, so engrossed were they in their own battle. The only results were a sore throat and skin burns from the dressing-gown cord I used, and my resolve never to try that way out of life again.

Then I ran away – not a wander this time – with my puppy in my arms. I spent the day in Epping Forest. Come night, cold, hungry and in tears, not wanting ever to return home, I dumped myself and my dog on Peter and his wife Micky. They took me in and kept me with them while Peter tried to sort out the mess in Barkingside. It was a relief to live with regular people and be a normal child. I can still remember the time there with them both and the feelings of security and confidence I had for a brief couple of weeks. I felt totally different. Micky now brushes away my attempts to thank her for her love and kindness at that time and for the long succession of evenings spent watching their TV (*Café Continental* was my favourite programme), being fed, being welcomed and made to feel that somehow I was wanted and worth while.

Returning to Longwood Gardens to Olive and Dad wasn't pleasant. Olive turned on me, telling me everything that had gone wrong was my fault. Although I know I was never an easy child to deal with, I felt this was unfair and turned to Dad for comfort and validation. I didn't get any. He was beginning to slip away to a place where neither Olive nor I could reach him.

I refused to call Olive mum, mummy or mother. I had been told by so many people, family and friends, what an incredible and saintly woman my mother had been that, having no real memories of her of my own, I enthroned her. She passed into the realm of fiction, a holy icon whom I worshipped but who bore little or no resemblance to any reality. To have called anyone else mother would have been an act of betrayal. Olive demanded that I should. Dad said to leave me alone. The dispute went on for a year or so until she grudgingly accepted my calling her by her name.

Poor Olive. Like me, she probably had no idea what had happened. She had arrived, escaping from an abusive marriage, full of hope at having found sanctuary with an old man and his shy, quiet son only to discover her refuge a madhouse. How could I like her now when Dad was so antagonistic towards her and she had taken over my place in my home? Why did Dad turn on her so violently? I had no answers then and I really have none now. What I do know is that my childhood ended with the arrival of Olive. Not because of her, though for years I thought of her, unfairly, as the wicked stepmother. The constant friction at home which filled my former peaceful refuge, as well as the double burden of high school and puberty, had much to do with it. Olive was just part of a turbulent passage into adolescence. And if at times I found my father embarrassing (and, to my shame, I did), poor Olive was to become totally unmentionable.

As unhappiness and despair over her situation took hold, much of Olive's initial energy and cheerful vitality ebbed away. She became grossly fat and very slovenly, and the larger she became the more stooped and shrunken my father appeared.

I passed the Eleven Plus exam with ease. No secondary school for me. The pressure to pass was terrific, and to celebrate Dad and Peter bought me my first wristwatch. I had an interview with the headmaster of Ilford Grammar School, the top high school in our area. A neighbour, the nice conventional Barkingside mother of two of my friends, came by and asked if I would like her to accompany me to the interview. Innocently I said yes without realising the implications or the hornets' nest I was disturbing. Quite naturally, Olive was insulted. Other neighbours were pulled into the row, taking sides. The woman and I were cast as villains. In the end Olive went with me. I failed the interview (for which I blamed her) and was sent to Beale Grammar, a second-choice school.

Memories of that awful school even now cause me to shudder. A sadistic Welsh gym master filled our days with fear and dread. Ordering us in gym class to stand at attention, he would walk up and down the lines of quaking boys and, with the back of his hand, flip our unprotected genitals. If he scored a direct hit and we bent over in agony, he would whack us repeatedly with a rubber-soled gym-shoe. Although a good gymnast, I was terrified of him and before his class I would force my fingers down my throat to make myself sick so that I would be excused. My continued absence enraged him, though. He took to coming into the lavatory and grabbing my hair as I crouched heaving over the bowl, and would bang my head again and again against the wall of the cubicle. That treatment forced me back into his class.

Our music master enjoyed beating our backsides with a broom handle. One of the songs he taught us amazed me so much that I have never forgotten it. The first few lines went:

> *Darkies let us sing a song,*
> *In de ol' plantation*
> *Sing it as we sang it in*
> *De days long since gone by.*

Even then I felt uncomfortable singing it, recalling Stanley's description of the callous, inhumane treatment of African tribes by Arab traders. The lyrics degraded the subjects of the song and we who were made to sing it. Would he have taught it if there had been black pupils or teachers at school? Probably. The level of awareness in the 1950s was abysmally low. I had a long, painful session with the music master after my voice broke, because I was his star soprano.

My escapes from school and home life were drawing, training for the track and field, and masturbation. After years of trying I eventually achieved a real orgasm but although I vowed, as the first delicious tremors subsided, that I'd do it all the time now, there was, as I found out, a limit.

Micky lent me her copies of *L'Officiel*, the magazine of the French fashion industry, and opened a new world to me: *haute couture*. The clothes, those superbly cut and tailored clothes, illustrated what excellence design could achieve. Balenciaga, Christian Dior and Grès were my favourites.

For the boys at school I drew naked women, with huge breasts and nipples and exaggerated gaping vaginas, fecund and earthy, far removed from the aloof and glamorously thin models of the fashion world. These drawings were eagerly sought-after and gave me a dubious popularity. One boy, a prefect, took me aside and asked me to draw a man for him with an erect penis showing under his shorts. This was handed over in great secrecy and I was 'honoured' by being allowed to put my hand in his trouser-pocket to feel his erection. This drawing proving acceptable, he commissioned many others, some quite intricate and involving several male figures engaged in the kind of things that had happened to me in our neighbour's garage.

By this time the sadistic Welsh gym master had left. His replacement, a tall, blond, younger man, became a supportive and helpful athletics coach who taught me the best position for the fast start and how to pace myself in the longer races. When training I felt free and powerful, that I was flying, effortlessly and easily.

He also discovered a cache of my drawings and gave me a lecture on how this 'kind of thing' would lead not to blindness, which I expected him to say (it was a standing joke, laced with fear, in school among those who had discovered the joys of masturbation that our eyes would explode), but to a sad and miserable life riddled with disease and ending in madness and a lingering, painful death. All of which confused and puzzled me. Somehow sex and drawing nudes was bad and would only bring trouble. But it felt so good and was so enjoyable. Whiffs of hellfire, the Baptist chapel three times on Sunday when I was at Thornton Heath, and my mother's admonitions rose up, and for a while I stopped.

At home Olive, obviously very unhappy, had an affair with a young man whose even younger wife made frequent and explosive appearances, turning up at our front door, screaming and shouting. Our neighbours, of course, came out to listen and decided this was the last straw. We were forced by gossip to uproot, to move to the east end of London. 'I worked all my life to move us out of the slums and now we're going back,' commented my father.

The flat in Dames Road, Forest Gate, brought back dim memories of Knight's Road. There was no bathroom and the lavatory opened into the kitchen. I was numb with shock and couldn't, as Olive suggested, 'make the best of it'. She had never felt comfortable in Barkingside. Now our neighbours were working class and didn't patronise us and look down on her. Her divorce was never mentioned. She was back on home ground.

I, on the other hand, was in a totally hostile environment where kids my own age wore hand-me-downs and my accent branded me an outsider. But there was one big advantage to our move. Still wearing the ghastly brown Beale blazer, I was enrolled in Leyton County High Grammar School for Boys, demoted from my A Form status to a C Form one – Beale obviously didn't rank high academically in the county. It's just temporary, I was told, until you find your own level. Well, I obviously did, for I stayed in the C stream, the lowest level, until I left for college. My behaviour had something to do with this. I had more minus marks and detentions in my first year than any other boy in the school. Later on I tried and succeeded in attaining a mass of plus marks and gold stars but to no avail. C stream I was and C stream I stayed.

Like most grammar schools, Leyton had traditions. We had houses, diaries, a large library for fifth- and sixth-form use only, quadrangles for the staff – all very similar to Beale yet without the cast of grotesque Dickensian teachers in command. There was the usual new-boy round of fights and wrestling bouts to establish my position in the pecking order. A few I won, though most were settled without resolution. I still giggled a lot – in fact, with the horrors of Beale behind me, I giggled a great deal more. I really acted up in my first year, but I was never beaten. The only time I was sent to be caned – a last resort at Leyton – I walked out of school. The headmaster had a withered hand so the vice-principal, a delicious title that I made the most of, undertook the task of flogging grey-flannel-covered young buttocks for him. I walked out and spent the summer afternoon swimming in the Hollow Pond at Whipp's Cross. The day was hot and the surrounding forest and lake virtually empty. As usual, no one missed me, something I found gratifying and also irritating, but I discovered I could wander again with impunity.

In that first year at Leyton I came into my own for a brief period as a track star, running and winning prizes for the school and county. I still dream of running; it's the nearest thing to flying I've experienced except in dreams.

My athletic career came to a sudden and complete end when I fell under the influence of Mr Rose, an English master at Leyton. Highly intelligent, dynamic and charismatic, his personality drew me into the school dramatic society. My interest in sports waned very quickly in spite of many pep talks from the headmaster, who eventually ordered me to attend a series of meetings. Grudgingly I did but deliberately and consistently lost every event in which I participated. I didn't take to being ordered about and I proved my point. No one asked me to race again.

The first production at Leyton in which I starred was Gogol's *The Government Inspector*. I was initially cast as one of the townswomen, while another boy, Michael Folkard, had the female lead, Anna Andreyevna, the mayor's scheming, social-climbing wife. After a few rehearsals I took over the part, for which Folkard never forgave me.

Around this time I had a faint aspiration to become an actor. I don't think I was too serious about it, for drawing was still my first love, but the idea of just being an actor seemed glamorous and exciting to my schoolboy imagination. But I had great difficulty in remembering lines, and this, on top of stage fright (from which, in various ways, I still suffer), proved my nemesis. Covered in sweat and with a spasming stomach I used to wait, shaking, in the wings. Yet dressing up as Anna Andreyevna was fun. Carefully made up with a wig and nineteenth-century crinoline from Fox's Costumiers, probably looking like Charley's Aunt, junior version, I was someone else. For the brief period before the play began and nerves set in, and afterwards before I wiped the greasepaint off and disrobed, I was in limbo. Definitely not me, an uncertain boy unsure of himself, but someone else, an exotic persona. Not a woman or a girl but, while the disguise was on, not a boy either. I existed in a place where I could behave quite outrageously without any of the usual social strictures to stop me. I was camping about, I suppose, though the expression was then unknown to me. Because I wasn't *me,* I could camp it up hiding in this disguise, and feel powerful doing it.

I remember now my dressing up as a child. Draped in my mother's silk kimonos and scarves, I used to act out fairytale fantasies in front of the large wardrobe mirror. I usually played a young prince fighting off and being captured by bandits, or a pirate chief fighting for his ship and life, my sword a long wooden ruler. The play-acting often involved erotic games, too, for with the scarves I made tourniquets and tight little coverings for my genitals. Binding my hands and feet together I struck renaissance poses *à la* St Sebastian, inspired from pictures in our encyclopaedias. Pleading for my life or bravely defying the cut-throats to do their worst, bound to the mast – the end of the bed – by a mutinous crew was very exhilarating and, while the play-acting lasted, empowering.

Whether I looked like Charley's Aunt or not I attracted several stage-door johnnies. A school governor and a youth employment officer decided my bum was for feeling up. There was also a boy a year or so my senior who, in a dark upstairs storage room, had quick and unspoken sex with me in my crinoline for the three nights of the play's duration. Then he ignored me as if I didn't exist.

The following year the school staged *Macbeth.* Naturally I read for Lady Macbeth but, lacking the timbre and stature for the part, I got Second Witch to play, a character study. A dear friend, Peter, as First Witch and Folkard as the Third made up our grotesque trio. I had far fewer lines to remember and those I had were in verse which made remembering easier. It was a riot to perform, as we crouched in hag-like ecstasy around a large black cauldron lit from within by a red lightbulb. Swaying and cackling in voluminous rags (costumes made by me and Olive from old net curtains dyed and sewn in layers on a caftan-like foundation), these were parts made in heaven for us, especially Folkard – perfect typecasting. Humpbacked and hideous, we enjoyed the experience tremendously.

That year at the first-night party, heavily made-up and in costume, my bottom went unfelt. Young boys as old crones were definitely not on anybody's lust list. The first-night parties catered and organised by the PTA were a sumptuous abundance of delicious and beautifully prepared food, a symbol of how seriously everyone regarded 'the theatre'. Peter and

Micky always showed up on our first nights. Their presence made me feel I had a family and that they were interested in what I was doing.

Someone had the brilliant and mischievous idea of touring *Macbeth* and combining it with *The Emperor's New Clothes*, set in ancient China, the cast made up of teachers, with us kids roped in for crowd scenes. It was to be not just a local tour around dark and empty local schools, performing in the redolent smells of musty gym halls, but a tour abroad, to Germany.

The crossing, the ferry trip from England to France, was a calm one. There were no big waves, no stormy English Channel to plough through, but I remember reeling as I stood on *terra firma* again after several hours of wild chasing about on board. I was in Europe. An uncomfortably long train journey, sleeping in our seats during the night, rewarded me in the morning with a window-seat view of the Rhine. Terraced slopes, quaint villages and towns, fairytale castles, barges on the river – everything was intensely foreign and exciting.

Our first stop was Wiesbaden and we stayed at the school or youth hostel. On other stops we lined up outside the local railway station, adults and boys, with our bags and suitcases like a group of shabby refugees, while German families picked out those of us they wished to take home. There was always a tense period of waiting. I was glad I never stood too long before I was chosen. This first day, though, we were free to roam. It was summer and hot and several of us went swimming near the weir. The water wasn't cold and the tree-lined valley made a dark green frame for the silvery stillness of the river. I took a photograph of an old house reflected mirror-perfect until our splashing broke the surface. I kept the black and white photo for many years as a happy reminder.

Returning to the hostel I found to my amazement and fury that Folkard had used my absence to open and unpack my suitcase. Olive had fashioned me a rather extravagant dressing-gown out of old pieces of material, specially made for the tour. I was rather proud of its damask flamboyance. Unfortunately it wasn't the regular article worn by the other boys, in plain or tartan flannelette, and its colourful and ostentatious design caused much hilarious comment and teasing. Also, and equally unforgivable, Folkard had taken out my diary and read it aloud to the amused circle of boys. I could imagine Folkard's sniggering and crab-like form declaiming with spiteful emphasis my most secret thoughts and passions. Probably I should have punched him out there and then, but then as now I seemed more able to leap to the defence of others more quickly and easily than I could for myself. Besides, I was totally thrown by his betrayal.

At any rate, I had some leverage – the key for our dormitory – and I locked everyone out. Folkard threw a little foot-stomping tantrum but I refused to budge. 'I can't trust you,' I said, 'and the door is staying locked.'

Later that evening, quarrels aside, we ate in the town square lit by candles and torches: teachers, townsfolk and boys at long wooden tables surrounded by old and, to us, wonderfully foreign buildings. A magnificent supper (in England, rationing was still very strictly enforced), crowned by a delicious apple torte, not quite a strudel, which seems in my memory to have run the length of several tables.

We toured the monument to Hercules at Kassel. The palace had been bombed and was boarded up. We stayed in tiny little villages buried in the Black Forest and moved on to Frankfurt where the bombsites were neat and orderly and rebuilding was proceeding at a far quicker pace than in England. The shell of the cathedral was similar in its stark ruins to the many Wren churches in London.

And somewhere on the tour, in a small village, I was picked out of the line-up by a jolly, round baker and his wife and their friendly, tanned son. They lived in a timber-and-plaster house which must have been four or five hundred years old, narrow and tall with leaded windows. The winding, steep and dark staircase, the landing and every shadowy room I entered was redolent with the warm, yeasty smell of baking.

Kurt, their son, was a year or so older than me, fifteen or sixteen. In his lederhosen, his strong brown thighs already fuzzed with thick blond hair, he led the way to the top of the house to his bedroom. It was a tiny room with a low sloping roof of thick dark beams and white plaster, an attic room with a panoramic view of the village and the surrounding forested hills; it seemed to float and the noise from the square was muted and far away. On the walls in frames or just held by tacks were photographs and newspaper cuttings. With his arm around my shoulder he explained them to me.

On a wood-gathering expedition Kurt had been attacked by a wild pig and had killed it with one blow of his axe. The event had made him famous locally. Several black-framed photographs showed him posing with his heavy square-toed, German shoes, lederhosen and white shirt contrasting his brown arms and thick throat; his axe was over his shoulder, one foot on the dead animal, a wide, confident, sunburnt smile on his face like a big-game hunter. In his limited English he told me about his adventure. His arm went from around my shoulders and encircled my waist; then, with a questioning 'Yes?', his other hand went to the front of my trousers and cupped my genitals. We were both shaking as we kissed.

The theatre company spent two nights in the village, two passionate and joyful nights. Kurt's bed was ancient and big, a goose-down cover over a feather mattress, and in it we tried every position and variation we could think of. So this is what it's like, I thought – this is what sex should be. The days of being an object, being used in the neighbour's garage, were forgotten in an explosion of sheer ecstasy. Kurt was well built for his age while I was slender, and although he easily picked me up and threw me around as we wrestled naked on his bed, we mutually shared and gave. Love was never mentioned although our eyes filled with tears when we said goodbye at the station. In front of everyone we were stiff and embarrassed; other boys didn't cry, so neither did we.

Although I'd had sex 'done' to me, nothing like this had happened in my life. I suppose by continually returning to the garage I had given my consent, a child's consent, hoping for affection or love or whatever, but this was reciprocal joy, urgent and necessary. Kurt wanted me to do this to him as much as I wanted him to do it to me. Pushing my head into his thick blond pubic hair I felt his tongue licking me as his hands opened my legs with noisy wet sounds, his face buried between the cheeks of my arse. The hair in his armpits, his pubic hair, all had a warm, pleasantly musty smell like his home. Once he farted in my face. 'Sorry,' he said, but it was okay. We both burst out laughing.

That first afternoon he took me up into the forest. We swam in a shallow pool, cool and clear and fed by an icy stream, and we fucked on warm, smooth boulders, the wet imprints of our bodies quickly drying on the lichen-covered rock. He showed me where he killed the pig and, lying on the grass in the sun, my head resting on his arm, I smoked my first cigarette and felt rather nauseous although I didn't inhale.

As I packed my suitcase, Kurt said he liked my exotic dressing-gown; in exchange, he gave me a pair of lederhosen, an old pair he had grown out of. I tried them on and in our short leather trousers we had sex, hurried and quick, for the last time. We corresponded for about a year; then he found a friend who lived outside his village and we stopped writing to each other.

Returning to England, returning home, was a terrible anticlimax. After a month's freedom being with regular, sane people I re-entered a mad-house. After staying in clean, comfortable homes, the dirt and filth of our slum was almost unendurable. After the excitement of being in Europe, Forest Gate and school were deadly dull; even drawing had lost its thrill.

Then things changed, somewhat for the better. We had a new drama coach. Mr Rose left and Robert Brown took his place. In my life I have met a number of interesting, even remarkable people. Robert Brown was the first of them. Quiet and shy and not very good at class discipline, he opened a door for me and pushed me through. I will always be grateful to that kindly, patient man. Realising that I had an insatiable hunger for books and that my reading was totally scattered and unfocused, he steered me to the classics. Through him I discovered the unsurpassed Penguin translations of Homer, Ovid, Tacitus and Juvenal, and the great French and Russian writers of the nineteenth century. In fact, through him the whole Penguin Library was suddenly there for me. Mr Rose had sneered at the birthday/Christmas present from Peter and Micky, a beautifully bound and printed edition of Boswell's *London Journal*. I had begged them for it and it was generously and lovingly given. Robert was interested in why I had wanted it, what it meant to me. The day-to-day life, meticulously noted, of eighteenth-century London, the stuffy, pompous and mean self-portrait that Boswell unconsciously drew of himself and of his friendship with Dr Johnson, kept me spellbound. Robert didn't sneer. He told me to read Pepys and Saint-Simon, copies of which, much edited, I borrowed from the public library.

I think Derek Jacobi had played Malcom's son in *Macbeth* and all us boys were in *The Emperor's New Clothes*. Derek and I didn't get to know each other in Germany although I was aware of him. He was one of the circle of giggling boys as Folkard went through my suitcase. But through-out the next year of occasional play readings, many evening and some weekend afternoons at the theatre and Robert Brown acting as a focal point, we became fast friends.

Tall and well built with sandy hair waved in a frequently combed pompadour framing a wide, rather spotty forehead, Derek had a presence and a centre of calm and command. A great part of this calm was certainly due to his mother's influence. Coming from a stable, conventional and loving family gave Derek an assurance, a confidence that was unavailable to me, coming as I did from a madhouse. He was thrown at times by my insecurity and the paradox between my being a well-spoken, well-mannered boy and the eccentricities of my dress and, at times, my behaviour.

I had been given a duffelcoat, not the usual kind with a floppy hood and wooden toggles instead of buttons, but an enormous stiff, heavy affair with a stand-up collar around which I draped a white silk scarf acquired from a second-hand clothes shop. I thought the scarf gave me a much-needed touch of elegance. Some time after the German tour, my black school blazer – a hand-me-down from the PTA – bit the dust and Dad bought me an over-sized brown woolly suit. Hideously embarrassed, I wore it to school. I must have looked very funny: the suit, a baggy eyesore, was far too big. Thank goodness I didn't have to grow into it as Dad suggested, for, badly made of cheap material, it fell to pieces after a few months.

I was very conscious of the difference between Derek and myself: conscious that he dressed well and I didn't; that he had a loving secure family and a clean and presentable lower-middle-class home while, to me, it seemed I was living in hell. Had I been able to say to him, 'We are extremely poor, my father is unhappy and old and looks even older, my

53

stepmother is fat, smelly and dirty and I'm ashamed to invite you home; I'm too ashamed even to mention it and them,' life would have been far simpler. But I couldn't. The reaction and comments of schoolfriends in Barkingside had left me raw and sensitive. My family was a subject never to be mentioned and my home a place never, ever to be visited.

In spite of my insecurities, we became friends. The fact that at times I was so insecure and embarrassed gave Derek an edge, a power over me that he often used. It would have been difficult to resist commenting on my bizarre appearance and Derek didn't resist. Realising how vulnerable I was, he used this to dominate our friendship.

Once in the schoolyard during a break he suddenly told me to jump. I did, cracking my head on the iron frame of an open window above me. Pretending it hadn't hurt I went on talking, suddenly aware of the looks of horror I was getting as blood oozed down over my face. 'Why did you jump?' Derek asked. 'I didn't think you would. You don't have to do everything I tell you.'

But at times I felt I did.

We played in Noel Coward's *Fumed Oak* together, not a school production. Hunched crone-like in a sagging armchair I played Mrs Rockett and Derek was my son Henry. Although I received a continual and generous amount of laughter and applause, this wasn't due to any histrionic ability of mine, but rather that I affected a terrible stutter to cover my inability to remember lines. Derek, quite rightly, was furious for I was often unable to feed him the right cue – and at times any cue whatsoever. 'You're hopeless,' he told me. 'You haven't got what it takes to be an actor. You might do all right in a revue but . . .' And he was correct in his assessment – he usually was.

Hampered by stagefright and a bad memory, why did I attempt to act? First, for me, being part of a small, select group, a group apart from the rest of the school where the peculiarities of my dress and behaviour were not so noticeable, was a lure; with acting I could become someone else and exist outside a life I thought wretched and impossible. And second, well, I must have shown some talent, and certainly plenty of enthusiasm.

And then there was the incredible privilege of going to the theatre, not only once but often several times a week, a privilege accorded to very few schoolboys anywhere at that time. Thanks to Robert Brown, the PTA and Mrs Jacobi, I was exposed to a world that was beyond any fantasy my rich imagination could have conjured up.

My theatre-going was something Dad could never have afforded: in those distant days a gallery seat in a London theatre cost two or three shillings, but tickets continually materialised and I never questioned where they came from or who paid for them. I was embarrassed and afraid that if I did the source would dry up. The theatre was so important to me, to my education, to an awakening of my spirit.

Regularly going uptown to London's theatre district with Derek, always, but always, waiting at the stage door for our programmes to be autographed, cemented our friendship.

We had a rather horrid game we played together on the underground. We would sit together and stare at the feet of someone sitting opposite us, our eyes gradually opening in horror. Looking at each other, biting our lower lips, frowning in mock consternation and shaking our heads sorrowfully, we'd return our shocked gaze to our victim's feet. By now they had noticed us and a nervous shuffling would begin as they attempted to hide their offending shoes under the seat, fighting their desire to look down and discover what ghastly calamity had occurred. Then, for several moments, we'd switch our gaze to the advertising slogans above their head before our eyes would return, drawn unwillingly, to their feet. We'd continue for several minutes (the hardest thing was not to laugh), until, worried and confused, the person would hastily move to a distant seat and begin a nervous and careful scrutiny. We would also move on and select another victim.

I saw my first ballet, *Les Sylphides* with Alicia Markova, at Sadler's Wells Theatre. I also saw her in *Swan Lake* at Covent Garden. I sat with tears streaming down my face in soul-touched joy at the ethereal elegance of the dancers, the music, costumes, lighting and scenery. I could never have imagined anything so beautiful. Never in my fourteen years had I seen anything so completely magical.

I became accustomed to Margot Fonteyn at Covent Garden – the Royal Opera House – partnered by Michael Somes, a very fine dancer and choreographer, but I never became accustomed to her dancing.

The Richard Burton–Claire Bloom season at the Old Vic had a permanent set, a classical façade by Tyrone Guthrie. Signing our programmes at the stage door, Claire Bloom was delightful, and Derek and I watched with a schoolboy's amazement when this beautiful, exotic young star, her long hair piled on top of her head and covered with a chiffon scarf, flitted across the road and got on a double-decker bus just like an ordinary person.

Richard Burton, even with pockmarks, was glamorously handsome, but his dry, clipped voice did not move me; Bernard Shaw's *The Apple Cart*, starring Noel Coward and Margaret Leighton; Laurence Olivier and Vivien Leigh in *The Sleeping Prince*. Donald Wolfit at the Haymarket, giving, for him, an extraordinarily restrained and moving performance as a priest. Then roaring and belting it out with a no-holds-barred Lear in a fine rain of dust from the flies and a less-than-adequate supporting cast at the Lyric, Hammersmith.

More Old Vic with another *tour de force* from Frank Thring, the Australian actor, playing Herod in Wilde's *Salome*. Robert Donat giving a subtle and delicate rendering of much strength as Thomas à Becket in Eliot's *Murder in the Cathedral*. Wilfred Lawson in Strindbergh's *The Father*, *Tobias and the Angel* with a young, handsome, half-naked Brian Forbes as Tobias. Cilli Wang, a Korean mime, rolling about a darkened stage as the World in conflict. These last three were performed at the Players' Theatre Club where Robert took me for tea and supper on many occasions.

I used to wait for the hand-on-thigh, come-on routine from him but I gravely underestimated the man. His interest in me was directed by the highest of motives; he saw in me a hunger and a talent and he fed them, he gave me his time, his knowledge, money and energy quite freely, wanting nothing in return. I eventually met his girlfriend and the three of us got on well together.

I saw many revues. Ian Carmichael in a dress as a manic red-wigged pianist coping bravely but hopelessly with an entanglement of bracelets. Hermione Baddely and Cyril Ritchard; Joyce Grenfell in her one-woman show with dancers. Thanks to Mrs Jacobi, Derek and I had front-row stall seats. According to Derek, I laughed far too loudly. It's quite likely.

Musical comedies: Mary Martin washing her hair on stage in *South Pacific* with Sean Connery unnoticed in the chorus. *Kiss Me Kate* at the Coliseum where I had earlier seen Dolores Gray in *Annie Get Your Gun*. *Oklahoma!*, from which the Folkard family walked out. They considered it very vulgar. I was mesmerised by its total physical energy.

And So To Bed with Bobby Howes; Michael Redgrave and Peggy Ashcroft in *Anthony and Cleopatra*; Edith Sitwell at the Festival Hall. A wonderful *Alice Through the Looking Glass*. I took Kathleen and her sister Patricia, and both were rather scared by the trial scene. Margaret Rutherford and Peggy Mount played the White and Red Queens.

Watching spellbound as Edith Evans' squarely facing the audience died slowly in *The Lady's Not For Burning* by Christopher Fry. Eliot's *The Cocktail Party* with Denholm Elliot; Edith Evans' *tour de force* in *The Chalk Garden* with Sybil Thorndike attempting to upstage her. The Roland Petit–Zizi Jeanmaire ballet, *Carmen*. And an incredible *Porgy and Bess* at the Stoll Theatre in High Holborn, with a young, slim and beautiful Leontyne Price.

Derek and I, often with Folkard in our wake, would get together in the schoolyard at every break or lie in wait outside the staffroom for Robert Brown. He had great patience, coming out, spending his well-earned rest talking with us.

Going home, Derek and I would walk to the Jacobi house and then I'd go on across Wanstead Flats to Forest Gate. It became almost a routine that on Friday evenings I'd be invited in for bacon and eggs. Mrs Jacobi bustled about providing a glorious 'greasy spoon' meal that I found so delicious. I didn't get much to eat at home and was always hungry. Derek's father was usually there but kept in the background. His mother was the dominant figure in their home, an end-of-a-row house similar to ours in Longwood Gardens. Unlike ours, though, it had a light, sparkling air about it, clean and shining and filled with his mother's warm energy. Out of all the mothers I've known, had I been able to I would have chosen Mrs Jacobi to be mine. I truly loved her.

After several hours in this warm sanctuary I'd walk back home unwillingly for a weekend of quarrelling and silent, furious drawing in my bedroom.

The school had planned a production of Synge's *The Playboy of the Western World* for the next summer but during rehearsals our leading lady, a plump blond boy with a beautiful face and white, white skin came down with appendicitis. It was decided by several of us boys that we should substitute a revue-style show in lieu of the cancelled play. Our proposal came at the last minute in a frenzy of scene repainting, writing and learning of new lines. In spite of our enthusiasm and our serious dedication to 'the theatre', it would have been a humiliating and total disaster had we been allowed to continue – thank goodness we were stopped.

But, at the time, I was furious. I seethed for a day or so then stormed into the headmaster's office without knocking. He and I had become adversaries and regarded each other as alien beings. A tall man, actually very good-natured and kindly, he took with his withered hand to ordering me out of morning assembly with great regularity. Sitting at the back of the school hall with Derek I used to give a running commentary on the proceedings with an accompaniment of giggling which enraged our principal. I would stand outside his office waiting for assembly to finish and for him to return and give me a solid fatherly lecture on school traditions, what was expected of me, often ending with a 'I don't understand why you gave up sports' refrain. I resented the fact that it was always me who was singled out.

Barging into his office that day I demanded to know why he had cancelled our show. I called him a weak-minded cripple and, I'm sure, many other things. We stood on either side of his desk, him ordering me out and me defying him. My behaviour was quite unforgivable – anyone else would have seen that I was severely punished. Fuming, I went back to class where, trembling, I related the confrontation to Folkard.

Later I heard the headmaster's story varied greatly from mine and perhaps in the heat of the moment, in the little childish tempest I brewed in my own teacup, I dramatised and enlarged my part. But whatever I said in that exchange, for once I didn't feel a victim. I expressed what I felt, probably not coherently, but at least I didn't turn away.

Soon after that event the headmaster called me to his office and gave a rambling speech: 'It must be difficult for a sensitive and artistic boy like you to accept the school's traditions,' – he was always talking about tradition. He continued the sports thing – 'a healthy mind in a healthy body' – sympathised about my home life and then, red-faced, abruptly asked if I was homosexual. Apart from never having thought about it, denying being a sissy was as far as I had got; the word, with its connotations of shame, of prison, of headlines in the worst of the Sunday newspapers, of being so horribly different and apart, startled me into a vehement denial.

This seemed to comfort him. There was some more about how talented I was. That, if I wished, when I left school, he would have a word with a friend who knew somebody who worked for Norman Hartnell – the Queen's couturier – about a possible job.

Sports cropped up again as he wistfully suggested that a few hours of practice a week would channel my energy into more seemly patterns of behaviour. This embarrassing interview was prompted, I believe, by Olive's discovery in my bedroom of some comic-book-style drawings and writings detailing sudden and horrid deaths to various women. She assumed, quite rightly (for I once considered pushing her under an oncoming train), that these symbolised what was becoming on my part an irrational hatred towards her. Taking them first to the headmaster, they were then sent off to goodness knows where, but the result was traumatic: a weekly session with a shrink at Leyton town hall and several extended interrogations at Maudsley Hospital, England's most famous clinic for the treatment and research of the truly loony.

Dad, who accompanied me to the hospital, went around quite happily telling the family that the doctors thought I was mad. I squirmed with embarrassment but, with his hand on top of my head, he smiled and assured me he knew I was quite sane, and that he was still proud of me.

The interrogations at Maudsley were bad enough, but those at the town hall were worse. They were conducted by a lady. In the 1950s there was a difference – Olive, my stepmother, was definitely a woman; Mrs Jacobi was definitely a lady. And the psychiatrist in her office at the town hall was absolutely a lady – she even spoke like one.

The confiscated writings and drawings and many examples of my other work lay before her. One of her first questions, Did I masturbate?, was answered with a loud shocked 'No!'. I couldn't answer the questions that followed: which hand did I use, which position, sitting or lying down, what fantasies? I sat numb in red-faced misery. She was a lady. It would have been bad enough if it had been a man, but my upbringing, memories of my mother and her admonition 'Don't do that, it's dirty', were omni-present. I could only squirm.

With my 'regular' drawings, which I had begun again after leaving Beale, I felt I was on safer ground. Though they consisted of men and women and men and men sexually involved, I could separate myself from them. In her dark suit and glasses she bent across the desk, earnest in her inquiries. She wanted to know why I exaggerated the women's breasts and nipples and why I also gave the phallically over-endowed men huge breasts and nipples, too. Perhaps I hadn't been breast-fed? Had I? I didn't know. I don't think so. Why hadn't I included women and women together? At fourteen the idea that such a thing occurred was beyond me. I was shocked and embarrassed that it did. She seemed disturbed that I bestowed on both men and women curly black hair on their shoulders, around their nipples, buttocks and hips, but left the genital areas blank or shaved. Again I had no answer. Before she tackled the comic-book stuff, I bowed out. I stopped attending at her warm, stuffy office, and while I expected a summons to return none came.

The whole matter was never mentioned again, except by Olive. I kept it all from friends at school. I felt my situation to be strange and embarrass-ing enough without them knowing I was thought a loony.

About this time the boy who had had me in my skirt and wig as Anna Andreyevna, and who was now a prefect, began summoning me for occasional sessions in the storeroom. There, on my knees, or with trousers lowered holding onto a shelf, I allowed him to use me. He made sure our contact was minimal and afterwards he demanded I clean him off using my handkerchief. He hardly spoke except to tell me what to do, and he always left first. During school he ignored me until I was needed. Although I was beginning to develop a free and independent spirit, I hadn't yet managed to rid myself of the lessons and habits learned and formed as a child. When commanded sexually, I obeyed. I was curious and horny and often enjoyed the sex – and I kept to myself the anger I felt about being used and dismissed. It hardly occurred to me to do otherwise, but this was about to change.

Olive was working in the canteen at the Mile End police station and she fixed me up with one of the managers. 'You'll like him,' she told me, 'He's very artistic.' This was a dead giveaway but, at fourteen, I hadn't a clue. He was a small, good-looking man with dark hair and olive skin who lived with his mother in an old council flat in Bethnal Green, east London. She was away for the weekend. We met in a café near the station. Sitting at a table in the back with our mugs of tea, he asked me, 'You're queer, aren't you?' The word meant to me someone who was old and gnarled, eccentric, a witch or some ancient crabby personage from Grimm or Hans Christian Andersen.

'No, I'm not,' I replied rather indignantly

'Yes, you are. You're a little queer boy – I can spot them a mile off.' He went on: 'Feel my prick. Come on, feel it, that's right. See, you've made it hard. You're going to have to do something about it. Come on, let's go.'

The tea unfinished, we left. He cooked us a large lunch of eggs, bacon, sausages, tomatoes and fried bread, then unlocked the door to his 'studio' where he took photographs of me first in my suit, then undressing to my socks, shoes and underpants with my little hard-on poking out and finally with underpants around my ankles, bending over and spreading my buttocks for close-ups.

Then he attempted to get himself down my throat. He was too big and I couldn't manage it, so, turning me around with much shoving and pushing and a lot of vaseline, he said, 'Come on, you can take it, it's not your first,' and did get it up my bum. He was very big and I'd never seen or had to deal with anything so large. As he came he shook so violently I thought we'd topple over, chair as well. When he pulled out I thought my insides would follow.

'Don't move,' he told me. I couldn't. My arms were holding me up, I felt my legs wouldn't support me – they shook and wobbled beyond my control. He handed me a dildo, instructing me to use it. 'Smile, lick your lips.' It was just like years before in the garage. The doorbell rang. 'Stay like that – my friend will like it,' he said. 'And smile at him when he comes in.'

Bending forward with one leg on the chair, one hand holding onto it, the large dark-coloured dildo firmly gripped tight so it wouldn't slip out, I felt awkward and embarrassed. He put on a dressing-gown and went to let his friend in. The other man was well dressed and well spoken. He walked around me several times. 'Very nice,' he said, 'a lovely young chicken.' He tilted my head up towards him and I smiled as instructed. Counting out several pound notes he held them in front of my face. 'These are for you, dear boy. *If* you're a good boy, that is.' He put the notes on a table and undressed. Covered in black hair and with a large belly, he looked very odd, for he kept his socks on.

He picked me up and sat me on his lap. 'Bring him off – he hasn't come yet.' Sitting on the friend's lap with his prick inside me I was masturbated while being photographed.

The afternoon went on. At one point they tied me up, binding my hands to my feet, and fucked me. Still tied up, the friend caned me, lightly at first, then harder. 'I don't want to mark him,' he said.

'It's all right,' the photographer replied, 'he won't mind. He's not going to tell anyone – are you?' he asked me. Of course, I said I wouldn't. The caning increased and I started to protest, then cry out. The photographs continued. 'Let's have some tea. You're being a very good boy.'

We sat in the kitchen and the photographer had me on the table while his friend used my mouth. 'Look what you've done,' he said, pushing his erection against my face. 'She can't get enough of it.' Perhaps their referring to me as 'she' or 'that', sore and hurting, I decided I'd had enough, or perhaps it was just the right time; anyway, I rebelled. The dildo had been replaced and, while I balanced on the edge of the table for yet more photographs, I decided to leave. Easing the thing out, I dressed and left. The two men tried to stop me but I was determined. 'Stupid little bitch,' the photographer said as I left.

I walked back to Dames Road breaking into hot, angry sobs, feeling their cum running down my legs. For the first time in my life I realised I had been used, treated like an object, and it hurt. To them I was a 'chicken', a 'she', a 'bitch', not a boy but a thing to be abused, paid and discarded. And I caught a painful glimpse of what had been going on in the Barkingside garage and I pushed the realisation away. It made me feel ashamed and dirty.

Back at school it was decided I should forsake maths and the sciences and concentrate on the arts. I think I was the only boy granted such a privilege at Leyton and I happily complied. Besides spending more time in the art room, the lack of a disciplined schedule meant I could wander off when I wished. The decision to exclude me from the maths class came about mainly through bad tuition. After my first algebra lesson at Beale the master asked us to raise our hands if we hadn't understood – I was the only boy in class who did. On being told to come to the front and getting my head slapped, the man extolled my stupidity loudly and at great length, punctuating his remarks with more slaps. I didn't bother after that. If I didn't understand I kept quiet, and my constant low marks were the result.

I was Catherine of Aragon in *Henry VIII*. I got some more laughs when the attendant page-boy, in his attempts to comfort me, kept pulling my wimple off.

The last production I graced was Christopher Fry's *A Phoenix Too Frequent*. Derek and I starred, me as the grieving widow and him as her maid. He undertook a Welsh accent and was tipsy and brilliant. As usual I forgot my lines. (The second half of the bill was Marlowe's *Faust*. I badly wanted to play one, if not all, of the deadly sins, but I wasn't given a chance.) I attempted to design a set for *Phoenix* and, with help from Peter, an artist himself, managed it.

61

I also made masks, enjoying the experience immensely, and painted a number of dreadful posters advertising Fry's play which I pinned up around the school. These posters consisted of two busty and scantily clad women – the widow and maid supposedly – draped over badly formed lettering, all executed in gaudy powder paint. No sooner had I pinned one up than it was taken down. For several days I produced and pinned until I was told to stop.

Derek and I decided we'd have the best wigs from Nathan's and costumes from Fox's. We spent so much money indulging our egos that corners had to be cut on *Faust*, but we didn't care.

Derek was understandably upset when I couldn't give him the right cues. Fooling around during rehearsals, playing silly buggers at the back of the hall, drawing Robert to the limits of his vast patience and beyond were what all schoolboys did, and together we egged each other on to more and more silliness. This was all well and good, but on stage Derek became a professional and my inability to remember all my lines exasperated him.

Robert, through a friend, gained admittance for our company for a backstage tour of the Old Vic theatre. The prop room, dressing-rooms and stage were empty, waiting to be explored. I was thrilled to be standing on the spot where the indomitable Lilian Baylis had sat during the evening performances, cooking her kippers on a gas-ring and hissing unwanted and unnecessary stage directions to a galaxy of stars. I had read how, in the days before the Second World War when she and her sister fought to keep the Old Vic and Sadler's Wells functioning, Lilian Baylis somehow attracted the great names of the English theatre. For her they worked for a pittance and suffered her continual interference, yet they returned again and again. Olivier, Gielgud, Edith Evans, Sybil Thorndike were the cream of a long and illustrious list.

In one of the property rooms, tossed on the floor with a pile of worn-out costumes and props, was a well-used sketch book. Filled with drawings, scribbles and notes – a veritable mine of ideas and inspiration – it was given to me by the man who was acting as our guide, telling me it was to be thrown away. It was the kind of book an aspiring young artist dreams of possessing, but I'd hardly looked at it before Derek stole it. On the train home Folkard asked if he might see it; and as soon as I gave the book to him, he handed it to Derek, who leapt from the train with a cry of triumph. I never saw it again. Furious, I turned and punched Folkard who retreated, snivelling, to the far end of the carriage. But nothing I could say to Derek persuaded him to return the book. That episode put a dent in our friendship.

Life at home went on much the same except that Olive took to attacking me with blunt instruments: a coal-shovel, brooms, a milk bottle. She was unhappy and I was unhappy and Dad stayed out of our battles. I felt she was a usurper and could not understand, given Dad's supposed loathing of her, why she was still with us. I made this clear. She had become very fat and smelled horribly. Together they resembled a Cruikshank caricature: him stooped and shrunken and her bloated and barrel-like; an odd couple. I was embarrassed to be seen with them. Yet I was fine walking along Forest Lane to the public bathhouse with Dad on Saturday mornings. He was my dad and, during those brief times, I claimed him. I fantasised that he'd win the pools and, after giving Olive some money, we'd go off and buy a house with a large garden and live together, just the two of us. If this happened I would never wander again.

Andrew was a seventeen-year-old boy soldier. Stationed at Woolwich Barracks, he spent much of his time at home just a few doors down from us. Blond, blue-eyed, muscular, stocky and compact with creamy white skin, he often spent hours working on a battered motorcycle in his parents' garden. I watched, enthralled, across the low fence as he stripped to the waist; his white skin pinkened under the late-spring sun and gradually became covered in black grease and oil. He was very open, waving and smiling and showing his white, even teeth. He didn't have any close buddies at the barracks and we became friends because we both read and shared a fascination with science fiction. We consumed hundreds of paperbacks together. I can still recall their musty odour and the smell of his sweat and feet as he lay on my bedroom floor reading. Of course I lusted for him.

One warm evening he brought a bottle of cider with him. Alcoholic cider. It helped loosen my tongue, enabling me to give a rambling, embarrassed, round-about monologue during which I eventually arrived at my purpose. We both masturbated – well, I knew I did and Andrew often pointed to his erection and the wet spot of pre-cum staining his trousers, complaining how he had to 'pull off' at least once a day. I said, blushing deeply and terrified of rejection, that perhaps, in a friendly way, we could help each other out. My expectations didn't go much further than that, although my fantasies did. To my relief and joy, Andrew agreed. Why not? For some reason we didn't get together that night but we made a date for the following evening.

The big brass bed with brass knobs on the bedposts that I slept in for a while had disappeared as mysteriously as it had appeared. I now possessed a narrow bed that sagged in the middle on which the two of us sat naked together. Andrew reached into my lap and stroked my erection. 'I think we should get to know each other before we start,' he said. Then, without giving me a chance, he leaned on me, pushing me over onto my back.

Over the next few months I fell in love with him. He was fun, he was kind and he was always ready for sex. Coming home late from Woolwich Barracks, he'd climb in through my bedroom window and wake me up in the middle of the night. It wasn't the uninhibited free-for-all as it had been in Germany, but our sex together was good. And we did exchange roles, although generally he took command.

Then Andrew told me he was engaged to be married. I knew he was seeing a girl occasionally, and that he wasn't going on with our relation-ship, although he said he'd miss our nights together. I felt stunned and cried a lot. I missed school; my absence went unremarked so I began wandering off again.

Then came the exams. I managed to scrape through with a pass in every subject and at a prize-giving ceremony was presented with a Reprint Society book of drawings by Leonardo da Vinci: a total treasure, a museum full of genius, exploration and inspiration.

That summer I took a job delivering Corona lemonade and managed to stay away from home, sometimes for days, sleeping at night on sacks in the depot. To be away from the continuing family fighting was bliss, and not seeing Andrew was an added bonus.

Derek and I occasionally went out together to the cinema and I was still invited for their Friday night eggs and bacon on a regular basis. One evening towards the end of summer we went to a dance in a community hall near Gant's Hill Station with two rather silly, giggling girls that Derek brought with him. We made a strange foursome. Derek spent most of the evening making pointed remarks about my appearance and behaviour. Embarrassed and uncomfortable, I felt excluded and wondered why he had invited me. Often, when I began to speak, he and the girls would interrupt me, breaking into songs from *White Christmas* which they had obviously just seen, then giggling together at unexplained private jokes.

Eventually, attracted by a tall, slim, dark-haired girl, I asked her to dance and then walked her home. She told me she was studying to be a dancer, let me kiss her closed lips and then announced: 'I can never see you again – my life is dedicated to dancing.'

I think the last time I saw Derek was at his house. His parents were out and, over tea, he asked me to dress up in his mother's clothes. I didn't need much persuasion. We were fooling around – it was a dare and I always accepted a dare. He took several photographs as I stood in the back garden, posing and leaning against the fence. He promised I could have copies when the film was developed but, quite suddenly, my life completely changed direction. Black and white photographs of me in his mother's clothes no longer interested me. Our friendship, which had become rocky and difficult, was pushed aside as I left behind my schooldays and became a student.

Walthamstow Tech

THE SOUTH WEST ESSEX TECHNICAL COLLEGE AND SCHOOL of Art, now upgraded to university status, is a strange, ugly building with a great pseudo-Grecian porch stuck on the front. It's an uneasy hulk set squatly next to the rather delicate art deco charm of Walthamstow town hall.

This building was my destination. Armed with an enormous bundle of drawings, I mounted the steps for my interview with Stuart Ray, the tall, charming, erudite head of art at Walthamstow Tech. The bundle included a series of *The Young Man and Death, Le Jeune homme et la mort.* Many pages of writhing (but clothed) lovers; many drawings of women in fantastic and very theatrical gowns; and, of course, drawings in the style of Aubrey Beardsley in pen and ink. Women with huge breasts, grossly endowed men, all with very hairy nipples, shoulders and hips – the type of drawings which had so disconcerted the psychiatrist several years previously.

Stuart flipped through them several times in silence, then assigned me to the dress department. I was accepted. I was going to be an art student! I didn't care which department I was assigned to, for my life, my real life, was about to begin.

Looking at my dad, sitting low and worn in his big armchair, I realised I was leaving. Although I hadn't actually left home (I could leave only with a grant, and a grant was two years away), I knew we were parting for ever. Parting in a way that his marriage to Olive had never parted us. I was about to become myself, and being myself was something I thought he could never truly accept or understand.

There'd be no 'Meet my fiancée, Dad', no wedding, no grandchildren to hold us together. The thought of introducing him to a future lover – and there would be lovers, I knew it with the certainty of youth – was absurd. Homosexuality was still punishable by law, and although I'd never thought of myself as being separate, I saw that to be truly myself meant leaving Dad behind. He had been my companion, my constant, for all my life. For years we shared the same bed. I loved him so, it hurt to see him – as I could clearly now from the edge of my new life – shrunken, old tired and locked into a miserable relationship. To understand that this was all his life had to offer, whereas mine was without limits, was profoundly disturbing. Yet there was nothing I could do.

I suppose everyone faces this kind of parting at some time: the leaving of the known, the seemingly secure; leaving love or what seems to us to be love – some kind of security at least – and stepping out into the unknown. No matter how exciting and full of unlimited possibilities the new life seems, there is also a feeling of loss, of emptiness, that never leaves us.

Stuart Ray had decided that dress design would suit me. Daphne Brooker, the gifted head of the dress department who guided and encouraged the talents of Shirley Russell, Don and Renée Robinson, Sylvia Ayton, Marion Foale and Sally Tuffin, welcomed me with open arms. I was the first-year prodigy who would get into the Royal College of Art in three years instead of the usual four. I had the talent. I was going to be a star.

And, according to Daphne, I could design brilliantly. I knew about Bonnard and Vuillard and Sickert and the Camden School of painting. I liked Picasso, had read books on Palladio. I enthused about Dior and Balenciaga, was in awe over the sculptural simplicity of Grès, knew about Schiaparelli and her flirtations with the Surrealists; had been to the ballet, the theatre and the opera. I adored Zizi Jeanmaire and Von Stroheim. I was the walking talking first-year sophisticate of Walthamstow – a real little snot – and I was going to the RCA in three years. I totally believed it. I had so much energy and an overabundance of self-confidence. It seemed as though we all had this youthful energy and we were certain of our strength. It was an energy that made us believe we could solve all the problems, and we were strong enough to be the answer. There was that feeling then, in England in the mid-'50s, a groundswell, still far out to sea, but building up to the tidal wave of new ideas and expression in the 1960s. 'Hope, hope, fallacious hope.'

A small problem arose, though. I couldn't sew. My attempts were a disaster, ludicrous in every way. Even after two years of intense effort, it was hopeless. At the end-of-the-year fashion show a tall, elegant, first-year student stepped out from behind the curtain and stood in front of the class, numb with embarrassment. She was modelling a coat I had done – and done is the right word. A good design in pink wool, it was a simple little A-line number with a rolled collar, but it needed fine tailoring, which was totally beyond me. My coat was a misshapen lump, veering wildly to the left, unhemmed; one sleeve was beautifully set, the other twisted and rumpled. The coat and the model's glazed eyes (for by now she was in shock) produced roars of laughter – my own included – and the poor girl burst into tears. Even my buttonholes, which sometimes approximated a certain neatness, were always grubby, no matter how many times I washed my hands. I just couldn't sew. But it didn't seem to matter and lots of people would help.

I was off and nothing could stop me. And so I fell in love. Well, it happens, and boy was I ready. For the first couple of weeks at Walthamstow I was photographed and drawn and sculpted by other students and staff members – intoxicating attention which I found flattering. Mary Frazer, an Australian student, was sculpting a head of me when Eric Hebborn walked in and asked if I minded him drawing me. He had just joined the Academy Schools and was teaching at Walthamstow one night a week. He says in his autobiography (*Drawn to Trouble*, 1991) that I thought he was 'making overtures' to me. What he doesn't mention, and he knew because we talked about it later, was all the behind-the-scenes preparation for our meeting.

He and I were set up by Nancy and Audrey, third-year painting students, who saw me as a possible though (heavens above!) not permanent affair for him. I was told about this great guy, what a fantastic draughtsman he was, how he'd really like to meet me. I was also told that he was getting over someone – or, rather, I was to be the getting-over bit – that he was still in grief over an affair, an intense platonic friendship with a boy at Walthamstow, a painting student called Howard. The youth was in every way an ideal: a handsome face and form, athletic and totally charming. They wrestled, fenced, went to parties and got drunk together, slept in each other's arms, and never had sex.

So Eric and I met when he was on the rebound. I was a consolation prize to be served up to take his mind off Howard who, now in his second year, was head over heels in love with Valerie, a young sculpture student. 'If you ever want to hurt me,' Eric said to me in the first months of our relationship, 'go to bed with a woman.' These words came out of the blue with no preamble. But I knew to what he was referring.

I was prepared and offered up as a distraction, something not to be taken seriously. I was in the dress-design department and he and his friends were painters. I should have written that in capitals: PAINTERS. We dress designers were made to feel that we were somehow socially unacceptable – but I would do for the moment.

As Eric finished his drawing, he invited me upstairs to the college canteen for tea and toast, which was welcome for I had hardly any money of my own. I walked from Forest Gate through Leytonstone to the college and back every day, about five miles each way, and often had no money for food or even a cup of tea. Although it was a long walk, I didn't care, and

I never thought to complain. Being at college was enough, more than enough. I was joyous. Being tired or hungry were things I never stopped to consider.

Over our tea and toast we arranged to meet and go to Chingford Mount at the weekend, where Eric was working on a large drawing of elm trees, using 303 nibs (he always used a 303 nib) and sepia ink. The following Saturday morning we met up and walked to Epping Forest.

I'm not a landscape artist. I delight in visiting the countryside, but I always feel relieved to get back into town. But despite my personal preferences, we both drew trees that day, Eric his elms, I an oak. We stopped for lunch and met a friend of Eric, Sidney, who had wandered along to see what was happening, and to report back to Walthamstow where, the following week, I was questioned minutely about the events of the previous Saturday. Later we went to a pub and got merry on several pints of bitter. Eric talked about art and himself. It was the first of countless evenings which followed the same pattern: a few drinks and then the monologue. Brilliant and funny.

That first night, and for many years after, I was enthralled. I'd never heard anyone talk like this, before or since. I was swept away, unprotesting, into Eric's world. One of his many gifts was that of magical storytelling. This, combined with a clear and powerful sense of his own importance, and his knowledge about art, carried his audience away into his reality – and a fascinating reality it was.

Later, on the grass outside the pub, illuminated by the headlights of passing cars, we rolled around in a passionate embrace. I was naked, Eric still clothed. I told him that I loved him. And I did. After that night I submerged myself in his world and began to lose sight of my own. Drowning in love, that's what I was; swept away and drowning.

Eric wanted a young acolyte to attend and worship at his altar of opinion, and I was more than ready to fill that position.

We wrestled and fenced in the corridors of the Tech, held hands and smooched, went out for a few beers after evening classes, and then, having once been caught by a policeman in a back alley behind some shops, usually went up to Epping Forest, after which I'd walk back to Forest Gate.

At weekends, my education continued: at the National Gallery, the Wallace Collection, the British Museum and the Tate. Eric talked and talked. His passion was for Rembrandt and Frans Hals. He was fascinated by the fact that Hals purportedly used only black, white, burnt umber and raw sienna in the majority of his paintings. I didn't care much for Hals but kept my opinion to myself. It wasn't needed. I was discouraged from looking at anyone else, my beloved Piero della Francesca included.

Rembrandt and Hals were *the* masters in painting, as were Leonardo da Vinci, Michelangelo and Raphael in drawing. I didn't disagree.

And during our excursions, Eric also often talked about Howard. I could plainly see how much he was hurting, how much this friendship had meant to him, how much pain its ending caused him. There is a bronze statue of a naked ephebus holding a gigantic sword, opposite Apsley House. This reminded Eric of Howard. Each painting or sculpture of an idealised youth we encountered brought Howard into being. At the Academy Schools, on a life drawing, Eric wrote:

> *'Tis true by chance you did beguile with tilted eye and faunish smile*
> *A youth who by man's ethic true must hate himself for loving you,*
> *with that strange love wrought by fate*
> *that ill deserves such thoughtless hate.*

The memory of Howard was omnipresent. I did what I could, said what I could, to help him heal while at the same time feeling intimidated by the constant reminders of how much Howard was still in Eric's heart.

And, of course, we made love. Horrible phrase. We had sex, far more to the point. In Epping Forest, in doorways, in bomb-sites (there were still plenty of those left), anywhere we could find a little privacy. We didn't have anal or oral sex – just Eric putting his penis between my thighs and coming that way. He was sexually inexperienced, and it didn't occur to me, at the beginning, to teach him, or to try anything different.

The winter months sped by. Then at the Tech one evening in the early spring of 1955, Eric turned to me and told me he thought it best if we stopped going around together, if we stopped seeing each other. He didn't offer any reason, just said he thought it was for the best. I was horror-struck, too shocked to ask why.

I had failed, love lost again. I was entirely and absolutely miserable, hurt and bewildered. It seemed as though this was a pattern I was setting up in my life, a pattern of loss and failure. My mother, Dad, the primary-school teacher, the soldier; people I loved who loved me back and then abandoned me.

For a long while I cried myself to sleep at night. My work went downhill. I would sit for hours staring at the wall, unable to think or draw. I was angry, too. Eric had promised me a permanent love, a life-long commitment. I had put my trust in that promise, surrendered completely to it.

Angry and hurt, I wanted to hurt him. He looked so calm and un-ruffled, as though I had never been a part of his life. I wanted to smash that smug exterior, to make him feel as much as I felt.

Looking back, I feel now that our initial break-up was caused by a combination of peer pressure, the fact that I wasn't the ideal youth of Eric's fantasies, and that I enjoyed and welcomed sex, something which seemed to threaten Eric throughout our years together.

The peer pressure came from third- and fourth-year painters who seemed upset by our relationship. Nancy Clarke took to kicking me as she passed me, and making sarcastic comments. At the first 'grown-up' party I attended, at Nancy's home, I became very drunk and was horribly sick on the lawn. I had been given a series of cocktails, mixed drinks, wine, beer and spirits, by Reg, a third-year painting student, who kept pushing them on me – just as a joke, he explained later, not that I really needed pushing. I was so ill that I had to spend the night at Nancy's, to her father's fury. I had no idea what I was drinking, how lethal it was, or what the effect would be.

After this unhappy début, I was banned from all painters' parties, even from Eric's twenty-first birthday party. This was enforced by another painter, a huge, ugly man called Don, and his girlfriend Margaret. Third- and fourth-year painters were too superior to mix with first-years like me, still less with a socially inferior dress designer. Even worse, I didn't hide the fact that I was gay. In 1954, even at art school, such things were supposed to be hidden. Did I have no sense of shame or guilt?

Eric, in his dark-grey worsted suit, his teaching suit from Burton's, with a maroon waistcoat and imitation pearl buttons, was exempt from any-one's scorn. This might be difficult for people to understand now, for so much has changed, but in those days Eric escaped social censure because in the bigoted and confused thinking of that time, even among fellow gays, with their silly 'Who's Claude and who's Maude?' routines, Eric was seen as the man. He was the doer, not the done; the supposedly masculine, not the supposedly feminine. That made being gay okay. For some reason, if you were the 'active' as opposed to the 'passive' party, you weren't (except in law) considered really homosexual.

But I made a great deal of noise at college. I had found a boon com-panion, a friend who accepted me without any reservations. This was Janet Deuters, who was also in the dress-design department. Janet with red hair and a total *joie de vivre* which matched mine; Janet who, with her amazing talents, became the first friend with whom I could talk freely. Janet and I shook the hallowed halls of Walthamstow Tech with our own unbounded enthusiasm and laughter. Together, life was all 'shrieks and floods', totally as it should have been at our age.

It was probably a combination of all these things that pushed Eric into our break-up. Then, just as suddenly, we were back together again. 'Perhaps we could see each other occasionally,' he said to me one evening. Later, in the middle of Wanstead Common, on one of the rare occasions when he accompanied me home, I gave him the best blow-job I could produce, thinking, 'Okay, mate, if you want to see me only occasionally after this, then you're an idiot.' Eric erupted with a howl (unusual for him, as his orgasms were, on the whole, restrained). He clutched my head with both hands and forced his penis down into my throat and held it there. It was the first blow-job I had given him and it worked. Threatened or not, Eric changed his mind. We were together again.

I was not under any illusion that Eric and I got together again solely because of that one act. We also truly needed each other, and we fitted perfectly into the roles our needs demanded. For me, he was the father who gave physical expression to his love, a teacher, a draughtsman of excellence, passionate and certain in his beliefs. For him, I was the young, adoring initiate, eager and willing to be absorbed into the mysteries of the Hebborn cult. I was sublimely happy but I never again totally trusted him.

My feelings of insecurity were underlined at a party in a student flat in Mount Pleasant. I had brought two bottles of my dad's parsnip wine with me and we were all pretty high when Fin, a friend from Walthamstow, a lovely brown-eyed boy with a sweet, gentle nature, came in crying. Eric had done something nasty to him, he said. They'd had sex. As Fin told me later, he was willing at first, but Eric had hurt him and now he felt ashamed.

I felt doubly betrayed and humiliated. Eric and I had committed ourselves, vowed everlasting love and faithfulness, and Fin was a trusted friend. I remember shouting and hitting Eric. His reply, reiterated many times over the coming years together, was: 'It was nothing, and I'd think more of you if you didn't behave this way.'

I didn't stop loving Eric, nothing like that, but now I was on guard, constantly on guard.

About this time two other things happened. Two warning lights went on, warning lights that should have attracted my attention. But, really, who notices these things in the early days of love? So I ignored them. A little voice said, 'Hello, what's this? What's going on?' But it was such a little voice, weak and far away. What was happening to me was so much stronger that I paid it no attention.

The first warning was that Eric gave me a present: a book from Foyle's bookshop, long before it was modernised, when there were still treasures to be found. It was *French Drawings at Windsor Castle* by Anthony Blunt, one of a series on drawings in the Queen's collection, published by Phaidon. On the flyleaf he inscribed a long dedication to me in which he wrote that, if we were to be happy, I would have to do what he told me. With this book and the inscription he said he loved me, he called me his lovely boy. He sat me down and, holding my hand, told me that he loved me dearly, and that I must obey him. He would be my guide and teacher in life and art.

The other warning came at a local greasy spoon, next to the bus depot. We were eating egg and chips when a handsome young man entered and stood by the door, gazing wildly about. His body movements were unco-ordinated and convulsive, and his mouth twitched. 'One day you'll end up like that,' Eric said to me. I was appalled and confused. I asked him what he meant. The man was obviously ill, and I felt healthy and confident with my youth, talent and love. What was he talking about? I would end up like that? It sounded too similar to the gym teacher's admonition. A flash of fear and dread went through me. *Could* I end up like that? 'You'll end up like that unless you do what I tell you,' Eric replied and went on eating. Subject closed.

I sat in silence. I was learning that when Eric closed a subject, it stayed closed. The extrovert part of me disturbed him. He wanted only my quiet, well-mannered side, a well-mannered, well-spoken foil for Eric's thick Essex accent and rather primitive manners. I also knew he worried that I might 'do a Howard' and leave him for a woman. My intense friendship with Janet made him uneasy. He often told me he didn't like women, that he felt uncomfortable in their presence.

Nancy gave another party. This time Eric wasn't invited but I was. Had I been less naïve, I would have realised this was odd. Nancy had a plan. Kicking and insulting me weren't enough, weren't working. I accepted the invitation in a spirit of defiance. Excluded from the painting students' parties, mortified by being left out of Eric's twenty-first birthday celebra-tions – I couldn't understand why he would want to have such an important birthday without me – I went along, with an 'up yours' attitude.

The party wasn't held at Nancy's home. I can't remember whose house it was, but I do know that I spent the night there in a bed with a woman, Josie Buchan, an attractive, well-endowed blonde dress designer who Nancy had co-opted to seduce me. Her plan didn't work. Josie did try but I made it clear that it wasn't on; I was in love with Eric. So we talked and then fell asleep.

Next day at Walthamstow the rumours were flying. Josie and I had shared a bed. This could only mean one thing: we'd had sex. From what Josie said that day, I realised I'd been set up. A trap had been laid, and, totally unaware, I'd fallen into it. Appalled, I waited for Eric's return from the Academy Schools. Nancy's plot seemed so mean-spirited. Whatever its outcome, it could only hurt Eric, after his traumatic parting with Howard. I realised how stupid and unthinking I had been. Eric was met by a con-tingent of painters, eager to expand on the gossip, and Eric believed them.

His fury, his anger and his bitterness were terrifying. I had betrayed him, betrayed our love. Perhaps that was the time for me to say: 'It was nothing, and I'd think more of you if you didn't behave this way.' But it didn't occur to me. Eric was in such pain. My energy was directed to comforting him, reassuring him, explaining what had really happened. Eventually he understood. The knowledge that we had been violated, that an attempt had been made to separate us, somehow drew us closer. We were the only gays, it appeared, at Walthamstow. At any rate, we were the only gay couple whose behaviour was open to public scrutiny.

In the first weeks of getting back together, late one Saturday night, Eric and I were in the doorway of the local post office, on a corner opposite the art store. A small van cruised slowly past and then stopped. Pulling up my trousers, I saw a man get out and come towards us. He had seen what we were doing – anyone passing could. Our behaviour was gloriously flagrant. Well, we were in love and we felt quite impervious to danger. From the way the man walked, a sort of swaying mince, and then from the way he spoke, I thought he was weird, somehow unbalanced.

'Hello, dears. Any trade round here?' he asked. His voice was high-pitched and in the light of the street-lamp his appearance sybaritic. A high golden pompadour, carefully waved, crowned his head. Surely he's wearing make-up, I thought. Yes, he was. There was a man who lived near us in Barkingside who was supposed to 'touch up' and this stranger standing in front of us had definitely gone beyond a discreet application of powder and rouge. He wore his overcoat like a cloak and the many rings on his fingers sparkled as he fussed with the upturned collar.

Thinking I was being sympathetic (I had been brought up to be sympathetic and friendly to those 'less fortunate'), I replied, speaking slowly and enunciating each syllable: 'Not around here, but Petticoat Lane Market opens early Sunday morning.' I assumed that 'trade' meant trading – that is, street traders, markets, street markets.

Eric stepped out of the doorway. 'I'll handle this,' he said. What he said I don't know, for as he talked he led the man back to his van.

'What a shame. Poor man,' I said when Eric returned.

This was my first exposure to a queen. There were to be several other encounters in the near future, none of them pleasant. Except that is when Quentin Crisp modelled for us in the life class. We students, trying so hard for some qualifying sophistication, had never seen or experienced anyone like Quentin. He was quite unique and extraordinary. With thick hair waved in a silvery blue rinse, eye shadow and lip rouge, painted finger and toe nails, he was totally in command of all his faculties. Never for one moment did I think he was less fortunate. Most amazing of all was his kindness of spirit and gentleness of manner at odds with his painted, rather severe countenance.

We circled him warily at first, as animals do on encountering a new and strange addition to their group. Finding him harmless, we welcomed him in. There were a couple of exceptions, bully boys – every college has them – who at first attempted to intimidate him, but Quentin was way beyond their juvenile bad manners and they retired confounded.

Naked except for a tiny posing pouch, the attitudes he adopted as a model were baroque and tortuous. He impressed us by his ability not only to hold himself at such excruciatingly twisted angles without moving for thirty or forty minutes, but to resume the pose exactly after a rest period.

During the two-hour break, between day and evening classes, Eric and I would hold hands and smooch in the corridor, the only gay couple among the 'hets'. Quentin, on passing, would stop and place his hand over his heart and slowly and exaggeratedly raise his eyes heavenwards. He knew Eric from the Royal Academy Schools and from him I heard the story of Quentin dressed in Edwardian fashion complete with bowler hat and rolled umbrella gliding along a London pavement. As he passed a large hole in the ground a workman stood up, his head and shoulders just above ground level. 'Oh look, a fucking fairy,' he called out to his mates when he saw Quentin. Quentin stopped, regarded the man for a moment then, raising his rolled umbrella, said: 'If I am a fairy then this' – waving the brolly – 'is my magic wand. Disappear.' Then Quentin glided away.

During the break in our relations Eric had discovered the gay nightlife of London with a new friend, an older man named Jürgen, a German. In Jürgen's tiny hand-made aluminium two-seater open-topped car with a leather strap around the bonnet, they explored the few gay clubs 'up west', in the West End, and a famous gay pub in east London, the D'Aragon Arms (known as the Duragon to its regulars).

I didn't like Jürgen at all. He was always touching me up and after a few drinks he told stories quite openly about being a guard in a concentration camp during the war, where he had forced young prisoners to have sex with him in exchange for food. It nauseated me. He bragged about it as though he had been doing the boys a favour, as though, because we were fellow gays, we would approve.

Usually, it was just him and Eric who would set out for an evening's cruise together, but sometimes I went with them. Gay clubs in the London of the mid- to late-1950s were furtively hidden away, disguised behind shopfronts, up several flights of stairs, or down in the basement. You had to be among the cognoscenti to know where they were. Boys and older men seemed to make up the majority clientèle, one group offering, the other buying.

75

One place we visited was located in a dilapidated nineteenth-century town house in the middle of Soho. Arriving late, we climbed steep, narrow stairs to where, behind a closed door, the club occupied an entire floor. The dim ultraviolet light turned our grubby white nylon shirts into sparkling beacons of cleanliness. Overcrowded, packed hip to hip, it was a perfect place for groping, which I found very irritating. Looking younger than my seventeen years, I was a chicken-hawk's dream, and was grateful for the presence of the large, dark, bearded, good-looking and totally masculine Eric. He would just loom at my side for the nuisance to fade. I kept close to him. This was alien territory, a foreign land waiting to be explored.

I was intimidated by the gatherings of queens, who, with shrill cries like flocks of gaily painted, omnivorous birds, would descend, flicking my long hair, pulling and poking at my clothes, expressing a hilarious contempt for my shabby art-student appearance. They took my shyness as disapproval, my inability to respond in any way as hostility.

I felt more under attack in those moments than at any time in the outside world. The rapid-fire repartee, the non-stop bitchiness, left me speechless and hurt. I was outraged at being referred to as 'she' and 'her'. I had spent too long fighting the appellation 'sissy'. With an idealised expectation, I had presumed that, among my own kind, I would be able to relax and just be myself. I was wrong.

Eric and I didn't dance together. Eric didn't dance. The club had a minute dance-floor with a baby grand piano on a somewhat shaky extension – the floor vibrated – built onto the back of the house, supported on wooden stilts. One night it collapsed. Fortunately we weren't there so we didn't know if it was occupied at the time, or if it also took away the pianist along with the customers in an avalanche of high-pitched screams and breaking piano wires. We simply turned up one night to find the club closed for repairs. As far as I know it never opened again.

One other club, in an alley near the Coliseum Theatre, deserves mention. Members had a key with which they let themselves in. Stairs led up to a discreet, well-lit room. Definitely upscale from the one in Soho. Jürgen knew the bartender, and when he was on duty we got free drinks. But there were fewer boys available for him and this kept our visits to a minimum.

Eric and I were more at home in coffee bars, which were then a novelty, made even more popular by the myth of possible discovery and fame as a pop or skiffle-group star. Like Lana Turner at the counter of Schwab's Drugstore in Hollywood, several young stars of the 1950s and '60s music scene supposedly started their careers in espresso bars. We visited The Nucleus, but its dark and shadowy recesses had a reputation for pot-smoking, and we definitely weren't into that.

Our favourite was The Gyre and Gimble, a high-ceilinged basement in Villiers Street, off the Strand. We'd sit on a bench in a corner by the long, steep stairs, down which young hookers and hustlers staged grand entrances. They would prance like showgirls on the wooden steps, to the applause of their friends. It felt like a bar from Isherwood's Berlin, seedy and impoverished, with everyone joining together as a family. Eric and I were part of a small court attendant on Ernest the Astrologer and Ironfoot Jack, last of the 'bo'miums' – two of the most colourful characters on the coffee-bar circuit.

Ernest spent most days in the reading-room of the British Museum where, even if he had no assignment to undertake, it was warm and comfortable. At closing time he wandered down through Soho, stopping at The Nucleus or The French Café in Old Compton Street, and usually ending at The Gyre and Gimble. A slight, grey-bearded man, querulous and effeminate, he was intensely absorbed in his work. A brilliant astrologer, he sat like minor royalty, writing voluminous charts in a meticulous script. He taught Eric astrology, giving him the address of the astrological store by the British Museum. With Ernest's guidance, Eric began a series of readings for fellow students at the Academy Schools. These were so revealingly accurate – detailing births, deaths, minor scandals covered up or forgotten – that Eric stopped. He wouldn't undertake a chart for me. 'I know what's going to happen,' he always said in answer to my pleas.

'But I don't, Eric.'

'Quite,' he replied.

Another subject closed.

Ironfoot Jack presented quite a different appearance to Ernest's. I often wondered why Jack didn't have an eye-patch; it would have been so appropriate. He was flamboyant in a large-brimmed black hat, black cloak, and the steel hoop attached to his boot which gave him his name. He insisted, with an energetic theatricality, on the demise of bohemianism, claiming he was the last surviving member of a once thriving international community.

Jack wasn't my idea of what constituted a bohemian at all: he was only vaguely literate and coarsely vocal, without any of the style or intelligence I associated with my romantic vision of Left Bank Parisian life. But so what? This was an experience totally different from the dreary battle-ground of home. Eking out our coffees, we sat and talked, smoking too many cheap cigarettes (Player's Weights), and mixing with real characters, real people. This was living.

I began posing in earnest for Eric. As we hadn't a studio I stood for hours naked in isolated parts of Epping Forest – not that, in winter, there were many people around. I even posed in the snow, standing on my discarded clothes, turning bluish-violet with cold. It was okay; it was for *art*. It was for Eric, whom I had set firmly on a pedestal. As far as I was concerned, he was the artist, the magical draughtsman, and I would have done anything to aid him.

Coffee bars, gay clubs, pubs, parties and work. For five days a week, from 9 a.m. to 9 p.m., we were at the Tech. Although we looned about (especially Janet and me) during the two-hour evening break, we worked. We worked weekends, too, out drawing with one another, pushing and extending our knowledge and ability.

Perhaps no time is as wonderful as the years at college. Freedom to begin to accomplish what has formerly only been dreamed of. Work, play, friendship and love.

Eric had a supporter and friend. What exactly her job was, and for whom she worked, I cannot remember, but once or twice a year, on quality embossed notepaper, she wrote to Eric, recommending that he apply for this or that prize. She always assured him that he stood a better than even chance of winning it, and signed each missive, 'believe me, Joyce Brown'. And we did believe her. For that summer of 1955, Eric applied for – and won – a landscape scholarship. With it we went to Maldon, Essex, on the River Blackwater, to 'tent it', to camp down on the marshes. Halcyon days, that first summer Eric and I spent together. Paradise, really – well, almost.

Maldon, 1955

 ERIC KNEW EXACTLY WHERE WE WERE TO STAY. LADEN DOWN with our tent and camping gear, rubber groundsheet, our art supplies, a frying pan and a few pots – the barest minimum necessary for survival – we stumbled off the bus at the top of Maldon Hill.

Passing The White Hart pub and several cottages we were soon in a narrow lane between hedges woven together as they had been for centuries, and laced with wildflowers. On our right, uneven and lumpy with Viking burial-grounds, a large untidy field slanted away to the estuary below. We huffed over the tiny footbridge spanning the railway and along past Beeleigh Oak, a huge gnarled old tree that, in spite of its name, was definitely an elm.

Then it was a good push and a struggle through an overgrown tangle of bushes and brambles that walled and sheltered a tiny grass-covered peninsula, a neatly cropped lawn surrounded by salt-marsh bordered in the distance by the River Blackwater. We had arrived, and claimed this totally private arcadia for our first summer together.

From Beeleigh Oak the ground dipped to our haven and from it a green gothic-ceilinged chapel of immense willow trees arched up and over a boggy area of black mud and fallen branches: our kitchen and bathroom. An iron pipe, rusty with age, had many years before been pushed into the bank and now jetted a crystal arc of pure spring water into a large enamel iron bathtub filled almost to the brim with liquid mud. Our lavatory was on the far side, hidden behind bramble bushes. We had everything we needed: we had each other, the campsite was perfect and the summer promised long hot days and warm clear nights.

We bought new-laid eggs, milk still warm and frothy from the cows, and butter at the farm. Freshly baked bread, fish still flapping from the boats, good, cheap cuts of meat, vegetables and fruit almost given away, all supplemented with the odd tin of baked beans. We ate well.

Early in the morning, naked – no pyjamas for us – and enjoying the dew-soaked grass on my feet, shivering sometimes in the pale sunlight straining through the mist, I lit the fire. There was always plenty of wood and Eric showed me how to stack it and keep it dry. With a roaring little blaze I quickly brewed the ritualistic first cup of tea of the day. Slabs of crusty bread thickly buttered together bacon and eggs tasting of smoke made our breakfast. Everything I cooked tasted of smoke, including the tea. Still naked, wrapped in blankets, we sat at the opening of the tent drinking from our enamel mugs; and after smoking the first cigarette of the day, we would crawl back under our blankets and curl up together until the mist had cleared.

Eric was a gentle, cuddly, warm teddy bear of a lover and, with no one to bother us, no social or peer pressures, that summer was a time of bonding. We were never so close, so happy or so carefree together again.

After washing and dressing, we tidied up our campsite and then spent the day painting and drawing, me posing for Eric. Naked against a fallen willow tree, hip slanted in a high Renaissance attitude against a branch, I stood for hours – days, really – in the middle of the bog, often thickly covered with mosquitoes. I only objected when I looked down and saw them hovering and settling on my penis. When posing I constantly got hard and then soft; it was a sensual, dreamy game that helped dissipate the stiffness and cramping that came from holding myself still for hours. Eric became cross and irritated if I moved and, after each rest break, took some time carefully arranging me back in exactly the same position.

While I posed I fantasised, plundering my childhood landscape of erotic games. I was the young prince bound tightly to a tree while the bandit chief drew my likeness to send it to my father with a ransom note. I wandered, too, through the previous night's coupling. Doing nothing but standing as still as I could my sexual imagination ran freely. Occasionally, Eric would stop drawing and, telling me not to move, would kneel and suck me slowly, deliciously, to climax while masturbating himself. Or, standing behind me while I held the pose, would ease himself into me, stroking me and biting my neck and shoulders.

Leaving our sanctuary we pushed up through the bushes back to Beeleigh Oak, turning right and passing Beeleigh Abbey, often through the open gates seeing old Mr Foyle of the famous bookshop in Charing Cross Road reading or taking tea on the terrace. A narrow, tree-covered tarmac lane led to where one part of the canal, the Chelmsford canal I suppose, ended in a huge pool of waterlilies and a vast, decaying eel trap. A little further and we reached our swimming-pool, Beeleigh Lock. Here I posed again, clothed this time, in a shirt, sweater and trousers, standing looking aimlessly towards the water.

Eric's paintings captured the overgrown bucolic calm of that summer. The silence broken, tempered with distant and muffled farm sounds and birdsong; a warm sensual abundance that matched our feelings for each other and amplified them.

Eric told me he was half gypsy. He accounted for his mother's often brutal behaviour by her marrying outside the 'tribe' and the loneliness she felt from being ostracised by her Romany family. One evening, in that marvellous luminous stillness after the sun had set and just before dusk, Eric and I built and lit a roaring bonfire for our gypsy wedding. We made a small cut on our thumbs and exchanged and mixed our blood. Binding our clasped hands tightly, his right to my left, and vowing to love each other forever, we leapt across the blaze. Still with our hands bound, we sat and shared a bottle of Cyprus sherry and rolled happily and drunkenly into the tent.

In our second week at Maldon we were invited to tea with the Cuthbertsons. Mr and Mrs Cuthbertson lived on a First World War cutter which he had once captained. In the Second World War he had taken the ship across the Channel under enemy fire to help with the Dunkirk evacuation. A kindly Scotsman with a deep and abiding passion for art, he was Eric's first instructor in painting. What I recall most clearly was the love and caring the Cuthbertsons had for each other. She looked at him with the eyes of a young girl and his frequent touch of her arm or her hand, a mere whisper of a touch, proclaimed his love far louder than any words could do. I felt overjoyed in their company. I saw their love as a long and golden reflection of the young and immediate passion that Eric and I were forming. I saw us romanticised, in old age, and in love; a lifetime of it built joyously, freely given and returned. And I felt secure taking his hand or arm as we walked home in the dark.

Eric's prize money came in three instalments and long before the second arrived we had spent the first. I wanted to go and pick fruit at the Tiptree Farms to earn some money, but Eric had a better idea. With only a few shillings between us, we set off early one morning for the tiny village of Goldhanger which nestled untidily under the sea wall. It was a long but enjoyable walk for, apart from a country bus, several cyclists and the occasional flash of a pheasant paddling furiously in a panicked burst of flight across our path, we had the countryside to ourselves.

We arrived hot and thirsty at Goldhanger's tiny green. Against the lichen and mossy wall of the churchyard, we drank and sluiced our heads under the village pump. Wet and dripping, we walked across the road and bought ourselves a homemade ice-cream each from the post office and general store. Almost in unison we both said how marvellous things taste when you're hot and thirsty and then, laughing together, said 'Snap'. It was that good. Our being together was that fine and good that summer.

Our destination was Mr Frost's two cottages on Fish Street. Eric had told me many tales about Crawshay Frost, Goldhanger's notable eccentric, who, before the First World War, had been an acclaimed nature photographer. During the war, shellshocked and traumatised, he was invalided out, and never recovered from his experiences. As a youth, Eric had often been hired as an artist and odd-job man by Mr Frost, who paid him generously. Our visit was in the hope of us being hired and receiving the same generous remuneration.

The garden surrounding Mr Frost's cottages resembled a plundered jumble-sale. Bushes, trees, even the front hedges were strewn and decorated with sheets, towels, various pieces of clothing, including underwear and socks, all in a condition of decay and hanging in skeletal shreds from branches and twigs. The ground was a palimpsest of books, more assorted linens, pots, pans, china (some of it old and fine), with knives and forks driven into the earth, their bone and silvered handles looking like a child's toy soldiers standing at angled and undisciplined attention, overseeing a mutinous and disarrayed campsite.

Mr Frost was not at home. We called, tried to get into both dwellings (their interiors looked to be as packed and disordered as was the garden), and eventually sat down next to a pile of what looked to be fresh bread, breaking off crusty outsides.

Our wait was short: Mr Frost, an elderly, thin, rather dirty white-haired man wearing a pair of stained shorts and a jersey, cycled into his garden in a distracted manner. He was delighted to see Eric but was also preoccupied. He had been feeding his geese along the sea wall. The pile of bread, about twenty loaves of it, which we had been eating, was for them. He bought the day-old loaves from the village bakery. No self-respecting countryman or woman would have considered putting day-old bread on their table. He boiled us up some tea and I was dispatched with two shillings (he counted the change on my return) to the post office for milk. Wrapped in thick grease-proof paper was a solid block of cheddar, green with mould but delicious and tart when we cut into it, slicing away the scabrous outer layer. Tea, bread and cheese: a simple, fortifying lunch.

Mr Frost proceeded with a monologue, a running stream of gentle and mildly stated grievances, a vocalised extension of a continuing, never-ending internal listing, a compilation of everyday bothers which kept him in a state of constant agitation. Goose eggs were being stolen and one day he would have to go and talk to the parents of the boy he suspected; it was a task he did not relish.

He had discovered an ancient landing-stage and was attempting to excavate a submerged Roman galley from one of the many mud-filled creeks nearby. He wanted to house his finds in a small museum but had met with strong local opposition. To find a storage place was important since several rooms, including the bathrooms in both his cottages, were packed with Roman remains. It was necessary to leave the sea-soaked pieces in running water to clear them of salt.

This lack of bathrooms had led to a recent upset with some friends who had come down from London. They had given notice of their impending visit weeks before they arrived and Mr Frost had ordered from Harrod's an abundant and sumptuous picnic for them. Obviously the guests hadn't seen their friend for some time and seemed a little put out by the wild disorder of his garden through which he had led them to the cornfield beyond. He had flattened a corner of wheat and, on a couple of horse-blankets, spread out wine and food.

All went well for a time until the ladies needed a lavatory. After visiting the house they returned shocked and dismayed. I can only imagine the well-bred urgent whispers. Mr Frost suggested the men use the bushes, explaining that he did frequently, and that the ladies take a short walk up Fish Street and relieve themselves behind the tombs in the churchyard. This suggestion broke up what must have been a difficult and awkward reunion. The ladies, insulted, departed accompanied by their menfolk, leaving Mr Frost alone with his feast. The incident had happened only days before and, showing us the flattened corner of wheat (the farmer was asking a preposterous recompense for the damage), we could see wasps and flies still gorging themselves on the remains of the food. Several unopened bottles of wine were lying around and, to our disappointment, they stayed unopened.

As Mr Frost recounted his story, he mixed all the events together, muttering to himself or to us that 'for the gentlemen it was acceptable but not for the ladies'. Then in the same breath he began a solitary discourse about the Spanish and a gift he had made to their embassy in Britain. He had sent them an old illuminated Spanish bible which he hoped would strengthen Anglo-Spanish relations and weaken the Franco régime.

From there he launched into telling us of a dispute with the vicar over organ rights. Mr Frost had paid for the repair of the church organ and insisted on playing it whenever he chose which, it seemed, was usually during the vicar's sermon. Mr Frost, according to Eric, would sail energetically into long and complicated fugues every time he thought the sermon boring or when the vicar strayed into what Mr Frost considered to be dangerous waters. The church militant was one subject that he attacked and submerged with great enthusiasm. Anything to do with militarism was anathema to Mr Frost, to be resisted with his very being. Naturally, the vicar objected vociferously, but to no avail. It was an ongoing power struggle.

Into these sagas he would weave constant mention of his toes, several of which were in imminent danger of gangrene, and he would display his bare feet, energetically waggling what appeared to be ten healthy digits. Eric told me Mr Frost slept with his feet dangling over the sill of an open window supposedly on doctor's orders, with a notice hanging from one asking visitors to pull only in dire emergency.

His last, but certainly not least, subject was the continuing battle with his next-door neighbour, the Major. The Major's domain was military in appearance and upkeep, with neatly trimmed lawns and hedges, exactly placed flowers in precisely shaped beds, and topiary birds smoothly shaved and moulded fronting his thatched Tudor cottage. The poor man must have felt he was living next door to the village dump with a madman as overseer. As Goldhanger was a tiny village and Fish Street no more than a narrow lane, they could not avoid meeting each other. Each encounter fuelled a battle that would never, *could* never be finalised. The combat had no middle ground where possible arbitration could take place.

But we had come to work and earn money. Mr Frost had a perfect job for us. Laid out in front of the open kitchen door were several mahogany beams ordered through local woodyards and a large satchel of finely honed steel chisels from Harrod's. Mr Frost, deeply disturbed by any stories about war, had come by what he thought would be a perfect solution of that awful Mau-Mau business in Kenya: art to soothe the savage breast. To get the Africans started, he had sketched out the wood scenes and motifs he thought conducive to a peaceful and pastoral life. To underline his point, these crude drawings of a plough, a smoking pipe and a cow were interspersed with other subjects to be avoided, symbols he believed promoted disquiet and death: a rifle, a bottle of gin and a naked woman. He intended that these pictorial guides and admonitions should be carved in bas-relief and sent with instructions to the tribesmen. For a week or so we made sporadic forays from our tent to Goldhanger, hammering and chiselling out Mr Frost's ethical pictographs as he directed our efforts. Each night we would walk back to our tent, hands blistered, happy with a pound or two in our pockets.

When the second part of Eric's prize money arrived, our visits stopped. We were free again. This instalment seemed to go more quickly than the first and, as the money diminished, we had our first real disagreement of the summer. I suggested again that I should go and work at one of the nearby fruit farms. Not only was I considering our current situation but I realised that I would need some money for the coming term. I couldn't and didn't expect Dad to pay for my studentship. I gathered that Eric somehow saw this as a bid for financial independence and felt threatened. No matter how many times I explained and tried to assure him that since we were together and I was living off his money, whatever I had in the future would be ours, not mine, he would not be convinced. He explained that he would win many more prizes and I shouldn't worry about money as he would make enough for both of us. He underlined this by telling me that he wanted me to be with him, that he *needed* me to be with him, and my going to work would ruin our holiday. I let myself be persuaded, and it set a pattern for our future together.

Other clouds hovered over our idyll. Two very swishy queens had discovered our campsite and haunted it for several days. They were both fat and greasy and I was repulsed by their effeminate gesturing, the constant 'my dear' that underlined almost every sentence, and angered by their referring to me as 'a chicken' or 'she'. Their intrusion on our holiday fuelled my anger. They took for granted a comradeship cemented by our mutual sharing of a common sexuality, a bond that neither Eric nor myself felt or wanted.

One evening I was tired and went to bed early, leaving the tent flap untied for Eric's return; he was visiting the Cuthbertsons. I was awakened by a none-too-gentle shaking. I don't know if they had seen Eric leaving and thought I'd be an easy conquest, or if in desperation had hoped for a foursome. Whatever, they were in the tent uninvited. By the light of a torch, before I was fully awake, they were showing me photographs of boys having sex together and drawings by Quaintance, a forerunner and major influence on Tom of Finland, and groping me under the blankets. On seeing the photographs I was excited, and although intrigued by the glossy black-and-whites, I was angry at their effrontery and their needy pawing at my body. 'No jammies for her,' one of them remarked. That was it. Leaping out of the tent, I ordered them to leave or I would report them to the police, a threat that I plucked from my childhood.

They met Eric returning from the Cuthbertsons. He was furious, accusing me of inviting them in for sex behind his back. Still seething over their unwanted intrusion I shouted back, insulted by his inference that I would be unfaithful. I was even more angry that he could think I was so lacking in discrimination that I would choose those two caricatures for my act of betrayal. We slept apart that night and for several days were distant and polite with each other.

A short time after this I returned from a shopping expedition in town and found Eric inside our tent with a young boy. This time, I exploded. Although they were dressed, I could see that Eric was sexually aroused. He had one arm around the boy, his hand under the hem of his shorts. The poor child – he was about fourteen years old – must have wondered who this fury was that leapt upon him and literally threw him out. Eric was very dignified, making me feel I had overreacted – which I believed I had until

I found that Eric had given the boy my treasured pair of sandals, and that this wasn't his first visit.

In the last weeks of our holiday we moved. We had an offer from a man who lived on a barge a mile or so downriver from Heybridge Basin. This was where the canal emptied through lock gates into the Blackwater estuary, and was another extraordinary place. Like much of Maldon and its surrounds, Heybridge Basin gave the impression of isolation from a world gathering up speed to rush into the second half of the twentieth century.

On the left side of the lock was a low promontory and in its centre, looking out over the estuary but screened from public view by tall, thick privet hedges, was a ramshackle clapboard tea-house, its white paint cracked and peeling, its many windows glazed over with layers of salt. Here we had our afternoon pot of tea and scones. The hedge kept out every sound except the cries of the gulls and the wind whistling through the telephone lines. The silence was amplified by an almost total lack of customers. Just as we had done on our marshland peninsula, we felt we were on an island, cut off and separate from the outside world. It was a strange, haunted place that drew us back again and again to savour its remoteness.

On the other side of the tea-house, tucked into a corner made by the promontory and the sea wall, was a shingle beach. This was unusual, since the Blackwater's famous mud was ubiquitous. Here Eric made another splendid drawing, again in pen and sepia ink, of the decaying and gutted ships and boats left to rot. The man from the barge approached Eric, admired his work and invited us to stay on with him. He wanted the panels around the inside of the craft painted with scenes from the war. He was willing to pay a small fee and to provide us with occasional meals. He made a superb goulash, thick and rich, and tasty chicken stews. So we moved in. He lived in a little cabin perched on the deck and bred miniature pomeranians. At the time of our stay there must have been twenty or more of them. A fluffy mass, they scampered noisily from one end of the barge to the other, defying my attempts at friendship. We had the cavernous interior to ourselves. Sparsely furnished with a few kitchen chairs and a pine kitchen table, two gas-rings powered by a bombola, it was all we needed. But it was the bed, a large creaky double bed, that persuaded us. Living apart, Eric renting a tiny room at Mrs Whittle's, and me at home, being in bed together was a rare luxury.

With Eric painting the war panels, I could sit at the table and concentrate on my dress-design assignment, keeping the sheets of paper free from grass and mud stains. Here I came under fire, however. Dress design was considered effete and of no value. It wasn't art according not only to Eric but to the rest of the painters at Walthamstow. Eric took exception to my neatly drawn and delicate watercolour-tinted pages of ideas for suits, dresses and evening-gowns. Why didn't I draw more freely and use charcoal or conté instead of a fine pencil or pen line? Why did I design clothes only for tall, thin women? Why not for short, fat women? Why indeed was I a dress designer, something his friends at the Royal Academy Schools found great joy in sneering at? Why indeed? Helplessly in love, I was swayed by Eric's dictates and my work suffered. I didn't care. I had something far more important in my life.

Moored against the sea wall, only a few yards from the barge, was a small, dilapidated pontoon, a landing craft angled at low tide on a mud bank which we bought for a few pounds. A previous owner had built a sturdy plywood superstructure over the shell of the boat. Narrow and damp, lit by day with four small windows and at night with a carriage candle lamp, it was our first home together. Knowing nothing about boats, we repainted the superstructure inside and out but neglected the bottom – not that we could have done much to it since the nearest dry dock was at Maldon, and the expense of towing and docking would have been too much for us anyway.

From a book of Dürer woodcuts Eric copied a florid piece of lettering. Because it was in German, we had no idea what it meant but in black paint it had style and elegance on our white front door. And in our little craft we happily spent the last part of the summer, working and loving together undisturbed.

Every day of that glorious summer seemed a total joy, a gift. We were in love and becoming closer and closer. I pushed whatever I didn't like or didn't want aside. I revered Eric; in spite of an inner voice that was still troubled and wary, but which I refused to heed, he was fast becoming a god in my eyes, and he did nothing to discourage my adoring deification of him. I was with a man who told me he loved me and that we would be together forever, and that for me was everything.

Walthamstow, 1955–56

THE AUTUMN TERM BEGAN. THE DRAWINGS I HAD PRODUCED in Maldon – thick, heavy painterly drawings with applications of gouache impasto, little detail and no indication of how the clothes I drew could be made – were greeted with outrage by Daphne Brooker, and I redrew them according to her dictum: pages of delicate pencil sketches coloured with patches of lightly applied watercolour and small swatches of fabric pinned to the corners. I felt satisfied with these. Daphne, an excellent teacher as far as the craft of making clothes was concerned, had tastes that, like her, were refined, middle-of-the-road and so middle class that I felt stifled. I had a continual stream of ideas that she rejected as being too vulgar or impractical. Whether they were or not, I never got the chance to find out.

Daphne loathed the new energy in fashion exemplified by *Harper's Bazaar*. Encouraged by the eccentric imagination of Diana Vreeland, Richard Avedon, working for *Harper's*, changed the way *haute couture* was photographed, brought high fashion out into the real world and in doing so changed the concept of frigid exclusion forever. Before Avedon, models were posed stiffly in tastefully elegant settings that had little to do with anything in the real world. Fashion was for the few and the privileged, and the general public could look but not touch. By photographing beautiful women in beautiful clothes in the street, at the circus, sometimes in very ordinary working-class settings, Avedon initiated the idea that fashion was for everyone. It was not a precious, delicate hot-house bloom to be viewed from a distance, but a strong healthy plant that could grow and thrive anywhere.

I remember a series of pictures of Suzy Parker, the beautiful red-haired American that Avedon photographed in Paris; one in particular stands out: gloriously voluptuous, her breasts round and full and pushing out from her dress, she is running down a dark street towards the camera. Alive and passionate, it thrilled me. 'It's not fashion,' Daphne said. 'It has nothing to do with fashion.' Certainly it had nothing to do with her own conventional approach, but for me it had everything to do with the sexiness, the immediacy of clothes.

We design students were expected to produce variations on the current fashions, pastiches of Dior that had none of the master's excitement or daring. I designed some strange clothes based on Goya paintings but with a definite bias towards the circus – nothing like the A-line then being pushed down our throats. I wanted to explore, to explode with the energy, the excitement of being alive, in love and in art school. The colours I used were gaudy with zigzags, polkadots and stripes. I had just discovered art deco, at that time really out of fashion. Fascinated by its anarchic, break-the-rules vulgarity, I wanted to use it. The clothes were bouncy with layers of frills, like the dress of a flamenco dancer but with extremely short skirts and exaggerated sleeves and little bustles. Daphne was horrified and tore them up. I was made to feel as though I had defecated on the altar of fashion; I returned to the A-line and plodded on grimly.

Back at college, I was seeing a lot of Fin. He had taken to launching himself on me without warning, and I would find myself thrown to the floor in silent, ostensibly desperate wrestling matches. Fin, his face red and strained with effort, would become frantic with a desire to pin me to the floor and hold me there. Neither of us would win or surrender, and the bouts would end as suddenly as they began. I enjoyed the wrestling, matching my strength against his, but at times the ferocity of his attacks surprised and puzzled me.

We played a lunchtime game, a typical boys' game of daring and bravado which would also, I hoped, cure me of vertigo. We would line up the waist-high cutting tables in the dress-design room, two or three of them on a level with the open windows, and launch ourselves into space. Only when airborne did we grab the vertical bar dividing the windows and swing back round into the room. Building up speed and working ourselves into a frenzy, yelling and shouting with excitement, we jumped, tempting fate again and again, feeling completely invulnerable in our adolescent daring. The secretary to the college principal, coming through the gates, saw my orange-jerseyed figure leaping out (the art department was on the top floor) and fainted. She believed she had witnessed a suicide, and our game came to a sudden halt after the threat of expulsion and a lecture on behaviour.

We again came close to being expelled after a spontaneous party in the college. One evening, several of us got together in the still-life room. The college was closed and, we thought, empty. Lighting a small fire on a sheet of metal, we sat around it, drinking happily. Ken Russell and his future wife Shirley were dancing about when our innocently illicit bacchanal came to a halt as the principal burst into the room. Taking his regular nightly walk around the building he had heard voices coming from the sculpture room in the basement and had discovered two half-naked students there, a boy and a girl, having sex. From them he garnered there was a party upstairs.

Next morning, suitably grim-faced, Stuart lined us up for a lecture. Having successfully pleaded on our behalf with the principal, he felt that he could righteously thunder over our misdeeds, but Stuart was an incapable Jove and our giggling was barely suppressed.

Jürgen came back into our lives. He had separated from his wife and taken a back room in a row of once grand but now dilapidated Edwardian houses graced with a large sign: The Cumberland Hotel or Cumber Ho. The sign, once neon-lit, was in as bad a state of repair as the houses. They faced a sea-green, tree-lined park, Highbury Fields. Eric and I occasionally spent the weekend there with him, the three of us sallying forth for a Friday- or Saturday-night tour of pubs and clubs. The Duragon became a favourite, with talent night a special draw. The master of ceremonies, a tall, fleshy queen, commanded the stage to introduce with quite unsubtle references to genital size and sexual stamina the latest acquisition to his stable of young men.

Unfamiliar with the microphone and changing key regularly when finding a note or phrase too high or too low, the would-be crooner gathered more good-natured ribbing than applause. 'Give 'em a chance, give 'em a chance!' shrieked the compère, torn between laughing at and protecting his chunky ward. Undeterred, the aspiring songster would return several times throughout the evening, his voice and confidence strengthened by ordeal so that by closing time he was often passably adept. Eric was welcomed royally by the young queens, but they never hid their resentment at my being with him.

Once, coming to collect us at Walthamstow, Jürgen had met Fin and become enamoured. I can't say 'fell in love with' as I can't envisage Jürgen ever being in love, ever able to free himself to give without question or thought. He was prone to crushes but I could always see his mind at work calculating, weighing out the pros and cons and making decisions based not on joy but on advantage.

We now were an unbalanced foursome on our nights out, with Fin by the evening's end usually drunk and helpless and Jürgen taking advantage of that. Back at Jürgen's, Eric and I could hear sounds coming from their bed – stifled grunts and Fin's occasional cry, muffled in the pillows or by Jürgen's mouth. Jürgen used to boast that he fucked Fin several times a night yet Fin told me he never did and added that he never kissed Jürgen, only allowing the older man to give him a non-reciprocal blow-job or come between his legs.

In the morning, Jürgen would pull back the covers on their bed and crouched or leaning over Fin, would noisily suck him off while my friend would pretend to sleep. This display for my benefit and Eric's was, I suppose, an attempt at claiming something which, for Jürgen, was unclaimable. The sound of their sex at night and the sight of Fin's slim brown body stretched out and then convulsing in orgasm stirred something in me which I refused to acknowledge as lust.

In our second year together people at college were beginning to talk about Eric and me. One lunchtime at the long table (the art school table in the college canteen) Howard began sympathising about the flak levelled at me. He had been subjected to the same snide remarks during his friendship with Eric. Suddenly Fin spoke up. 'I think I'm going to try homosexuality for a bit,' he declared, bringing the general conversation to an embarrassed halt. He had spoken the taboo word out loud.

'I can truly recommend it,' I replied, trying to be flippant but inwardly furious – 'try homosexuality for a bit', as though he were contemplating a new painting technique or a diet.

As Fin spoke he stared at me with what seemed to be an undeclared challenge that I completely misread. I wanted to hit him – and did, soundly, several days later during one of our wrestling matches. I was so angry that I hurt him. Afterwards, in a rush of guilt, I walked away, unable to apologise or offer comfort to the huddled, groaning figure on the ground behind me. He limped around for several days and, at last, unable to bear the silent reproach in his eyes, in his whole demeanour, I apologised though without saying anything about why I'd hurt him or why I'd felt so angry.

Eric's promised prizes hadn't materialised and, desperate for money, I took a morning job delivering newspapers. This meant getting up at 4.30 a.m. for a two-hour jaunt around the better parts of Forest Gate. Classes didn't end until nine in the evening, and after an hour of beer-drinking at The Bell pub, then sex and my walk home, I was only getting about five hours' sleep a night. The job came to an abrupt end when, after a weekend spent posing naked for Eric and two friends from the Slade School in their unheated attic studio behind Mount Pleasant post office, I developed a bad cold which turned into bronchitis.

Fin came on a visit with good wishes from Janet, Sylvia Ayton and Josie.

Eric entrusted Fin with a note to me and a cotton bag on a cord to go round my neck. I never found out what the bag was stuffed with – a gypsy's cure, was all Eric told me. The note was rather formal, instructing me to wear the amulet around my neck and to throw it away when I was well again. It would absorb whatever was wrong with me and must not be opened, since this would release the illness back into the world. The note ended with his love. I was sure that Eric's charm had cured me but it was the only time he used it, although I had several more bronchial bouts over the next few years. Fin stayed for several hours and, neither of us being in a talkative mood, just sat holding my hand in the silences between his recounting the happenings at Walthamstow and at his home.

In a few days I was well but jobless. A more efficient paperboy had taken over during my absence.

We dress designers were given painting lessons by Maggy Greene, of whom we were in awe. Good-looking, poised and elegant, her voice a sophisticated drawl which came to us through clouds of cigarette smoke, she eulogised the sensual pleasure of bathing with her lover. To our amazement, she recommended we try it with our lovers. Conducting her discourse with elegant strokes of her long cigarette-holder, she was to us, far more than anyone we knew, the epitome of style. She informed the class that although my paintings were ahead of the rest at that moment, it would be easy to overtake me. According to Maggy I was a dilettante, a word used often at Walthamstow. In almost the same breath she informed us that I would be in prison before I was twenty-five. 'What for?' I demanded, surprised and dismayed. Her pronouncement, uttered in a low, affected drawl, shocked me. 'Oh, just about everything,' she replied, smiling.

For a moment I was back in the garage, frightened, until I realised the rules had changed. There were no grown-ups to threaten exposure. I was free. Free, I thought, to be what I wanted.

During the summer term I allowed that deliciously intoxicating freedom to overwhelm me. I made a pair of skin-tight red satin trousers and wore them with my hair bleached white, a pale-green silk shirt, green eyeshadow and bare feet, becoming what I believed to be the incarnation of bohemianism.

In the England of 1956 my appearance must have been startling. The very most our conventional dress code allowed were Teddy Boy variations on the omnipresent suit, but apart from a few truck drivers giving vent and one refusal to serve me in a pub because I was shoeless, my bizarre appearance went unremarked. Had anyone made a connection between this sudden flowering and my sexuality, I would have been surprised. I considered my appearance to have everything to do with being an art student, and the thought I might at the same time be celebrating the repressed feminine side of my nature never occurred to me – and the idea would have been hotly denied or dismissed should anyone else have suggested it.

One Saturday I returned from an early shopping trip to find a note from Eric. He and Fin had gone to Maldon to check on our boat. It seemed a long way to go for sex – but if it was for any other reason, why hadn't they waited for me? I got very drunk and by the time they returned I had passed out. This time I made no scene. I was too hurt and kept my feelings hidden. Eric had promised me a monogamous and ideal life, without secrets, truly 'making love'. But this seemed so blatant and totally at odds with everything he had said to me about our life together.

The term 'making love', for me then and now, has little to do with the sex act. It signified, and still does, two people coming together and the day-to-day learning to trust, the constructing of affection and love, making a life. Sex is a part of this – a healthy and happy part – but to call the sex act 'making love' denigrates both it and the more important building of a union. As the angel says to Barbarella, 'Angels don't *make* love, they *are* love,' and I thought of Eric and myself as angels, albeit earthbound ones.

The next time Fin and I had a wrestling bout we had to be separated. I had hit him in the face and the blood ran from his nose down his chin. We fought as if we were going to kill each other. After this we adopted a strained and formal politeness which continued even on our nights out.

Fin and I were encouraged to walk about naked in Jürgen's room. I felt like a tart: two naked boys putting on a show for a couple of punters. It was so unlike the times when Eric and I were alone, when I was completely relaxed and natural without clothes. But Eric insisted so I complied. He began a drawing, a composite of Fin and me merging, our faces and bodies together in one image. It was never finished.

One rainy evening when the four of us had been drinking the sweet Cyprus sherry that seemed then to be his wine of choice, Jürgen suggested Fin and I have sex together while he and Eric watched. Had we been sober I'm sure Eric and I would have ignored him. As it was, Eric concurred with Jürgen's proposal, the two of them urging us on. Rubbing our bellies together, kissing hesitantly in an awkward embrace, I began to hump Fin, bending my knees a little and easing my erection between his thighs. This excited him and his kisses became passionate and deep, sucking and chewing at my mouth. I pulled away and got dressed, sitting by myself for the rest of the evening.

Highbury, London N5

WE TRIED TO RECAPTURE OUR FIRST SUMMER TOGETHER, switching between the tent and the boat. Although during much of the holiday we had a great time, we couldn't match the euphoria of the previous year. Besides, it rained constantly, a typical English summer of cold damp days and colder nights. Shut inside the narrow confines of the boat – or worse, the even smaller tent – we eventually gave up and stayed with Jürgen. I made a token show of resistance but soon realised that if we wanted to be together and dry we had no other choice. Fin had left and there were just the three of us again when Jürgen took us on outings into the countryside and down to the south coast.

One day we drove up the Thames valley to Cookham. Settling Jürgen in a pub, Eric and I descended upon Sir Stanley Spencer in his tiny red-brick Victorian terraced house. I imagine it was his daughter who let us in. Spencer greeted us as though we were old friends and led us upstairs to a room that had been turned into an inconveniently small studio. I found it unbelievable that no one – no patron, no organisation – had come forward to find a decent workspace for him. In the last year or so of his life he was given a studio, but it was decades late.

Spencer was a mural painter at heart. He and Diego Rivera seem the only important exponents of this major aspect of the visual arts in the twentieth century. Yet whereas Rivera is known internationally, Spencer's genius and reputation haven't as yet crossed the Atlantic. Both painters had an intense idiosyncratic vision and style and both were anecdotal, but I feel Spencer had a lyricism and a passion not found in the Mexican's work which link him to a direct line of great Florentine painters in the Early Renaissance. From his Slade School paintings, his richly monumental self-portraits of 1913, the early *Resurrection* in the Tate Gallery, through the *Burghclere* and *Clyde* side murals to a *Crucifixion* completed in 1959, the year of his death, his energy and passion were rarely diminished.

Spencer often bewailed the weakening or loss of his vision but, though it occasionally faltered, it never left him. His 1959 *Crucifixion*, with its acknowledgements to Bosch and Breughel, show how clear and forceful it was even near death. The painting is cut in half by the horizontal bar of Christ's cross. Christ has his back to us. His head is turned, grim-faced, to the sky while a grinning goblin of a man with a tasselled red stocking-hat, nails in his mouth, hammers Christ's hand to the beam. A shrieking thief throws himself forward towards the figure of Christ in a effort to escape. Another executioner, also with nails in his mouth, his arm curled around his head, hammer in hand, stares at the struggling thief with pig-like anticipation.

On the ground is a massive figure of Mary, almost part of the hill itself. She lays her face, sorrowful and resigned, to the stony soil. In the background are the roofs and walls of Cookham, a group of villagers leaning expectantly from the windows of one building.

The painting crackles with the electric energy of a much younger man. The composition is a series of angles and cantilevers, with the bars of the three crosses making a crazy, jagged half-circle, all balanced by the upright posts. Each figure, from the man nailing Christ to the tense expectancy of the viewers at the window, vibrates with a pulsating force. Only Mary and Christ are quiet: Mary, earthbound in her grief, and Christ, who anchors the painting, his upward gaze transcending human emotion, awaiting the miraculous reunion with his father. Separate and apart.

Spencer was working on a large canvas when we visited him. It was almost the height of the room but was rolled up at each end, leaving only part of it visible. The subject was Christ preaching at Cookham regatta, and it was still unfinished when he died. In the foreground we could see a man in a cap carrying oars and a mop, and behind him Christ leaning forward in an Edwardian straw chair. Meticulously squared up, Spencer had outlined in pencil the complete painting from smaller working drawings.

He brought out sheet after sheet of his red chalk and pencil drawings to show us. Women in long dresses of the 1930s and men in shirt-sleeves and braces. Couples embracing in punts and standing listening to the sermon. We were shown several of his 'pot-boilers': realistic, meticulously painted views, sparklingly observed and realised with an affection that, however much he might dismiss them, glowed in every detail. While they form a definite pictorial record of the English countryside and village life during the first half of the century, they are also powerful and exciting paintings.

We drank tea in the kitchen and he told us the now famous story of how he posed for the 'legs' in a painting his first wife did of their maid.

Although nothing like him either physically or in the way his life and home were organised, Spencer somehow reminded me of Crawshay Frost:

both were eccentric and both had an internalised vision of great intensity – Frost's vision, though traumatised and broken by his experiences in the First World War, and Spencer's strengthened and made certain.

In my third year at Walthamstow I was awarded a grant, a weekly stipend of three pounds. With this to finance my rent, food, painting materials and pleasure, I left Dames Road and Dad and moved into the Cumberland Hotel in Highbury, north London. My room was the central space of a second-floor room, partitioned with thin sheets of plywood to produce three narrow corridors. A bed, wash-basin and gas-ring were completed by a minuscule wardrobe wedged against the bed.

My neighbour on one side was a man from Pakistan. Day or night and in a very strong accent, he would spontaneously break into a rendition of a Johnnie Ray song, 'Just Walking in the Rain'. He accompanied himself by stomping on the floor or pounding the partition. The singing would bring on a fit of coughing and hawking, each sound graphic and clear through the flimsy plywood. But I had left home and could deal with anything.

The 'room' on the other side was vacant for a week – and then Fin rented it. Several nights later, sitting talking on his bed, he leaned towards me. 'Please,' he said, kissed me and burst into tears. I held him as he cried, stroking his head and rocking him like a baby. As his tears subsided into choked hiccoughs, he began laughing and kissing me. It was like taking a mirror image, a darker image of myself. Although facially we weren't alike, physically we were very similar. Fin's dark pubic bush matched my blond hairs. Our erections were the same length and width, and when I entered him, it felt that I was somehow entering myself.

During the night, as we lay sweat-covered and panting in each other's arms, he promised not to tell anyone. But it was a promise unasked by me for I knew I must let Eric know.

In the morning Fin refused to speak to me. I was totally confused and upset by his silence and not looking forward to the evening's confrontation with Eric. Surprisingly, though, Eric took the news calmly and instead of our usual trek to Epping Forest he returned with me all the way to Highbury. Knowing that Fin was next door and that he could hear everything, Eric made a great deal of noise in bed that night, his claiming of me. The next day he decided to leave Mrs Whittle's altogether and take a large room at the Cumberland. Using the whole of my grant as rent in advance and Eric's wages from his weekly class at Walthamstow, we reckoned we could manage. As Eric and I made plans to move in together, Fin moved out of the hotel and went back to live with his parents. We were friends

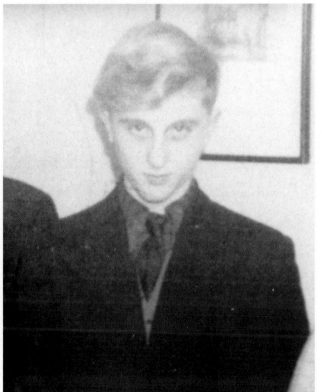

ABOVE LEFT
Me aged two in the garden at
Knight's Road, Silvertown,
1939

ABOVE RIGHT
A pageboy at Frank and
Mary's wedding, Barkingside

LEFT
Me aged fourteen or fifteen
at Thornton Heath

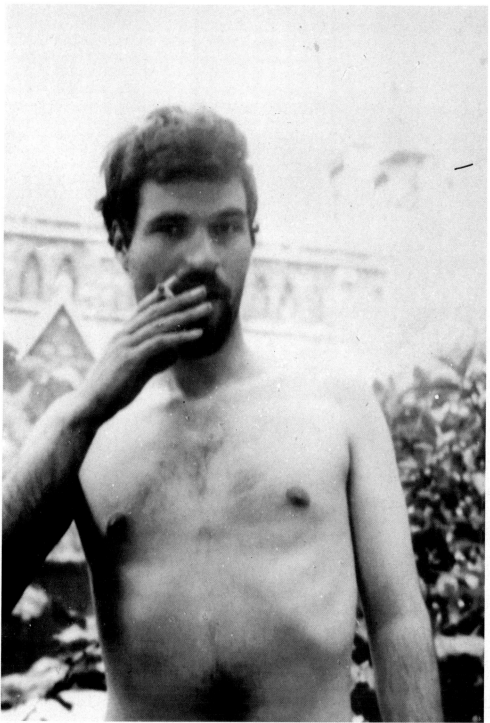

Eric in the front garden of the Cumberland Hotel, London, 1959
(photo: Collection Janet Deuters)

OPPOSITE
Looking rather sulky – and I'm *not* wearing eyeliner, London, 1959

OPPOSITE TOP
Sylvia and Janet at the
window of 'our' room,
Cumberland Hotel, 1960
(photo: Collection Janet Deuters)

OPPOSITE BOTTOM
Janet and me dancing in Park
Lane, 1961
(photo: William Kempster;
Collection Janet Deuters)

ABOVE
Janet, Eric and Mr Davis in
the front garden of the
Cumberland, 1959
(photo: Collection Janet Deuters)

LEFT
Marie Gray and friend,
Piazza Navona, Rome, 1966

Eric, Janet (in shadow) and me in the 'Pompeian' room, Piazza Paganica, 1963

La dolce vita, 1964. A party at Paul Cooper's flat. From left to right: Janet, Anne Francine (American actress), me, a British friend, Ferrill and two friendly Italian boys

again but still distant, with Fin unwilling to discuss what had occurred between the three of us.

Eric and I rented a large, bay-windowed front room with a view of the vicarage across the road. As we had no curtains and never thought of obtaining any, this became a two-way exchange. Our single beds 'for two gentlemen sharing' (our landlord's description of us) we arranged end to end in an L-shape. There was a wash-basin, a gas cooker and a gas fire against the far wall where the fireplace had once been, and next to it a cupboard for crockery and food. Not much was stored there since as soon as we bought any food we ate it.

On our first night together we found our beds alive. Even after much searching we couldn't trace our attackers who, obviously not having eaten for some time, came out in swarms to feast. In the morning, after much scratching and interrupted sleep, small itchy red bites speckled our bodies. We called in Mr Davis, thinking it had to be fleas, but our landlord told us the invisible army of the night were bed bugs. With much chuckling, he sprayed the underside of our mattresses with a mixture of DDT and paraffin, annihilating the problem.

For some unknown reason, Mr Davis allowed us to rent this big, well-lit, airy room for three pounds a week. He informed us that he had considered dividing it up to make more skinny corridors like the one in which I had been living, since this division would bring in an extra pound or two. Before any agreement was reached, though, he took us for an interview with a mysterious figure, Mr Pinkus, owner (so he informed us) of the Cumberland conglomorate. Mr Pinkus appeared on rent day in the ground-floor front room. Languid and soft-spoken he, like Mr Davis, seemed intrigued by us. We handed over my entire grant as payment in advance. As Eric said, this at least guaranteed a roof over our heads, and I couldn't argue with that.

As Eric's prize money was slow in making its appearance, we were soon forced to ask for some of our advance back. Mr Davis found this amusing. No one, according to him, had ever paid so much in advance, and certainly no other tenant had reclaimed their money so quickly.

Mr Davis always insisted he was only a hired manager, caretaker and odd-job man, but it didn't take Eric and me very long to unravel his cover. The mysterious Mr Pinkus, we worked out, was his older brother, whose sudden absence for several years, Eric believed was the result of a prison sentence.

Mr Davis was an extraordinary man, full of energy and good humour, obsessed with money – obtaining it, not spending it. A Dickensian character who, though at odds with the London of the 1950s, had found a niche for himself in Highbury, he played his role as manager with verve and enjoyed his own eccentricities as much as the foibles and adventures of his tenants. 'By Christ, gentlemen,' he would announce, always knocking before he entered our room, to regale us with yet another epic tale of the Cumberland: tenants leaving in the night owing several weeks' rent, or hospitalised after a fit or an overdose, or the successful suicides who sometimes were not discovered for a week or longer.

Apart from a never-ending scuttling through his domain, unblocking baths and lavatories, arguing with tenants, clearing out the rooms and possessions of the departed and the dead, Mr Davis had no life of his own. He lived in a small cubbyhole under the front steps which, after the sudden and unexplained departure of his brother, became the Manager's Office, graced with a sign painted by Eric.

Several times a month Mr Davis could be found in the back garden destroying furniture left behind at the close of a street market. One afternoon, after a titanic struggle to bring a baby grand piano through the basement, I watched enthralled as he attacked it with a sledgehammer. When the elegant black instrument was reduced to a heap of splintered wood and tangled wire, he stepped back, smiling and sweating. 'By Christ,' he remarked, 'no one's going to play that again in a hurry.'

Another time I came up on him, hammer in hand, he was in the final stages of demolishing a large seventeenth-century chest. He made me pay before he would allow me to retrieve two sweet female caryatids, slightly weathered, carved in oak. One had a keyhole in her stomach. The remains of several other figures lay smashed into the ground with the rest of the cassone. He would attack sideboards, chairs, armoires, chests of drawers, destroying them and afterwards making a celebratory bonfire with the remains. I found pieces of several neo-classical chairs, ebonised and gilded with a broken claw foot, and splintered bits of delicate inlay.

Apart from a chronic shortage of money and the resultant lack of food, life with Eric was good. Once we existed for two weeks on spaghetti and cheddar cheese. The highlight of that fortnight was a soup made from boiled potatoes, milk and an Oxo beef bouillon cube. During that time we walked halfway across London to reclaim a few shillings a fellow student had borrowed. Naturally he didn't have any money but he did have a couple of eggs, which Eric and I shared with him.

Being hungry seemed a natural extension of my childhood, and with Eric as a companion we turned our quest for food into an adventure. Once he picked the lock on our gas meter, retrieving handfuls of shillings and sixpences. Instead of spending wisely or restocking our empty larder, we took a number 19 bus into town and feasted on escallope, spaghetti, chips and rough red wine in the white-tiled cellar of Jimmy the Greek, celebrating a break in several weeks of privation.

'Well, then, by my life, what's this, gentlemen?' asked a shocked Mr Davis with the empty gas-meter box in his hands. He often left the collection of gas money for several months so he could enjoy the weight of pounds of silver coins in the canvas bag he carried with him. At first we attempted to deny it but eventually confessed. I was puzzled by his attitude. There were no threats, no demands for immediate repayment; he seemed amused. 'I never expected this from you gentlemen, by Christ, I didn't,' were as far as his admonitions went.

Here in our room with a view, Eric and I were truly making love and building a new life. We did our laundry together and shopped in the High Street, partners in volatile domestic bliss. I bought *Plats du Jour* and an Elizabeth David cookbook, and eventually learned to cook well.

Peter Greenham, a successful society portrait painter, was a visitor (i.e. a teacher) at the Academy Schools, and had become a friend of Eric, who invited him to dinner. I stretched my limited skills and prepared what was for us, in our straitened circumstances, a luxurious meal.

The evening began well. Peter regaled us with stories of his eccentric aunt who had conceived a loathing for people with red hair. She kept a supply of ripe tomatoes by her open window and would throw them at any titianed head which passed by. We had bought several bottles of cheap but good red wine in Soho and this helped the evening along, and perhaps fuelled what came next. I cannot recall the starting point, the spark that ignited the ensuing eruption, but suddenly Eric and I were fighting. The table was overturned as, in a scattering of food and china, we rolled onto the floor. Crying out that I was leaving for good, I ran out into the street, praying Eric would come after me. He did and held me in his arms, telling me he loved me. Reconciled, we returned, expecting to continue the evening. To our amazement, Peter had left. We couldn't understand it; there was dessert, a creamy trifle, to come, as well as unserved coffee percolating and a minute amount of cheap brandy to go with it.

I took Maggy Green's advice and bathed once or sometimes twice a week with my lover. The large Victorian cast-iron bath, shared by approximately twenty other tenants, needed a thorough cleaning before we could use it, with sheets of newspaper spread out on the filthy floor. Once installed, we were lavish with our money, feeding it into the gas meter to ensure a constant and plentiful supply of hot water.

Janet and I left the dress-design department and joined the painters. After two years of intimidation by Eric, I was surprised to find, when I announced my decision to change, that he allied himself with Stuart and Daphne and the college principal, all of whom lectured me at great length on the inadvisability of forsaking what, I was informed, could be a glittering career. Janet went through much the same ordeal without the extra pressure from Eric.

Once I actually began painting, Eric initially proved to be helpful and instructive and then he would suddenly turn and in a fury tell me to go and paint somewhere else. He twice threw my easel, palette, brushes, paintings and drawings out the window. Maybe it was the subject matter. I had started on a series of lovers – heterosexual, of course, all the images of love around us were heterosexual; I never thought to question this, I just accepted the status quo.

My lovers series disturbed Eric profoundly. 'All you ever think about is sex!' he would yell. Totally unaware that these images of men and women passionately entwined could be seen by him as a threat to our security, a sign that I might be interested in women, I blithely continued.

Eric was having his own problems. When he moved into the Cumberland he had accidentally left behind at Mrs Whittle's a large pile of drawings under his bed. Mrs Whittle (who viewed Eric as a prospective husband for her daughter Mary) had thrown them away. Most of his early work and drawings of Howard and me were lost. Eric, understandably, was distraught. Apart from writing a letter of fury and scorn to his ex-landlady, as I did, there was nothing either of us could do. Thankfully, the Maldon series and the drawings of elms on which he was working when we met were stored at the Academy Schools and so escaped destruction. But I mourned a long, intricate drawing covering two or three sheets, full of whirling planets and stars amongst which I danced and leapt, naked and joyous. It was the only mystically fantastic drawing I remember Eric attempting.

In my first year at Walthamstow, Eric had painted a full-length life-size portrait of one of the students, Donald Upchurch. Using a Frans Hals palette of earth colours, it aroused a good deal of comment, both for and against. The drawing of the figure was admired but the dark, Old Master flavour was at odds with current favourites Sickert, Bonnard and Vuillard and their pastel colours.

At the Cumberland Eric turned the canvas round and painted a portrait of Fin's girlfriend on the back. Homosexuality having been tried and found wanting, Fin had decided he was now firmly heterosexual. On several occasions he and this girl appeared and spent the night in Eric's bed. Fin would behave as Jürgen had, making their coupling noisy and public; another claiming. In the mornings, like a handsome little game-cock strutting his erection across the barnyard of our room, he'd pee in the sink (we all used the sink – the lavatory was two floors up) before rejoining his girlfriend in bed to have sex. I wanted to watch but Eric wouldn't let me. Fin's attitude was a very definite 'up yours' to both of us, but he used our room because it was the only place he and his girlfriend could go. I should have found the situation embarrassing but instead it seemed vastly amusing.

For Eric's painting, Fin's young woman wore a blue-and-white striped dress and Eric chose an impressionist palette and technique in an attempt to win approval from his critics. Wedged between the high windows and the canvas, with no space for him to step back and view his work, the portrait, in spite of many reworkings, proved a failure. Layers of thick paint applied with a palette knife submerged his fine drawing. Early one morning we carried it up to the Academy Schools and there, with space to step back and consider it, it became clear how unsuccessful it was.

Undeterred, Eric produced a series of impressionist-inspired pictures of our room. With our wash-basin and white cupboard underneath, the bay windows with a view of the park beyond, a nude of Nancy by the gas fire and an exquisite still-life of Victoria plums in a bowl (which was later stolen), all radiant with light and colour, these interiors proved very successful. They gained Eric admittance to the Royal Society of British Artists. Proudly, and rightly so, he told me that he was the youngest artist ever to be accepted. Yet he wasn't happy with the paintings. Sneering at the selection committee and at his work, he called the paintings meaning-less trifles, a sop to the Walthamstow Sickert School.

Janet and Sylvia Ayton arrived for a visit one weekend afternoon and, delighted by the rural decay of Highbury, took a room a few streets away. Late on Sunday nights, Eric and I, lugging the huge transistor radio Peter had given me, would creep into their place and the four of us would listen to the latest hits from America on Radio Luxembourg. It was the only station in England that played them. Eric surprised and delighted me – for he had no interest in music at all – with Elvis's 'Teddy Bear', a single which I played repeatedly. I thought of him as my big teddy bear, cuddly and warm, but our displays of affection had to be kept strictly private. Once, as we were crossing the deserted courtyard of Burlington House, I took hold of his hand. 'Don't do that. People are watching,' he said. Looking around at the many windows, all seemingly empty, and still holding his hand, I replied, 'People! People! I don't care if people are watching!' But Eric's white-lipped, grim face silenced my exuberance. That some idiot policeman could caution or arrest us for holding hands or kissing in public never occurred to me, though I think Eric was more aware than I was.

Jürgen moved into the far end of the Cumberland, settling in with two boy hustlers, Lenny and Syphilis Rose. Rose, slim and blondly beautiful and only recently released from prison for fucking near Brighton racetrack, carried his queerness like a banner. Angry and defiant, he battled each and every day face on with a hostile world. Lenny, his none too bright stooge, shuffled behind his beautiful, angry friend, a sluggish wake to a dazzling comet.

I wanted Eric to draw them, especially when they were joined by another hustler, a dark and handsome boy we called the Black Widow, who was on the run from the army. The trio added a touch of ersatz glamour to the squalid eccentricity of the Cumberland that I felt should be noted and captured. I even thought a series of drawings of them and other boys would make for a good exhibition. My suggestion was quickly stamped on by Eric, who thought the idea grotesque and the boys repulsive.

Eric had begun work on a major painting, a life-size portrait group, eight feet by ten. I am at the centre in a Van Dyck pose (one, in fact, that the painter had Charles I adopt) with my left hand over the clasped hands of a young woman. Looking modest and forlorn in her hodge-podge student clothes, hers is the only figure not looking outwards. I'm still not sure that holding a woman's hand wasn't Eric's unconscious fears subtly expressed – his fear of losing me to a woman. Fin is there, in an awkward unsettled position, his arms bent, his hand held palm outward in a half wave as a tentative greeting, peering out from behind another student.

Eric painted us in the Academy Schools, formerly the stables of Burlington House, under electric light. The yellowish glow created havoc with the colouring and when the picture was taken upstairs to the daylight of the Academy salon, the alizarin crimson and garish greens and purples of the shadows completely unbalanced the picture.

He feverishly reworked it, again losing much of his fine drawing under the heavily applied paint. I thought it magnificent, the play of the light masterly. The quiet melancholy of us young men pausing to regard the viewer, our figures slashed by a diagonal of light, is strong and imposing. Painted fifty or a hundred years earlier, it would have garnered certain admiration and comment as a fine student work, but when exhibited in the Academy Schools show, it was mostly derided or ignored. I felt so angry and hurt for Eric and for the painting – they meant so much to me. Eric's style and the Old Master conception and execution, were totally at odds with the burgeoning movements in painting. 'Kitchen Sink' ideas were already passé and the New York School was opening eyes and minds with abstract expressionism and tachism. After the intense energy and hope with which he had produced his big portrait group, Eric was shaken by the almost total indifference shown towards it by others. He had thought this would be the first step on the stairway to success.

Eric was confused and depressed. In a desperate last effort of his student years, I helped take the portrait group canvas off its stretcher and turn it around so he could paint a pastoral, a mix of Puvis de Chauvannes and Courbet, on its back. In the place of the group of moody young men and one dumpy, self-effacing woman, Eric painted a group of naked young women in a green, sunlit landscape. But the figures and the landscape never coalesced. The realistically painted women were at odds with the invented landscape: both were anachronisms out of synch with contemporary life, produced using old-fashioned formulae. Eric was seeking an avenue, an arena in which he could display his many gifts, but, chained passionately to seventeenth-century Dutch painting, his great talent was proving almost a hindrance to him.

The big portrait group and the landscape having failed to gain the attention and the Prix de Rome in painting which we had both hoped for, Eric took Sir Henry Rushbury's advice and entered his wood engravings for the Rome scholarship. Sir Henry was then keeper of the Academy Schools and an admirer of Eric's work. Eric, Jürgen and I took a stall for a couple of weekends at a Hampstead open art show. We had framed a set of the tiny black-and-white prints, hoping to sell them. The subjects, taken from Gainsborough, Brueghel and several of Eric's own drawings, failed to find either an audience or a buyer. They were old-fashioned but not 'old-fashioned cute', they were not pretty and not in colour. Another disappointment.

I had acquired a German edition of the collected works of José Guadalupe Posada, and I raved about the energy of this brilliant Mexican engraver. Eric dismissed him as crude and amateurish, but Posada's subject matter fascinated me: Death as a partner in our everyday life – not as a 'grim reaper', the ever-watchful, never-sleeping shadowy attendant on our every breath, but dressed and acting out our life with us. I started to incorporate *calaveras* into my drawings of lovers but Eric found them 'unhealthy' and, under pressure, I stopped both the lovers and the death drawings, only tackling the subject again thirty-seven years later.

With his engravings and Sir Henry's support, Eric gained the Prix de Rome. Although rejoicing in his success, he was nevertheless hurt that it wasn't his paintings that had won the prize for him, telling me he felt less winning the engraving scholarship. We had believed the portrait group would somehow propel him into the limelight, setting him on the path to certain fame, attracting the equivalent attention that Moynihan's group portrait of the teachers at the Royal College of Art had produced.

Eric and his work meant far more to me now than my own. Absolutely immersed in his world, my own work became submerged in my efforts to support him. Eric's life, his hopes, his dreams, his day-to-day struggle, filled my world. I was the rapt worshipper, no longer an initiate, happy in ministering to the Artist. My teddy bear he may have been, but in return he demanded complete devotion and a disavowal of my own creativity. The chain was around my neck and I allowed him to lead me anywhere.

We sold our boat to Nancy and a new friend, Patsy Brogan, who was to move into the mysterious Mr Pinkus's room in the Cumberland. For me the craft felt soiled after Eric and Fin's visit, and since then I'd taken little pleasure in staying there. Having only repaired and repainted the super-structure while totally neglecting the hull, its condition was shaky. The two women moved in and in a few days, with curtains and cushions and little ornaments, had transformed the interior. They then decided to have it towed downriver to Tollesbury. It sank in mid-stream. The power boat they used moved too fast and, against an incoming tide, the tow hook was ripped out, taking part of the structure with it. Both Nancy and Patsy were aboard at the time and almost went down with the boat, only being rescued at the last moment. Although neither Eric nor I witnessed the disaster, the two women described it to us furiously, detailing every slow, submerging moment. The boat was eventually refloated and arrived at Tollesbury only to break free of its moorings during a high tide some time later and impale itself on a stake in the mudflats.

We left the Cumberland and moved into a tiny four-roomed seven-teenth-century cottage at the far end of the High Street, Janet and Sylvia taking on our old room. Gwyther Irwin, then enjoying popularity as a tachiste painter and printmaker, was our landlord, and kept the downstairs front room as a hideaway for himself. I enjoyed the energy and invention of Gwyther's large canvases, his assemblages of torn posters and cal-ligraphed white shapes bursting against a blackened ground, but once again I kept my opinions to myself for I could see Eric was seething and confused by Gwyther's success. Jealous, bitter and frustrated in his own attempts, he seemed to begrudge others their triumphs.

A standing portrait of me painted in the Mount Pleasant studio, with a white shirt, tight jeans, thick-soled suede shoes and my old duffelcoat draped across my shoulders, was shown at the Royal Society of Portrait Painters where it was well received and stood out in welcome contrast to the stodgy mass of dullness that made up the rest of the exhibition. Again, I suggested to Eric that he embark on a series of portraits of young men, some clothed, some not, but the idea got lost in the paintings of the large group and its aftermath.

I caught Eric on two occasions having sex with the Black Widow who, after serving a short sentence for going AWOL, had been thrown out of the army on account of his sexual preference. Another time, talking to Peter Greenham, I discovered that Eric had been lying when he told me he was having dinner at Peter's and then spending the night there. When I confronted him I felt like a shrew, and Eric's refusal to discuss these shabby digressions and his dismissive 'I would think more of you', only heightened those feelings. Compounding my insecurity, Eric began to weave his 'I can do what I like, you must do what I tell you' maxim into our fights. The arrogance of these sentiments shocked me, but I was so needy, in love and under his influence that I was helpless in my confusion.

Eric decided to walk to Italy during the summer. Having no money he approached Mr Davis, who unexpectedly guaranteed a loan of one hundred pounds from his bank. We parted in tears. I was positive that this was the end of our relationship. Eric, eager and excited, savoured the journey and adventures ahead of him and I allowed my fears of loss and abandonment to overwhelm me. On our last night together I made him draw me as I lay on our tiny Victorian chaise longue, two watercolours in red and black chinese ink, erotic and very free.

Eric wrote to me throughout the summer months, which I spent, chaste though tempted, exploring London's cafés and bars with a young ex-boxer and his girlfriend, a part-time hooker. His letters detailed his arrival in Venice where he met David, an American painter, entrepreneur and networker, and became part of the social whirl in that beautiful city. David introduced him to Peggy Guggenheim who attempted to seduce Eric rather obviously by offering him the penis from a Marino Marini bronze in her courtyard. Unscrewing the phallus, she pressed it into Eric's hand, telling him the heat of Venice was concentrated in that bronze member. Eric, finding himself in a position which most young aspiring male painters would have begged to find themselves, gave her cheek a modest kiss and returned the phallus to her.

On his return to London Eric looked splendid: muscular, tanned and very healthy – a Mediterranean god. I had never seen him so lean, handsome and strong. Walking several hundred miles across Europe with a knapsack on his back had transformed him. This physical metamorphosis had also restored his self-confidence. I was white and a bit underfed in comparison, which he didn't comment on.

We spent the first few days of his return in bed. His energy and stamina were the stuff on which myths are made and although my bum became rather sore I wasn't about to complain. Somewhere on his tour he had obviously explored new sexual techniques. Our sex together had always been good but kind of unadventurous, Eric preferring variations on the missionary position. Now, surprised and delighted, I found myself in new and exciting positions, locked in the most passionate coupling of our years together. It seemed as if we had held ourselves in all summer, waiting for this reunion. Suspicions came later.

To me, Eric's return set a seal on our love. Other than to be with me, there was no reason for him to come back to London. I took it as an affirmation of faith and trust, and when he set off again for Italy our leave-taking, although tearful, celebrated our relationship. Anticipating the years ahead, Eric elaborated on a future life together when, as a rich and famous artist, we'd buy a house in England and spend holidays in Italy. Holding me in his arms, he recounted his dreams and desires and they became mine. I too dreamed of a large house where, as a perfect 'wife', I would give sparkling lunches and candlelit dinners.

When Eric returned to Rome I moved back to the Cumberland. Months before, in an excess of intimacy, Mr Davis had taken us down to the basement. The white-tiled kitchen and large, old gas range were still in place at the back, but at the front of the house a steel-lined door guarded Mr D's treasure. With a flourish he turned several locks and opened the door for a few seconds so that we could briefly see inside, before locking it again. The floor of the large room, its bay windows barred, was covered in thick layers of ten-shilling and one-pound notes and silver coins. This was his 'extra' money, he explained; not wanting to declare to the taxman, he just threw in, as he had been throwing in for years.

Since then, Mr Davis had found himself an attractive young woman, Veronica, and had emerged from his hole under the front steps and set up house with her in the hotel. He had found another hiding place for his 'extra' money and the former Ali Baba's cave was vacant. In this dark, cavernous basement I lived very happily for the next few years, even lending it and the large double bed out to friends for the night or the occasional weekend.

The Royal College of Art

I WORKED EXTREMELY HARD FOR THE COLLEGE ENTRANCE exam and Eric supported my efforts in a very positive and constructive way, expertly offering advice and helping me with all my paintings. I had amassed a pile of drawings including many of lovers and death but these he chose to ignore. The general opinion of the selection committee, Carel Weight and Roger de Grey in particular, was that my paintings were too pretty and very Walthamstow; they admired the drawings, however, and especially liked a large panel of lovers embracing around the rusticated exterior of the Gothic church across the road from the Cumberland. These drawings and my entrance exam essay (answering the question: 'What influences and experiences decided you to become an artist?') gained a place for me.

This exam was held in the college canteen, formerly the ballroom of a large porticoed house. The room was full of eager young aspirants doggedly seeking one of the most coveted painting scholarships in the country.

I had no idea whatever about who or what or how things had influenced me. Always since my earliest memories I had felt passionately excited by drawing, so I simply began my essay with a description of me sitting on the lavatory and pencilling in on a stiff sheet of pine-scented Ital lavatory paper two mice cuddling each other. My essay then came to a complete halt. There seemed no possible connection between this childish scribble and the series of drawings of lovers I had recently abandoned. Facing a complete block, I wrote about sex. Part fiction and part fact, I had a great deal of fun detailing some of my experiences and emotions – not the confusion and dread I sometimes felt but instead a cockiness and bravado, an attempt to get the attention of the judging committee. Long before the others finished, I got up, walked the length of the room, handed in my paper and left for a coffee. A year or so later a fellow student told me he was astonished at my demeanour of complete and utter confidence. At the time of the exam I had no doubts at all about winning a place. It was one of the few times I had complete faith in myself.

Afterwards Fin joined me and was also surprised at how little time I had spent on the essay. Janet should have been there with us, too. She had initially been accepted for the entrance exam out of the hundreds of applicants. But when Stuart discovered that Fin had not been accepted, he was incensed. He wrote to Carel Weight, head of the painting school, to inform him that Fin was the most brilliant painting student at Walthamstow, and that he should be given a place. Stuart's interfering letter – adding that his opinion was backed by the rest of the staff at Walthamstow – cost Janet her chance that year. I was mad when I heard the news and, grabbing Janet, marched her into Stuart's office, berating him for what I considered was a quite unforgivable action. Then we marched out again, slamming the door behind us. The doors at the college were heavy and solid and mounted on well-oiled hinges, made for such dramatic entrances and exits.

About ten minutes later, thinking I had left much unsaid, I slammed back to Stuart's office and finished my harangue. I've always found it easier to fight battles for others. Unlike my own, their issues seemed so clear.

Several days later, walking past the weaving room, Janet and I saw Stuart Ray leaning against the door. At first we thought he was eavesdropping but as we passed and he slid slowly to the floor we realised he was having a fit. Carrying on our conversation I walked down to his office and quietly informed Mr Brown, the secretary, that Stuart needed attention.

Fin gained his place at the RCA. I couldn't blame him for accepting it – *I* would have. My anger was directed solely at Stuart. Fin married his girlfriend and to everyone's amazement gave up painting and joined the army. I wasn't to hear from him until years later.

In 1959 the RCA was scattered haphazardly through South Kensington. It filled a number of buildings in different locations, resulting in a wide variety of style and comfort. The painting and printmaking schools were upstairs over the Victoria and Albert Museum, which meant we students had the complete run of that vast treasure house.

Months before, Eric and I had discovered a shop dealing in japonaiserie in the middle of the tiled extravagance of the Sicilian Arcade, which runs between Kingsway and High Holborn, almost opposite the Central School of Art, one of the Royal College's rivals. Here, for pennies, we bought fine but worn or slightly damaged prints by Hiroshige, Hokusai, Sharaku and many others, stirring in me an abiding interest in Japanese art. Somewhere I still have a watercolour by Eric after a Hokusai print, a torchlit night scene of men carrying a coffin-like box, attempting to gain entrance into a locked and barred house.

The Japanese section at the V&A, partitioned by wooden screens and wheels, had a neglected air. The slightly dusty display cases were all unlocked and I passed many hours during my studentship opening their glass lids and unlocked drawers, taking out prints, carved stone and ivory *netsuke* as though they were my own collection. I always returned them carefully. Another student, I found out later, showed less restraint. According to Carel Weight, this student had let slip several samurai swords tucked under his duffelcoat when passing the porter's lodge. The luckless student's room was found to be lined with a collection of Japanese art. Not content to have them to himself at the museum, he obviously needed them around him – not to sell, just to admire.

I spent weeks behind the screens, undisturbed, making large black chalk drawings of a set of Utamaro women draped in heavily patterned kimonos.

The dress-design school where Sylvia, Sally Tuffin and Marion Foale studied, was situated in an elegant house in Ennismore Gardens, a ten-minute walk from the painting school. And a series of sheds housed the sculpture school in the grounds, I think, of the Science Museum. The library and design school shared two houses with the college canteen and administration in the Cromwell Road. Disorganised and eccentrically inconvenient, the spread also made us feel we owned the area, that this bit of South Kensington was our territory.

David Hockney and I were the two most noticeable 'queer' guys at college, and before long we developed a friendship, though not a close one. There was a movement, short-lived and disorganised, to ban queers from college dances, as we were always partnered by the best-looking girls. Janet was my 'official' partner but Sylvia, Marion Foale and Sally Tuffin were also in our gang, and the sight of us escorting them, dancing with them and enjoying ourselves caused much resentment among the 'straight' guys.

David drooled over the young, slim lead singer of a rockabilly group who intoned in a dead-pan, nasal American accent the complete Everley Brothers' songbook while doing a subtle bump and grind. He dressed to the left, his tight trousers revealing a large helmet head and balls. I propositioned the young singer for David but although I dragged David across to talk to him during a break, I don't think any later meeting ever took place between them.

Eventually, accompanied by Janet and David, I bought myself a suit in a dark and conservative charcoal-striped flannel from Carnaby Street. The trousers, worn over my pale suede winklepicker ankle boots, were regulation tight. The jacket, a 'bum freezer', was very short, ending just above my arse. I also dressed to the left and displayed my all like a matador. 'It's a bit revealing,' remarked a shocked David. 'Don't you think the jacket could have been a bit longer?' David (at the time a strict vegetarian) was espousing 'equality for the sexualities', and I have to thank him again as I did then for stirring and starting a long-delayed awakening in me of protest and anger at millennia of sexual discrimination. I had never felt that I was discriminated against; the appellation 'sissy', I thought, had more to do with my physical appearance than my sexual nature or sexual preference. I still ascribed the very rare confrontations that occurred to my being a somewhat slender – well, skinny – ephebus and an artist.

Apart from the abortive attempt to ban us from college dances there were a couple of other incidents. David came to me one day upset and shaking. Someone had stolen – had been stealing for some time – his paints and brushes, and now his pin-ups of boys showering cut from American magazines had been burnt. I told him to report it to Carel Weight. He didn't, so I did. Carel was shocked and sympathetic but there was little he could do.

At a year's-end critique of our paintings, Laurence Alloway embarked on a savage, homophobic attack on several of my paintings. He didn't seem interested in their pictorial quality – as I remember they weren't that good – and concentrated instead on the subject: a series of semi-abstract, Keith Vaughan-influenced male nudes. They were actually paintings of Eric, showing him reclining on one arm or with his hands behind his head, brown and muscular and lean, memory paintings of him on his return from his cross-European walk. They were the only wholly open homosexual paintings in the college and I was proud of them. What infuriated Alloway ('these disgusting paintings sicken me') was the glowing cadmium red penis shining out semi-erect from each canvas.

He contrasted my paintings with an elegantly witty picture by David, *Adhesiveness*, and during the entire hour or so returned again and again, attacking my work. Several of my fellow students, including David, sympathised with me later. It appeared that an allusion to homosexuality wittily camouflaged was permissible but my kind of open, salutary expression was completely anathema, an accursed creation.

In 1956 Lord Wolfenden published his report on homosexuality, arguing for a change in the law to decriminalise it. The maximum penalty for buggery was still life imprisonment. Being caught in the bushes, in a lavatory, in any public place with another man meant a prison sentence and the possible ruination of a life and career. The police were even given powers to enter and seize bedding, sheets and towels if neighbours complained of 'indecent behaviour'. As E.M. Forster wrote, 'What the public really loathes in homosexuality is not the thing itself but having to think about it', having to notice it.

Apart from very few clubs and pubs, there was virtually nowhere for the average man to go to look for another man – a mate – or to find momen-

110

tary sexual release. In *A Class Apart*, a book of photographs by Montague Glover with a commentary by James Gardiner, there are several pictures taken around Trafalgar Square in the 1930s which show both young and older men offering themselves, some for money, others simply for sexual companionship. In the 1950s the locale changed to Piccadilly Circus but with an almost identical line-up. Once, waiting for Eric at the junction of Piccadilly and Regent Street, a West Indian offered me money – he just walked up and said, 'I'll give you three pounds.' I was seventeen and, thinking I had been blessed with an unexpected and generous charity, replied, 'Really, gosh, thank you,' only to realise then that I was being offered money for sex. 'I want to get my cock up your tight white bum,' he said stroking himself.

The English creed, 'do what you want as long as you don't frighten the horses', truly applied to us. As long as we led an enforced furtive existence behind locked doors and drawn curtains, as long as we kept our true nature hidden and denied our own existence, as long as the public could ignore or pretend we weren't there, then those of us who didn't stick out were tolerated or patronised. Should we ever let a chink of light through this wall of bigotry and dismissal, we could expect the world to stamp on us hard and quick.

Once, at a party, Sylvia and Marion Foale were dancing together. Stylishly dressed, elegant and lovely, I couldn't help but remark: 'They're beautiful. They look like a photo of lesbians by Brassai.' Marion's boy-friend went berserk when my comment was relayed to him later in the evening. Sylvia and her boyfriend and Eric and I were about to drive away when Marion's irate young man rushed out, screaming, kicking and punching the car, trying to get at me. The others wanted to drive off but I climbed out and calmed him down. 'No, I didn't call them lesbians,' I told him. 'I said they *looked* like a photograph of two lesbians dancing. I didn't think either of them *were* lesbians – the idea had never entered my mind.' Mollified, Marion's chap shook my hand. A narrow escape. I had brought the dread subject out into the open and, worse, being a queer, my remarks about lesbians had included someone's girlfriend. I was lucky.

David Hockney introduced me to Walt Whitman's work. Later, I found the volume of the collected poems I had bought ripped in two by some obviously literate red-neck. But these isolated incidents are all I can remember, and although they were enough, the fact that there weren't more I can only ascribe to an almost total ignorance of homosexuality.

I lent David my copy of Cavafy, translated by Rae Dalven. Although I still find many of his poems infinitely sad, the images of casual and hidden passions and of a declining culture are universal. His genius is as relevant today as it would have been two thousand years ago. David never returned the book and eventually I bought myself another copy.

Although David and I were friendly, we weren't close. It was Janet who, in my second year (at last having gained the place she deserved in the painting school), formed the linchpin in my relationship with David. They became fast friends and, because of my friendship with Janet, I was included. It was with her, for example, that I gave David several erotic photos for his birthday from a collection a friend was selling. The boys and teenagers, healthy and happy, were obviously revelling in their sexuality, sucking and fucking each other and grinning and showing off their assorted flagpoles, erect and hard, with little bottoms round and smooth being spread, kissed and penetrated for their own pleasure as much as for the camera. Taken in ordinary suburban settings, acted out on settees and unmade beds, they captured the joys of youthful male sex.

David took the collection out into the small back yard the better to see it. He was stunned and kept murmuring, 'Oh my, oh my.' This was long before his first trip to America and was probably the first time he had seen erotic photos. (At that time no sex magazines were available in England other than the nudist *Health and Efficiency* type.) He chose several rather chunky boys enjoying each other and reluctantly returned the rest.

I remember discovering a little shop near Ilford High Street that sold *Health and Efficiency*. I bought a copy and kept it hidden under my mattress, naturally. With one exception, all the photographs, fuzzy black-and-white snapshots, were of women. The exception was of an ordinary-looking man, standing on a towel in front of some bushes, his penis showing. A penis was something I was quite familiar with but it thrilled me to see one in a magazine.

In my second year I was awarded a scholarship to Italy. Accompanied by Carel Weight and Roger de Grey (who was later to become president of the Royal Academy) and several other students, we arrived in Florence in the dark after a hellish journey. I had spent a night vomiting in a lavatory, my head in the bowl. I had drunk several glasses of red wine at the French railway station while waiting to board the express. The dinner I had shared with my friends, which we'd bought from the épicerie in Brewer Street, was rich with ham, sausage and various cheeses, again washed down with more red wine, and would have been digestible had I not topped it all off with a generous half-glass of iron tonic prescribed by our good Dr Leibson in Highbury. My undoing.

E.M. Forster could have created the simple, tiny whitewashed hotel room on the top floor overlooking the piazza and church of Santa Maria Novella. With a view of pine- and cypress-topped hills poking up behind the roofs and towers of the city, it was perfect. Florence and Tuscany in April: walking in the rain, drinking from small bottles of grappa (to prevent colds, of course), awash in the High Renaissance. Those ten days or so were spent on a high better than alcohol or any drug could induce.

I was dressed in my 'Italian' gear. Pale suede winklepicker shoes, skin-tight trousers, my hair long and over my ears, with a beautiful white sweater Eric had brought me from Italy, and a short thigh-length cream raincoat, I expected to see replicas of myself everywhere. The Florentines, alas, were extremely formal in their dress; *la bella figura* was all, and expressed itself in very English tweed jackets, shirts and ties, grey flannels – all very proper. I stood out like a brazen beacon, which is exactly how I felt on my first night out.

The two other students I was with left to go on an extended bar crawl so I walked back to the hotel along the Arno, gathering a crowd of excited and vociferous Italian men around me. Pinching and squeezing my butt, grabbing my crotch, sliding their hands under my sweater, shouting and gesticulating, they obviously thought I was a male prostitute. Totally bewildered and completely unable to deal with so many hands, every time I stopped walking to defend myself I was pushed back against the embankment wall and assaulted. Their attempts to undress me or at least get their hands under my clothes, 'to cop a feel', excited them, and they were becoming rather violent and hysterical. The sanctuary of the hotel, when at last I reached it, was truly blessed. For the rest of our stay in the city I never went out alone at night. In London my appearance went unnoticed or at least unremarked upon. I looked like many other art students in my jeans or my odd gear. Italy was conventional in comparison, and my appearance an affront to that conventionality. Everywhere I went I drew some comment, and the Italians, unlike the English, comment loudly and openly in a wonderfully operatic manner.

When our short scholarship ended I took the train down to Rome and the British Schools to see Eric. He wasn't there when I arrived. I sat and waited an hour or so in his studio and then went to look for him. By the entrance to the dining-hall was a group of students and I asked them if they had seen Eric Hebborn. One well-built man, clean shaven and with thick black hair, small eyes and thickly sensual lips answered, 'No, he's not been here today.' I walked a few steps away and turned back. I recognised Eric's voice but not his face. Without his beard he was unrecognisable but his voice, with its traces of an Essex accent, was unmistakable.

The next week was miserable. I was in Rome and Eric was ignoring me. Wrapped up in an affair with Gianni, a beautiful Sicilian boy, he told me he was very busy – and besides, he said, my appearance embarrassed him. I accepted this until I met Gianni. Eric had been desperately trying to keep us apart, but one day Gianni came to the schools unannounced. My appearance might have been strange in Italy and certainly it provoked a great deal of attention, but when I saw Gianni – dressed in a bright lavender fluffy mohair sweater and tight pants similar to the ones I was wearing – come swaying deliciously up the steps of the British School, Eric's protestations of embarrassment seemed a trifle thin.

Gianni and his friend-lover Ugo gave a small party for me and I taught Gianni to dance. After all the guests had left Ugo suggested he and I go into the bedroom so that Eric and Gianni could be alone. I declined in my best English manner, hurt and confused. It was my only defence, and Eric and I left together.

The rest of my stay was awkward and embarrassing. Spending most of it sightseeing with a fellow student, I saw little of Eric. I couldn't blame him for his affair with Gianni. The boy was very good-looking and sexy and any self-respecting queer would have been attracted to his southern Italian beauty. But being dismissed in such an offhand manner I found humiliating. I was angry, too, at Eric's lack of style, his inability to deal with a situation he created, and for his finding fault with me in his ineptness. He felt guilty and so blamed me for his feelings, blamed me for existing, at least in Rome.

Glad when the week came to an end, I returned to London bubbling. If I could be pushed aside so easily now when I was young and healthy, what could I look forward to in the future? Eric had already made remarks about how I wouldn't age well. On our first holiday in Maldon while we were sitting on the churchyard wall waiting for a bus to Goldhanger, he drew an exquisitely cruel caricature of me in old age. Stooped, shrunken, balding, pot-bellied with a grossly enlarged Smith family nose, the entire figure was an affront to my youth and devotion.

I was now twenty-two, deeply in love and profoundly insecure. Instead of taking responsibility and dealing with the situation, however, I allowed the ground rules that Eric had laid down for our relationship, my love for him and my insecurity to govern me and did nothing – nothing of any value, that is.

I felt lost not only in my personal life but also in my work at college. I had embarked on some really bad paintings and had just about stopped drawing all together. Alloway's attack had disturbed me but Eric's judgement on the moral bankruptcy of my lovers drawings and the 'all you ever think about is sex' litany was an extension of my mother's 'don't do that' which combined to undermine my self-confidence. I tried still-life drawings and some in the life-room going from one side to the other, the model being just a part of an interior landscape of students and the paraphernalia of an art school. But these didn't interest me and it showed.

Jürgen had persuaded Mr Davis to open a club and install Jürgen as manager. He named it The Lucifer. Situated in the basement of the Cumberland adjacent to my room, at first it was a success and relatively untroubled by violence. Eventually a gang of Finsbury lads took charge, and Friday and Saturday fights became common.

Patsy Brogan and her boyfriend Mike, a colossal, good-natured Irishman, were having a drink one Friday when a fight broke out upstairs, spilling down the narrow wooden staircase into the bar. Furious at having his pre-dinner drink interrupted, Mike put his pint down on the counter, ran to the bottom of the stairs and, as the fighting boys came down, he just picked them up and threw them into the air behind him. When there were no more gang members trying to get in, Mike joined Patsy at the bar, finished his drink and together they went on for the fish and chips Patsy had warming in their oven. As she served Mike, a plate of hot food in each hand, she saw one half of a pair of scissors sticking out of her boyfriend's broad back. Her scream of rage could be heard in the street. Still howling, Patsy tore into The Lucifer and demolished it. Grabbing hold of the carefully cut 'Italian' hairstyles, she ploughed through the bar, smashing heads together and leaving twenty or so stunned and bleeding youths wondering where this avenging virago had come from.

Patsy and Mike didn't stop the gangs from using and fighting in the club, though. That came about when a real gang moved in, an adult and dangerous gang connected in some way with the Kray twins, Ronnie and Reggie, who for years dominated the criminal underworld of London. The brothers were often mentioned: 'We should get Ronnie to come down here. He'd like you,' I was told a number of times. We had no idea to whom they were referring. The club now had an enforced quiet and emptiness.

On Wednesday afternoons – the free afternoon set aside by the college for gallery viewing and getting to know and influence people of importance in the art world – Janet, Sylvia and I often descended into the red-lit underworld of The Lucifer. The three of us and the four or five gang members who were always there made an unusually large crowd in the now-deserted bar. We would be welcomed and entertained like old friends. The 'governor' – a large, heavily built man whose jocular nature matched his smile – adopted us: 'You don't have to worry about nothin' with me around.'

We had no idea that these were dangerous people. Their life and their attitude to life were so completely different to ours. Innocent and fascinated, we allowed ourselves to be charmed by them as they, in turn, were intrigued by us. Gangsters and art students made for a strange mix. We had never met gangsters and they had never met students. Polite, friendly and generous in supplying us with drinks (rum and Coke was our favourite), I saw them as the addled, slightly ridiculous but nevertheless harmless mob in *Big Time on Madonna Street*, the Italian film starring Vittorio Gasman.

Although the gang had moved the nuisances out and civilised the place, Mr Davis was heartbroken at the loss of his customers. The gang spent freely but their small numbers could not compete with the sellout crowds that drained the bar dry over previous weekends. He attempted to close the bar down but, after being taken aside for a 'little chat' during which a few bottles of spirits were broken, he changed his mind.

One night I discovered that Dougie, a small, well-built but plain young man, was the gang's one-man collection agency, and that he carried and used a cut-throat razor. This knowledge was rather important to me as for several weeks on a Thursday or Friday night he and I toured north London, visiting a round of bars, restaurants and clubs in which our reception and treatment bordered on the obsequious. Dougie carried a briefcase and always had what he called a 'conference' with the manager or owner while I sat there clueless, enjoying more attention than I had ever expected to receive in my life.

Dougie flirted with me but offhandedly – it was a joke, a game, and I accepted it as such. As he changed gears in the car his hand would rub against my thigh, 'Oh, I *do* beg your pardon,' he would say and then laugh. He opened doors for me and his hand cupped my bum: 'Oops a daisy,' and another laugh. 'Oh, excuse me,' and he'd grin. I realised that he was sending me up, mocking me, but in a gentle and comradely manner without a trace of hostility. As he parodied my accent, the smile on his face was without malice, the smile of a friend.

One evening he stopped the car outside a club near Hampstead and went inside without his briefcase, leaving me waiting for him in the car. He returned rather quickly. We drove around for a bit then parked next to a railway siding. Smoking and talking, he asked me questions about my work: how I began a painting, if I drew on the canvas first and then used colour. Did I fill the drawing in, he wanted to know, and was puzzled when I told him I used the sketch only as a guide. Where did I get my ideas from? Again he was confused when I told him an idea just arrived and I built and expanded on it. Then he unzipped his trousers and took out his cock. It was erect. 'Well, I've got one – where's yours?' he asked. We tumbled into the back seat with much kissing. When I was completely undressed he pulled down his trousers and turned on his belly, half kneeling, half sprawling, and said, 'Fuck me! Come on, fuck me!' a command that surprised me. The two halves of his butt in the darkness, divided by a cleft filled with a thick mass of black hair, pushed up to receive me. I strained to gain entry, Dougie swearing quietly to himself.

'Push out,' I whispered, hoping to aid our efforts, and my cock slid in. He was tight.

'Jesus Christ. Fuck!' Dougie cried out.

'Are you all right?'

'Yeah, just don't stop,' he replied. Slowly he relaxed, opening out, and came at the same time as me, bringing himself off over the seat. 'Ooh, what a mess!' he exclaimed as he cleaned up with a handkerchief. We smoked another cigarette.

'That was my first time,' he said. It came out as a muffled confession as he sat staring straight ahead. I didn't know what to say. 'So, let's do it again.'

This time entry was easy, his arse slick and wet with my cum. 'Yeah, fuck me. Yeah. Fuck me,' was his constant demand, and when I came he pulled himself away, turned me over and fucked me with short, deep strokes, his hands twisting and pulling on my nipples, his fingernails biting into my skin.

We dressed and sat smoking in silence. He leaned forward and to one side and let out a long, loud, wet fart and laughed. 'Well, I've done it. I'm a queer now.'

'Getting fucked doesn't make you a queer, Dougie.' I heard a note in his voice that needed reassurance.

'No? Well, what does then?'

I had no answer.

'I've been wanting to get fucked for years,' he said. 'Don't you go telling no one.'

'I won't.'

'No, I mean it. Not no one.'

'Okay, I promise.'

'Okay, then.'

Later, racked with guilt compounded by the realisation I wouldn't, *couldn't* tell Eric, the thought of secrecy making me even more wretched, I told myself I wouldn't have sex with Dougie again, that I wouldn't have sex with anyone other than Eric.

In the middle of the following night Dougie reappeared, banging on the steel-lined door of my room. 'I thought you'd never wake up. What's all this armour-plating about? Making a bomb shelter, are you?'

I told him it had been Mr Davis's treasure trove. 'He's barmy, that guy, really barmy.'

Dougie had brought a vibrator with him. 'I use it on the old trouble when I don't feel like doing it to her.' I knew enough rhyming slang to decipher 'trouble' (trouble and strife) as wife. 'Apples' (apples and pears) meant stairs and 'use your loaf' (loaf of bread) meant use your head. The secret rhyming language was developed during the nineteenth century in London's East End.

I got the naked Dougie on his back, a couple of pillows under his hips, and took him very slowly, taking time to sit on his face and let his tongue fuck me before shoving my cock down his throat, almost choking him. During the necessary cigarette break, Dougie grinned, raised his bum and let out another loud, wet fart. 'My arsehole feels fuckin' huge. Well, I'm a brown-noser now, and a cock-sucker. If that don't make me a queer, nothing will.'

'Dougie, nothing makes you a queer. You are or you aren't.' I'd been thinking about this since the previous night.

'All right then, do me with the dildo.' He rolled onto his front, raising his hips. 'If I am then I am. Fuck it.' I pushed the vibrator into him. 'Oh yeah, that feels so good.' Then I took over. 'Oh yeah, so does that.'

He left before morning and soon after I was informed about his occupation. Razors terrified me. Since my childhood days of using Dad's cutthroat, I had seen a man attacked with razors on the downs near Brighton. Surrounded by several men, he broke free, crying out, his hands covering his face, the blood running between his fingers as he stumbled across the short grass to the road.

When Dougie next invited me out on his rounds, I declined. My fabricated excuses weren't accepted and I told him the truth. 'Don't worry, I'm not going to cut you or nothin',' he said in an attempt to reassure me. But I didn't want to be an unlucky bystander, so our nights out were off. He still came to visit, though, and I was still feeling guilty. Attempts at rationalisation didn't work. My 'well, if Eric can do it, so can I' didn't convince me at all. Dougie attracted me. He wasn't good-looking but his body was firm and muscular. Not in love with him yet lonely, confused and horny, I would wait expectantly for his visits. I had vowed to be true, to be faithful to Eric, so I was feeling profoundly disturbed. Worried about Dougie's razor and wracked with guilt over our sex, I nevertheless couldn't help smiling: I was a gangster's moll. Not that the thought was any comfort at all, but I found it amusing, silly as it was.

One evening as Janet, Sylvia and I were having a drink, a boy rushed into The Lucifer, white-faced and hysterical, asking for help. He'd just killed his girlfriend during a quarrel. The gang offered no support and I found their cold indifference shocking. The three of us were horrified. This was their reality: murder and discarding a friend in need. Janet and Sylvia sent the boy across the road to our vicar – it was all we could think of.

Eventually Mr Davis closed his club. The gang paid one last visit, smashing chairs and tables and breaking bottles of spirits, and then they were gone, Dougie with them.

In my third year at college, my last year, we were given little cubicles to work in and left alone. I had been painting a series of large, abstract interiors – sort of in the style of Braque – with Eric pictured naked sitting or standing, as much a part of the interior as the furniture. Also included in these paintings were items I'd picked up at the street market which took place every Saturday morning by the junction of the Holloway Road and Upper Street, one of hundreds around London. At the end of the day the sellers usually left behind what they couldn't sell for the garbage trucks. Some even held miniature bonfires, consigning to the flames beautifully carved furniture, expertly made in mahogany and oak and other fine woods. These were destroyed not to placate some theocratic madman (or in Mr Davis's case, a salve for a frustrated, dark passion – a need to expiate an internal raging that could find no other outlet) but as a result of plain economics. The big houses of London, built for the emergent middle classes, were now out of fashion and being turned (like the Cumberland) into rooming-houses, flats or simply being demolished. The furniture that once crowded the spacious rooms now saturated an uninterested market. To store such items cost money and, anyway, there was plenty more modern stuff to replace them. So when the markets closed and just ahead of the bonfires and garbage trucks, I would swoop down and choose pieces of japonaiserie – cabinets, desks, tables made of bamboo and lacquer, inlaid or gold-leafed; all unwanted and just light enough for me to carry back to the studio and use in my pictures. Their reprieve was brief for when I had drawn and painted them they were left outside for either Mr Davis's pleasure or for the garbage men. I didn't have the space to keep them.

Unhappy and dissatisfied with these paintings, I began a series of small, intense drawings of screaming men in thick black conté and pencil. Mostly standing hunched forward, their muscular bodies tense, their hands clenched into fists, their heads thrown back in a silent howling, these images just flowed out of me. I had no idea what they were about, but once I started these pictures of rage and pain, I couldn't stop. Like Mr Davis, I needed an outlet. Unable to express what I felt except in misdirected spurts of anger, and incapable of using my power to take responsibility, I unconsciously used my talent as therapy. With Eric away, without either his expert advice or his dismissal of my inner voice (so effective in stopping me working), these drawings grew and flourished.

Forgery

WHEN ERIC FINALLY RETURNED FROM ROME, IT WAS A coming together and a recommitment of our love for each other. Eric seemed to crave reassurance, to need me to let him know how much I loved him. He appeared lost: the plans he had outlined two years ago, his schemes for fame and fortune, hadn't worked out, and he drifted around Highbury and the Cumberland depressed and with little energy.

I was overjoyed to have him back. Although still hurt by his behaviour when I had visited him in Rome, and guilty over my morale-boosting fling with Dougie, I rejoiced that we were a couple again, and I believed him when he said he loved me. The end of the college year was in sight and I was working like crazy. I kept my paintings and drawings at college. Eric didn't show any interest in seeing them and I wasn't prepared to be deflated or knocked off-course by any side-swipe he might throw my way.

When the graduation show took place I wasn't happy with my paintings but the screaming men did give me some pleasure and pride. If the quality was uneven, I thought, they at least were intense and strong.

After the graduation ceremony I met Sir Anthony Blunt for the first time. Eric had related to me how they had become friends in Italy, but for me it was just another (albeit illustrious) name from a part of his life that I viewed with suspicion and distrust.

Sir Anthony took us for a drink in a pub near South Kensington tube station. I can't remember much about what he said. Scathingly elegant about the graduation, we students were forced to wear caps and gowns, yet he appeared, in spite of his position and accent, to be rather anti-establishment. He very obviously had the hots for Eric. But here I knew I was safe as Eric didn't like older men.

Although at first I didn't show my drawings of screaming men to Eric, when a couple of them were framed and hung in an exhibition of student work, alongside drawings by David Hockney and Ron Kitaj, the pleasure

I felt overcame the reservations I had and I dragged Eric to the college to see them.

'They're obscene. They're disgusting and they make me feel sick,' he said, echoing Alloway.

It was an abrupt personal and critical punch to my solar plexus and although over the ensuing years I drew occasionally, to all intents and purposes I gave up. It was impossible for me to express myself and to go on living with Eric at the same time. I had a choice and I chose to live with my love. It was as simple and as difficult as that.

Eric seemed not to have produced much in Rome. The indifferent reception to his big painting still preyed on his mind. There was a series of free copies, monotypes, in black printing ink from Goya's *Tauromachia*; a small and lovely copy of a Giorgione, *The Picnic*; another small, brilliantly coloured view of the gardens of the French Academy from the Villa Medici; and some small Roman landscapes. Together with a few etchings and drawings and one strange picture – almost primitive, and unlike anything else by Eric (a painting of Howard lying under a tree with some men peering at him) – these appeared to comprise the total of three years' study.

It was an unhappy period for both of us. Our long student years were over and it seemed we could look forward to nothing better than a teaching job for the rest of our adult lives. And yet here Eric shone, for as depressed as we both were it was him, the cuddly warm teddy bear Eric, who, first thing in the morning, would make tea and then, sometimes nude, sometimes only in a pair of Y-fronts, would make me laugh and give the whole day a shine. He'd perform quite involved imitations of Fonteyn and Nureyev dancing, introducing them as 'Margotte Fontyne' and 'Rudolpht Nuroiyuv' in a broad cockney accent, then he'd pirouette and prance until, no matter how grim I was feeling, he'd coaxed and coerced me into hysterical laughter. His favourite was 'baby on potty' which he would announce straight-faced then squat and mime a baby's surprise, delight and then disgust at the vast amounts of body wastes it was producing. Then he would rise slowly, looking at the imaginary over-flowing pot with amazement bordering on horror, and walk away, very dignified and upright, sniffing and wiping his fingers distastefully on his stomach. He was a brilliant mime.

Always very kindly and solicitous when I had bronchitis, nursing me back to health, Eric was a gentle lover as well – sometimes too gentle, too passive. We laughed uproariously together at the many English comedy films from Elstree and Ealing. Humour and kindness alternated with a didactic, authoritarian imposition of his will, but I loved the playful side of him and I treasured it. I still do.

The long summer holiday stretched ahead and survival was uppermost in our minds, for we had little money. But Eric had a plan. The friendship between Eric and Mr Davis was now strengthened by a very juicy and succulent carrot that Eric waved in front of the landlord's nose: investment in art, something he could do with the hoard of undeclared money that now filled several large iron safes in the locked room. Eric writes disparagingly about Mr Davis, and certainly at times I found myself disliking him with an intensity that was disturbing. Venal would be a polite description of our landlord, yet at the same time he was occasionally surprisingly generous to us both, for our part our dealings with him were often completely dishonest. 'Serves him right,' Eric would say as we swindled him, but to use his greed as a reason for our deceit was only compounding our actions, not making them right.

Who suggested the first forgeries? In Eric's studio at the British Schools in Rome, Sir Anthony, on seeing several copies of Poussin drawings by Eric, had remarked that if they were on old paper they would easily pass as originals. Eric had bought a couple of books on famous forgers such as Van Meegeren, as well as a biography of Lord Duveen, the famous dealer who had relied heavily on the expertise of Bernard Berenson. So the kernel, the seed, of forgery and forging had been planted a couple of years previously.

We decided, quite arbitrarily, to try a couple of Augustus Johns. We had no stock of the original Whatman paper with its distinctive watermark that he used, so we bought the best sheets of paper available and cut away their watermarks. Using several books on John from the local library, we found ourselves the proud possessors of two Augustus John pencil portraits. One was of his wife Dorelia wearing a large-brimmed hat and the other was of a child, a boy, based entirely on a drawing from the Chatsworth Collection by Bartolommeo Schedone. We took them to Edmund and Don who ran the bookstore and framing business in Upper Street, by Canonbury Square, and had them elegantly framed and matted.

Again, I can't remember which gallery bought them but it could have been the Redfern or Agnew's – certainly it was one of the well-known galleries in the Bond Street area.

We both worried about signing the drawings. Unsigned works may be attributed to anyone, but forging a signature is a crime and neither of us was in doubt about the consequences should the fakes be discovered. We also knew that Augustus John always signed his work and that without the signature they would be valueless, so we crossed our fingers, said a prayer and Eric scribbled in John's name. It was done and we were on tenterhooks until they were sold. Then, illogically, we breathed a sigh of relief and relaxed.

Some years previously Jürgen had concocted a scheme to rob the Post

Office. Using different addresses and names he acquired four or five Post Office savings books. Eric carefully entered false deposits and faked a stamp for each. Of course Jürgen was discovered and imprisoned and Eric and I endured a couple of hours of intense interrogation in our cottage. One of the policemen – both were in plainclothes – took me upstairs to our bedroom where, after emptying out on the floor all our cupboards and drawers, punched me repeatedly in the stomach in an attempt to make me confess to being Jürgen's accomplice. Eric was receiving the same treatment downstairs. So, under no illusion about what we were doing, our fears of being caught and punished were mixed with an excitement and glee.

This experience gave Eric an edge and he began drawing and painting again. Mr Davis sat for his portrait, a pencil drawing first, then a painting. I posed for several drawings and a forty- by fifty-inch canvas as a nude in a Goya Maja pose, hands clasped behind my back. I thought I looked rather like a skinned rabbit but didn't say so. I was just happy to see Eric working.

We had shown the unframed drawings to Mr Davis who dismissed them scornfully and told us that we had thrown away the forty-odd pounds Eric said we paid for them. Yet when he saw the cheque made out to Eric for several hundred pounds, his excitement and interest grew and Eric and he became bosom buddies. Closeted together, taking long walks and meals at Mick's café in Highbury Park, Eric told me he was drawing our landlord carefully into a well-laid trap. Relating each day's conversation, he delighted in the idea of conning Mr Davis while at the same time building up a collection of art for him – and for us.

Eric's new plan was for us to become dealers in English watercolours and drawings. While buying for Mr Davis, Eric altered the receipts, adding to the price and using the extra money to buy works of art for ourselves. These we would stockpile until we amassed a sufficient amount to start our own business.

He also made meticulous copies of the best watercolours we bought with enough variations to make them individual works. Altering the view, adding or subtracting figures and changing the direction of the light, we kept the originals and Mr D received the fakes.

It wasn't long before we began to build up for Mr Davis and ourselves a decent assembly of nineteenth- and twentieth-century paintings, drawings and fakes. Most of our collection we lent out to keep safe from Mr Davis. He saw art only as an investment. What we bought for eighty pounds he could possibly sell for double or more, and this was his only pleasure in them.

I found a painting of *The Lady of Shalott* in a small auction house in the Holloway Road. I forget the name of the artist but the picture, painted in a pre-Raphaelite style, detailed and brilliant in colour, depicted her lying in a boat, her long hair trailing in the water floating down to Camelot. The frame, a magnificent piece of Victorian Gothic, beautifully carved with pointed arches, heavy with gold leaf, was in mint condition. We had meant to keep my purchase for ourselves but our East End financier surprised us while I was unwrapping it. The first thing he wanted to do was smash the frame – 'Make it easier to store, by Christ,' he told us. It took a great deal of arguing on our part before we eventually persuaded him to leave it intact. He just would not see that the fame was an integral part of the picture, that without it the value would drop enormously. He could not see that the frame itself was an object of beauty. When we insisted it was valuable he kept it, but grudgingly, and I made him promise that if he did take it off he would sell it to me and not smash it.

Don and Reneé Robinson hung many of the pictures in our collection in their elegantly restored house in Highbury Terrace, across the Highbury Fields. Surprised and delighted, not questioning Eric's excuse that we had no room to store them, they covered several walls with works by Varley, Cox, De Wint, Cotman, and so on.

We decided to move out of the basement. There was no way our imagined candlelit dinners could influence or impress anyone down there. Patsy Brogan and Mike had left Mr Pinkus's front room in the best-kept part of the Cumberland. Eric persuaded Mr Davis to let us have it and a back room for a nominal sum and to furnish the front room for us or, rather, to pay for a thick, bitter-chocolate brown, all-wool Axminster carpet and pale tea-coloured velvet curtains.

From the back garden we retrieved a huge, thickly varnished oak side-board and a matching chest-high, glass-fronted cupboard which, when topped with a slab of dark green church marble, served well as a drinks cabinet.

While Eric continued his seduction of Mr D, I took all the furniture, including a delicate early Victorian settee, two rosewood armchairs, the carved oak sideboard and cabinet out into the garden where I stripped off the varnish and beeswaxed them.

We had found an old pine tripod table with an oval-shaped hinged top. Compared to our other pieces it was crudely carved, but after I stripped, sanded and painted it a flat black, Eric took over. He copied a photograph of a red figure painting on a cylix of Achilles and Patroclus, and when the burnt sienna oil paint dried and was polished, an ordinary table became a very elegant object admired by everyone who saw it.

I stripped all the wood inside the room, including the door, the frames and sill of the bay windows and the simple slate fireplace. Eric wanted wallpaper but I persuaded him that the white paint acted as a background to the dark carpet, the polished wood and the many pictures. The chairs and settee were upholstered in a thick off-white cotton, and as our oval table proved too small, we bought from two new acquaintances (Leigh and Frank in Camden Passage) a small seventeenth-century refectory table in good condition. The room looked splendidly understated: polished wood, thick dark carpet, white walls covered in beautifully mounted and framed pictures, it was all elegantly tasteful and slightly luxurious. Using this room as our springboard, we were ready to take on the world.

These were the years of the Twist and 'Swinging London'. Well before their advent, while Eric was in Rome, Janet, Sylvia and I had held a party at the Cumberland in a downstairs room. Our decorations consisted of several rolls of lavatory paper made into streamers suspended from the centre of the ceiling and pinned to the walls to make a billowing canopy.

We scrubbed out a medium-sized zinc bathtub which we filled with cheap wine and brandy and several tins of strawberries, a potent brew. During the preparations, as I was clearing out the assorted debris from the room, I trod on a nail which pierced the sole of my foot. I needed help to remove it. Mr Davis held my arms while his cleaning man gripped the plank and pulled it out. 'Oh, stop making such a fuss and help me,' Janet commanded. So, with a couple of aspirins washed down with red wine, the pain disappearing into a mellow glow, I did as I was told.

The party was a great success, one of those historic parties that become minor legends. Several hundred students from the Slade, St Martin's, the Academy School, RCA, Guildhall, and so on, turned up. It spread out over the back gardens through the hotel into the front garden.

I excused myself late in the evening and went out on a tour of pubs and clubs – with whom I'm not sure. In the morning, with a ghastly hangover, I woke up fully dressed, my foot painful and swollen. Removing my shoe was agonising. Jürgen drove me to the local hospital where I had a tetanus shot, then took me back to Janet and Sylvia's for aspirin and sweet milky coffee in a big china mug held in shaking hands.

When the Twist arrived in London, people would break into quick little renditions to emphasise and underline their conversations, or practice while waiting for a bus or in the cinema queue. I can remember the first time I saw the dance performed one night at David Hockney's flat in Powis Square, by a young American man, a solo performance – not that one needed a partner. 'Everyone's doing it in the States,' he said, swaying up and down, backwards and forwards. Bully for the States, I thought, I shan't be imitating them. But of course I did, swept away in the craze as was almost everyone I knew: packing ourselves into dimly lit rooms, sweating on an alcohol high in a frenzied salute to Terpsichore. The muse of the dance would, I think, have been genuinely puzzled to see us, our bodies convulsed and gyrating but our feet fixed firmly to the ground.

Jazz clubs and the local *palais de danse* were the nearest thing we had to discos, and jazz was on its way out – traditional jazz, that is. Modern jazz, Thelonius Monk, the MJQ, Chet Baker and Gerry Mulligan were in, really cool and hip, though we didn't use those terms. We three had seen *Jazz on a Summer's Day*, the film of the 1958 Newport Jazz Festival, and took part in many arguments about Chuck Berry. A general consensus held that, being a rock'n'roller, he had no place at the festival. We argued in his favour. His riff, totally libidinous, mockingly irreverent, personified a sexual energy that struck a chord in us to which we could not but respond. Then Anita O'Day sang under the bright afternoon sky, beginning her session in front of a sparse and almost indifferent audience, pulling them to attention with an affected stylish, razor-sharp delivery of 'Tea for Two' – what better for a summer's afternoon – and 'Cold Hearted Hannah, the Vamp from Savannah, GA'. In a vast-brimmed picture hat and a tight dress that blossomed out below her knees, she became in those few dazzling minutes my equivalent of Garland and Streisand – an idol to be treasured. The entire film is an evocation of past days lost in summers long gone.

While I was living in the basement of Cumberland I became close friends with a short, powerfully built man, J.B. Ten or fifteen years older than me, he left home in his early teens to escape his mother, who loathed books and reading. She threw his books away and broke into violent rages when she caught him with one. We shared our books and he lent me records from his collection of jazz, actually giving me two albums of Anita O'Day which, through overuse, finally gave out. Sitting with him in his room off the High Street, I first heard Bessie Smith and Billie Holiday. We went to concerts at the Astoria in Finsbury Park, which had a Spanish village built around the ceiling: when the house lights went down it lit up and illuminated open, shawl-draped windows and a starlit sky.

J.B. fell in love with the wife of a friend of ours, an ex-student of the college. Sitting at the little café-kiosk in Highbury Fields with tears running down his face, he confessed his love for her and the fact that he always fell in love with married women.

One afternoon he came to Janet and Sylvia's room for tea, bringing with him one of the most beautiful young men I have ever seen, his brother, A.B. Full of life and energy, with a cockney's cheek and impudent sense of humour, his first words to me shocked his brother. 'I could go for you,' A.B. told me. J.B. hadn't realised I was queer and the term 'gay' was not yet in circulation. 'Course he is!' affirmed A.B. against his brother's protestations. J.B. had several arguments in Highbury over the question of my sexuality and one serious knockdown fight. This was a revelation to me, as much as my being a queer was to J.B. We had never discussed my sexual preferences. I never hid or disguised my attraction to men but nor did I trumpet it aloud. I assumed he knew and he assumed I was straight.

A.B. was a gigolo with a select upper-class clientèle. I'd read Colette and about Cora Pearl, the girl on the red velvet swing, but I couldn't imagine gigolos, romantically European figures, existing and thriving in England as A.B. definitely was.

That afternoon he entertained us with detailed accounts of several of his sexual exploits, beginning with a highly placed official in the Bank of England. This man would lie waiting for A.B. in a darkened bedroom. I imagined this in vast Soaneian proportions, the bed an elegant regency four-poster. Across his still and recumbent body he draped a lacy black silk negligee. After a couple of cigarettes and a drink in an adjoining room ('I always like to keep them waiting then they're really itchy for it,' A.B. said grinning), he'd undress and walk to the foot of the bed, then slowly, very slowly 'to get the old wanker going', he'd pull the negligee down and off the recumbent figure. Standing on the bed over the man and mas-turbating, he directed his jetting semen onto the man's chest and face. Still without speaking, he wiped his hands and collected an envelope with his fee from the side table, dressed and left.

Another client, from the House of Lords, liked wearing black stockings and black high-heeled shoes while having his bottom spanked by A.B. We listened with open-mouthed absorption and, for me, utter incomprehen-sion. I couldn't understand fetishism. Too young to have developed any of my own, I found the sexual revering of an inanimate object bewildering.

We invited the two brothers to the next college dance and although A.B. flirted outrageously with me, pulling me into a cubicle in the gents for some heavy necking and a good feel-up, it was Janet that he went home with, spending the night in my double bed.

Highbury, like so many other areas and boroughs in London, still retained much of its former village atmosphere. The short, narrow shop-lined High Street was a meeting place. We knew Italian Mick who ran the café, and the big fat Cypriot, a really good cook with an awful English wife. He made chicken, rice and lemon for us, sold us rough red wine in thick china cups and always submerged his thumb in our soup leaving a dirty print to stream back into the bowl. Mick's wife cooked regular eggs and bacon and made simple salads served with thick pink slices of home-cooked ham. The people in the grocer's and post office (who looked like characters from *Goblin Market* illustrated by Arthur Rackham) were always helpful, friendly and sympathetic. The chemist, a man in his thirties, a pre-yuppy, attracted to Janet and Sylvia, asked me countless questions about them when he discovered I wasn't their boyfriend.

Highbury seemed to us a magnet for eccentrics and eccentricity. A frequent visitor to our room introduced to us by Jürgen was Lucy B. Lyte who, dressed in crimplene slacks, a bulky windcheater and a knitted pixie cap, saw auras everywhere: even the squat red Victorian pillar boxes each had their own individual aura. She drove the other tenants of her rooming-house to a frenzy, for she would leave large Spanish onions halves, a dozen or more, around the building to absorb the toxic emanations from lavatory-bowl cleansers, bleach and furniture polish. The house would stink of onion but, despite threats and complaints, Lucy persevered. At nightfall she could be found cross-legged facing a newly selected tree – she chose a different one every evening – talking to the gnomes, elves and dryads, especially the dryads who were always benign, unlike the gnomes and elves who, often rude and unhelpful, would at times make her cry. She was a member of the Theosophists, had met the founder, Rudolph Steiner, and she produced sheets and sheets of watercolours representing auras of us, the trees, houses, lampposts and, of course, pillar boxes.

When Eric and I first moved into the Cumberland, the room behind us, formerly Jürgen's room, was occupied by a middle-aged Irish woman, Mrs Johnson, and two brothers from Jamaica. Mrs Johnson was tall, bosomy and solid with jet-black hair pulled up into a *casque noire*, in appearance the proverbial barmaid or even madame. The brothers, her 'chaps' – one about twenty years old and the other three or four years younger – allowed their lives to be organised and managed by her. All three worked, but Mrs Johnson made sure they handed their weekly wages to her for banking after a certain amount was subtracted for bus fares, cigarettes and a few beers. They all shared a double bed and made noisy sex. The brothers laughed a great deal, especially when their motherly mistress was angry, capering around jeering and teasing her as she stood screaming on the little black and white tiled balcony overlooking the garden. In spotless white under-wear, which shone against their muscular black bodies, they would jump up and down, their laughter rising above Mrs Johnson's coarse Belfast accent. Their humour would eventually infect her and the three of them would retire for a bout of house-shaking sex.

Mrs Chatterley de Guest, Yvonne, worked for a detective agency and had her own cards printed: 'Discreet investigations undertaken'. She used a friend's phone as no one in the Cumberland had one of their own. '*Et voila!*' she would cry out, snatching the black beret from her head and replacing it with a neat trilby perched at a jaunty angle. 'Now, my disguise is complete. Am I a man or a woman?' It was difficult to tell. Wearing trousers, small, shiny boots and her belted raincoat, she had an ambiguous appearance. Not androgynous with a sense of mystery and allure, just

John in London, 1973

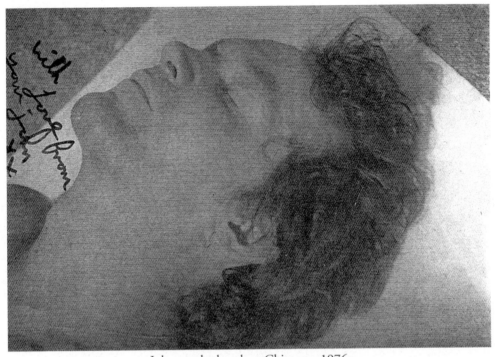

John on the beach at Chiarone, 1976

The two of us at Vulci, 1977, and (right) John in our flat in Putney, 1976

John at an Alternative Miss World, London, c.1977

John with his journey of the spirit, Commonweal, 1987

Hand-painted dress, 1973–74

Fabric designs, 1976–77

RIGHT
A drawing of John in one of my kimonos,
1976

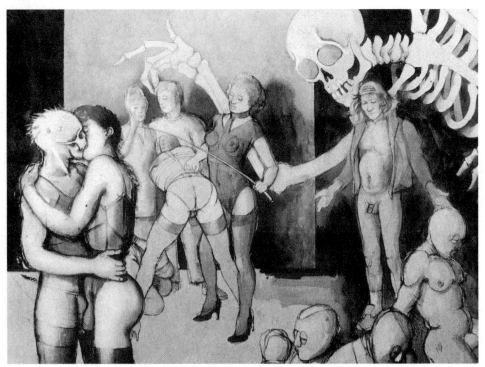

'And if I never love again', sex club, Los Angeles, watercolour drawing

Sex club, Los Angeles, watercolour drawing, 1995

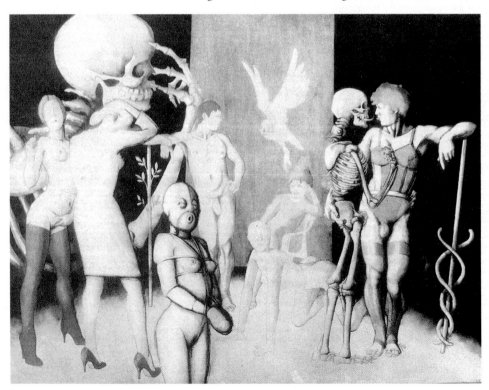

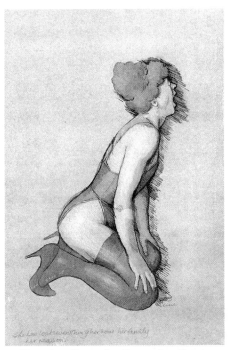

Drawing from the *Screaming Queen*
series, 1995

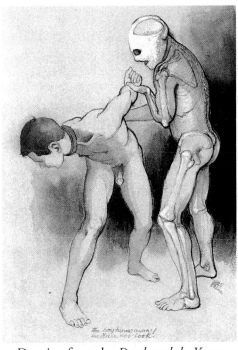

Drawing from the *Death and the Young
Man* series, 1995

Drawing from the *Death and the Young Man* series, 1995 *(Collection Edward Lucie-Smith)*

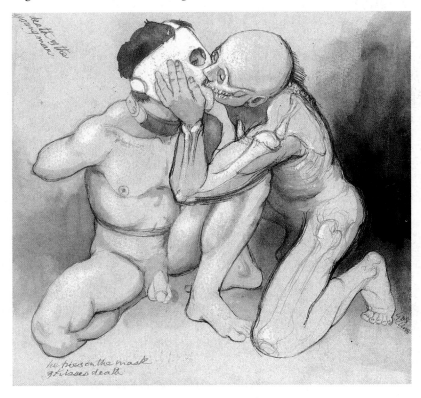

Tony Ward, actor and model, in *Hustler White*, 1995 – one of the sweetest, most charming and genuine men I've met *(photo: Rick Castro)*

rather odd. She covered mainly divorce and adultery cases which, so she claimed, meant hours of surveillance, especially trailing the suspects. Her boyfriend Sid, a shabby balding man who sniffed, was, according to her, the finest violinist in England. We never got the chance to give an opinion as he never played for us.

There was also Elin, a middle-aged Welsh woman and Rosicrucianist, who, with her young boyfriend, decided to stay in our room for weeks and weeks. And shortly after their departure a tall thin man moved in until I moved him out. At this time we never seemed to have any money and these people, unwelcome though they were, at least fed us.

Then there was Ruby, dear old Ruby. In her late seventies or early eighties, she had returned to the house in which she was born. She lived in the basement room, the scene of our great party, and filled it with large dark pieces of furniture that somehow escaped Mr Davis's hammer. Mahogany sideboards stood on oak tables touching the ceiling. Chests of drawers and wardrobes had been pushed and fitted together, leaving only a narrow pathway between cliffs of polished wood along which we shuffled and squeezed, to a large table on which stood yet another table under which she ate, or to her narrow bed with a sink and gas ring next to it. This was Ruby's subterranean home where she entertained, making cups of tea and boiled eggs for anyone able to sidle into her jealously guarded cavern.

In spite of her age Ruby took great trouble with her appearance: she was the most extravagantly dressed eccentric in Highbury, the most extravagantly dressed woman I've ever seen. Over her short cropped sparse grey hair she placed a woolly orange wig that quite often slipped around on her head. Under the weight of large straw or felt hats, decorated with flowers, it moved quite freely with a life of its own, and she spent a good deal of time readjusting it. She wore powder and rouge, applying both generously over the previous day's layer. Washing or bathing were not high on her list of priorities. Around her neck she wore several gold-coloured chains which, with time, left a thick greenish tide mark. Wearing off-the-shoulder blouses, she bolstered a flat chest with a feather pillow hung low near her gold-belted waist.

Ruby affected long and flowing skirts, often wearing two at the same time over many petticoats. When one pair of stockings failed her, she would pull another over them, giving her thin legs a distinctly knobby silhouette. Petticoats would come unhitched and trail behind her like a bridal train as she stepped quite daintily in gold sandals along to the shops. I remember her in her large straw hat on a swing hanging from the branch of a blossoming May tree in the back garden of the Cumberland. With the spring sun behind her, in a warm afternoon haze, her skirts and petticoats afloat, she looked like a Fragonard.

129

Eric drew several portraits of her sitting (like the portraits of Mr Davis in our basement before we moved upstairs) on an old carved wooden chair. 'Be put away, you should, for doing stuff like that,' she commented on seeing the large nude of me. Ruby was even less impressed by Eric's drawings of her but she kept posing as Eric was paying her. He caught the pain and fear, a look of hopelessness that was hidden behind the grimy, gaudy and stubborn exterior. Ruby was a fighter, pugnacious and determined, yet she knew she was engaged in a losing battle. Under siege in her basement stockade, she fought bravely. For her there was no friendly death but an implacable enemy to be resisted with every fibre of her being.

Downstairs, under our room, there lived Dennis, a well-educated, well-spoken man in his thirties, tall with a fresh schoolboy face. He was bald on top but with hair grown long at the sides and swept over the crown of his head in a highly lacquered flap he appeared, from a distance, to have a full head of hair. He existed in one of Mr Davis's partitioned corridors. Dennis's lover was the Cumberland handyman. Their mating was far louder than Mrs Johnson and her lads.

Once, in the middle of the night, woken up by bangs and thumps, groaning and screaming coming from under us, I thought someone was being attacked, if not murdered. Pulling on a pair of jeans, I rushed downstairs. Eric refused to get out of bed, telling me I was stupid to interfere. I was – but with the appallingly loud cries desperate in their intensity and the banging reverberating up through the floorboards, I felt I could do little else but respond.

Knocking on Dennis's door I asked if he was okay. 'Go away, we're fucking,' he snapped back. Assuming I was doing my good samaritan bit and rescuing someone from a fate worse than death, if not death itself, I returned rather grumpily to bed.

'What was going on?' Eric asked.

'Dennis and his chap were having sex,' I replied. 'Honestly, though, they might have some consideration. I thought he was being murdered.'

'Probably will be if he doesn't look out,' commented Eric.

Dennis wasn't murdered, unless of course one considers suicide as the murder of the self. Dennis attempted suicide many times. Whenever an ambulance drew up outside and the attendants rushed down the steps of the basement area, our first thought was: 'Oh, dear, Dennis is at it again', and we'd lean out to see him strapped to a stretcher being borne away.

Once, covered in a confetti of pills and still holding the pill bottle, he gave a faint wave to us, though I can't say he managed a brave smile. Whatever he was fighting, I knew these attempts were a cry for attention, but Dennis rebuffed any offer of help.

I had noticed one summer when visiting Janet and Sylvia – Eric and I were staying in the cottage – that on opening the front door there was a rather strange and unpleasant smell. Janet said she had noticed it several days before but couldn't find the source. The stench was ghastly. We'd never smelt a dead body before but we knew without a doubt that this was the odour of a decaying corpse. We went in search of Mr Davis.

The landlord, when cornered, admitted that the smell was strong and pervasive – not that he appeared concerned or even prepared to find the source. Only with the threat of us calling in the Health Department did he act, almost immediately finding at the top of the house in a squalid attic room the body of a man who had taken a turned-on, unlit gas fire to bed with him several weeks previously.

'Oh, it's not nice. Really, by Christ, it's not nice. I mean, well, now, I'll have to fumigate. It's gone through the floorboards. I don't know; they come here to die, if you ask me.' Mr Davis smiled. 'No, not nice at all, it isn't.'

At least two or three times a year the police, followed by an ambulance, would turn up and a covered body would be borne away. There was no particular interest in this ritual, no families turned up to claim property or to ask what had happened. Lonely people in little sordid rooms, finding they had exhausted the possibilities of their lives, ended them quietly and without fuss. That is how Dennis eventually left, carried out as an anonymous bundle on a stretcher.

And in this place, among this collection of amazing and extraordinary people, Eric and I decided to launch ourselves. Not having the money to move to a more respectable abode and needing Mr Davis to fund us, we were stuck.

Our refurbished front room was more than two aspiring young men on the climb up and out of poverty could wish for and it impressed everyone who came to visit. Of course, the hallway and stairs were a bit dingy and appeared even more so after entering our tasteful sanctum.

The back room served as our bedroom, kitchen and bathroom, and Eric's studio. At first thinking that somehow we would be able to design and arrange it so that it would be viewable, I painted it white with a simple black art nouveau design around the central rosette in the ceiling.

Both rooms had large plain stone fireplaces. Above the one in the back room I painted in grisaille a Renaissance-cum-art deco frame for a portrait of a woman posed as Diana the Huntress with a translucent rope of pearls around her neck, probably by Lely. Two naked young men stood on a black-and-white tiled floor very much influenced by Luca Signorelli, muscular and slim with *trompe l'oeil* additions of flies and birds. Eric grumbled but I insisted and persisted. It was to be the last painting I attempted for many years.

131

Finally realising that to open the back room to visitors was totally impractical, that there was no way to hide our bed and wardrobe, although the paper and unfinished drawings of Eric's forgery could be stacked, it remained definitely a part of the Cumberland, untidy and a little sordid. Although we began a bathroom, a small addition to the black-and-white tiled balcony, it was never finished and the shower tray became a litter tray for the many stray cats that haunted the gardens.

Underneath the back room lived a small, malevolent elderly Irishman and his retarded son. Before our arrival he had run the house on military lines, posting notices and generally interfering with the other tenants. When our front room was finished, but before the arrival of the curtains (which were being lined), the uncovered windows gave a view in the evening into a world, gently lit by several lamps, that had long vanished from Highbury Grove. This glimpse of opulence drove the Irishman into a frenzy. Banging on the door, he demanded we cover the windows and told us we were 'promoting a disorderly house'.

Soon after, when Sylvia had come over for tea, he burst into the back room, shrieking at Eric and me as we stood in shock. Although he didn't use the word 'queer', he told us that he could hear us at night, he knew what we were and what we were up to, and that if we caused any more trouble he'd go to the police. Sylvia leapt, literally, to our defence. Eric and I were speechless. Jumping in front of the Irishman, she shouted in his face, 'How dare you! You should be ashamed of yourself! I'll go to the police and complain about you making threats and harassing people. Go away!'

This confrontation came at a time when we had heard of two young men we'd met, friends of friends, who, on complaints from neighbours, had been arrested, their bed-sheets taken away for examination. They were charged with buggery; charged with just living and loving together. One of them hanged himself, unable to face the 'terrible disgrace' of being caught in an act of love with another man. We were honestly quite scared and I think with Eric's beginnings in forgery we were nervous about everything. Keeping Mr Davis happy and avoiding exposure as forgers and our attempts to start our own business were all taking their toll. This confrontation with the little man from downstairs panicked us. Eric decided that all the letters he had written to me, the journal of his European walk, which also detailed his sexual fantasies about us, must be destroyed. I took the opportunity to dispose of some photographs of Gianni, several quite sexually explicit, which Eric had brought back with him. I still regret burning those letters, though.

Also in the flames went a series of erotic drawings of us both, slightly idealised in pen and ink, small energetic drawings – 'attitudes of love', Eric called them. They showed us both rather athletically and energetically engaged in sex. Eric had drawn himself over-endowed and myself – for the sake of aesthetics, he informed me – very under-endowed.

My diary was also burnt. I had kept it only spasmodically but it contained many richly described evocations of our sex together in and out of bed. Eric felt it must go.

The nudes of me – those without erections – were kept. Viewed simply as studies of the male nude they were harmless enough.

Also consigned to the flames were my paintings of Eric and all the drawings of screaming men. I was less unhappy with their loss than I was over the destruction of Eric's work. It meant more to me, was far more important than my own, and yet in one sense I was relieved: burnt, they were no longer a source of contention between us.

All traces of our private life went into the bonfire and I mourned the loss. I wanted to seal everything up in a parcel and leave if for safekeeping with my brother or Janet and Sylvia, until such time – if there ever was one – when we would be free from bigotry and prosecution. But Eric was adamant.

This was his first exposure to bigotry and to homophobia and it frightened him, it frightened us both. Hiding behind his 'butch' masculine appearance, he looked to the world at large completely heterosexual and that was how he liked it. Much later, financial security gave him the confidence to be openly gay, but during our time together we made few close gay friends and our homosexuality was closed to the public. In fact, Eric seemed to shy away from any real intimacy with others. For me, he tolerated Janet and Sylvia, but I never saw him use anything but his public persona in company.

I was asked to provide some drawings for an Oxford undergraduate magazine. The editor had seen my work at the RCA graduation show. As always when I work, I concentrate on what I'm doing to the exclusion of everything else. Eric, of course, found fault with the subject matter – male nudes, hunky and chunky and semi-abstract in brush and black Chinese ink – but I persevered, gritting my teeth and ignoring him. For the first time, somebody wanted my work apart from my brother Peter, and the feeling was good. Then one evening Eric erupted.

I had not been out shopping. I had not cooked dinner and, even worse, I had not been fussing around him, not paying attention to him for several days. I had been totally engrossed in what I was doing. Jumping to his feet he kicked over the jar of water I was using, spilling it across my drawings. I hit him and he hit me and we had the most tremendous row. The old Irishman downstairs could definitely hear what we were up to.

Much later, in bed, Eric told me – he did not explain – what he needed from me, what was expected from me, what my role was. He was working to make something of us and he needed my complete attention, my constant support. Told that I had a brilliant eye and that I should use it not on my own work but in aiding him, he said he needed every moment of my time so that he could work in peace.

What was I doing? Restoring pictures? I could do that any day. And my drawings, they were disgusting and a waste of time, an indulgence when I should be, *must* be, supporting him.

Everything Eric created was passed by me; from the incipient doodle to the finished product I was expected to comment, criticise and praise. He needed meals on time, cups of tea regularly, sandwiches, cigarettes, clothes cleaned and pressed. He was asking for a full-time cook, valet, studio assistant, servant and dogsbody, though I didn't see it. Eric said he needed me and that was enough. As a child I had been trained to obey, and although as an adult I had a strong will, a rebellious spirit, these were subjected to an earlier discipline and to my need to be loved.

Eric drew a 'Rembrandt' for Mr Davis and several Constantin Guys water-colours, 'ladies of the night', and a couple of Sickerts. Recovering his spirit, he decided to have an exhibition. I selected a wonderful collection from the early pen-and-ink landscapes to studies of the cast room at the Academy Schools as well as nudes of me and landscapes of Rome. Together we went through them again and again until the selection was narrowed down to about forty, of which roughly fifteen we had matted.

Eric made an appointment at the Redfern and a couple of other galleries in and around Bond Street. No one was even slightly interested. I was furious – they were beautiful drawings. I couldn't understand anyone rejecting them.

Eric, quiet and bitter, began drinking again. Years before, after the failure of his big portrait group, now hung in Dr Leibson's large Victorian house, Eric started drinking heavily. There were several accidents in bed and after the last one I told him either he stopped or I wasn't sleeping with him again. It was bad enough to go to bed with a drunk but impossible when he just vomited, so inebriated he couldn't get up and use the bucket I placed by the bed. My threat succeeded and Eric stopped. This time there were no late-night incidents but he was nevertheless drinking heavily and continually.

Peter Greenham came round to dinner and the conversation turned to Eric's attempts at a one-man show. Eric had been drinking a great deal before and through dinner and now, sitting by the fireplace nursing a

Swedish brandy bowl almost half full of VSOP, he burst into tears, his body shaking. I held him, angry at the people who had rejected his work and hurt him so badly.

I got him interested in illustrating and translating the Lorca *Gypsy Ballads*. The book of Posada woodcuts was consulted and used as a basis for several of the engravings. Posada's *calaveras* of Don Quixote provided the inspiration for Eric's large engraving of Death dressed as a matador riding a bull, galloping across the bleak stormy landscape. Eric appeared to draw the energy and passion from Posada's earthy engravings and transmute them to his own more sophisticated style. The finest prints in the *Gypsy Ballad* sets are those most clearly connected to Posada. I also made him draw me. I had begun to loathe posing but he wouldn't hire other young men so, wanting him to work, I was his model again. But he refused to continue painting. 'No one wants my paintings so why should I bother,' he moaned. I worked very hard to get him to start again but it took several years.

And there were the boys that I had to deal with. One day I interrupted Eric humping the Black Widow in a tiny corridor room. Returning early another afternoon from the college I found Eric and a young Irish labourer – a pretty, muscular young man, short with black hair, blue eyes and a white firm body – together in our basement just before or after having sex. I didn't ask. Then there was another Irishman, a student at the RCA, whom I demolished. Eric saw him at a Friday-night dance and became enamoured, meeting him secretly but not secretly enough, so I attacked him. Eating lunch with a friend in the RCA canteen, I saw the youth enter. Filled with fury, I climbed onto the table and bellowed: 'There's that Irish queer who's trying to pinch my lover. Look at the sneaky little bugger. If he doesn't stop I'm smashing his face in!' The poor man, face white with shock, now the centre of attention, gave a loud cry, fled and was trouble no more.

An Italian arrived one day, a young man who looked like I imagined Dante might. Eric was his *amore*, he told me. 'Oh, really,' I said, and took him to find Eric. I left them to talk alone but returned to find Dante on his knees, his arms around Eric's legs. I sent him away. We both were glad to see him leave. Eric recounted that the Italian had fallen in love with him at the British Schools. Eric had fled to a small village, Anticoli, in the mountains, to get away from him. The young man had burst in upon him one night as Eric was sleeping in a little studio room, breaking open the door and attempting to stab him with a knife. The police and Dante's family were called after Eric had subdued him and he was taken to a convalescent home. Very unsympathetic, I took the high moral stand of serve you right for playing around.

The final straw was when David Hockney came to dinner at Janet and Sylvia's with Mo McDermott. Mo and Eric disappeared together for over an hour and I pretended I didn't care. Later I tried for the last time to talk to Eric. 'How could you do that?' I asked him. 'I felt totally humiliated. Everyone knew what you were up to. What would you do if it had been me?'

Eric, as always in such situations, withdrew, became still, pompous and cold. 'I'd leave you.' He said the words quietly and with his lips white and thin.

'Eric, it's so unfair.'

'Life is unfair.'

I gave up. No fighting, no shouting. I walked out and spent the night with two friends, Bridget and William Kempster, deciding that if Eric could have other men so could I, but I wouldn't be found out; obviously I couldn't be found out.

A few days later at the original ICA Galleries in Soho I met a man from the American Embassy and for several months carried on an illicit affair with him, sneaking out when Eric was teaching at Watford, and making lots of casseroles, casoulet and stews that needed little preparation and much slow cooking; I had to make sure my household duties were not neglected.

The break-up of our relationship had begun. With real communication between us quite dead and with my affair necessitating lies and deceit, it didn't stand a chance. I was beginning to grow up, chafing at the rules Eric had laid down for me. I loved him but I was beginning to feel stifled, beginning to need a life of my own. But the thought of leaving him never occurred to me; whether it should have or not, it didn't.

Packington Street

IN THE MID-1950S, IN SPITE OF THE HUGE REBUILDING programme put in place by the new Labour government, London was still a shabby and bomb-scarred city. The prosperity of the 'New Elizabethan Age' was not yet apparent. The centre of London was fog-blackened. The famous 'pea-soupers', despite the Clean Air Act of 1956, still floated across the city, from Hampstead Heath in the north to Greenwich in the south.

During those student days Eric and I, on our long walks, had noticed a curious 'circus', parallel to Charing Cross Road; memorably depicted in Dickens's *A Commercial Traveller* and his *Sketches by Boz*. The whole area was still oddly Dickensian: picture restorers, antique dealers, art galleries. And among them were old Welsh dairies, Italian cafés and shops catering for what was then still a heavily populated area.

Through the dusty windows of one shop we could a see tumble of marble and bronze; busts and statues, some damaged, others in pristine (we thought) condition. There were also architectural bits and pieces: columns, shields, urns all thrown together, it seemed, as though unwanted.

On these walks Eric had struck up an acquaintanceship with a 'pavement artist', the sort of untrained person who had the ability to reproduce, literally, upon the flagstones of central London, exactly what he saw. Known as 'Rem', this crazy old man wore a floppy beret which he believed typical of his hero, Rembrandt van Rijn. It seems that he had once been fêted by the Dutch government as a simulacrum of the original.

Talking with him by his pitch, we noticed a stooped and elderly man walking by with an armful of folders stuffed with prints. He had a mass of grey hair and bushy eyebrows. He passed a coin to Rem. 'He's worth a fortune,' said Rem as the man walked on. 'Places all over the place, stuffed with stuff, if you get what I mean.'

We decided, for God knows what motive, to follow him. He turned into Cecil Court, a little alley linking Charing Cross Road and St Martin's Lane. We watched as he unlocked an iron-grilled Victorian gate and then opened the glass-panelled door to his lair. Pushing past a penny-farthing cycle he closed the door behind him. The sign above read LOUIS MEIER, 'THE OLD CURIOSITY SHOP' itself. Many times we had stopped and looked in through the dirty windows at a disorderly mess that looked like the prop room of a film studio. Attic and Apulian Kraters and vases, most broken or repaired, but a few in excellent condition; an Egyptian sarcophagus, masks, prints, frames, Victorian dolls in grimy fancy clothes, all heaped and piled together. Dusty and cobwebbed, it was as though all the sweepings of history were crammed to the ceiling in an West End Aladdin's cave.

We had barely entered the shop before Mr Meier, advancing like a battered and ageing fury, pushed us out again, declaring in a Swiss accent: 'Something for nothing, that's all you want. Rembrandts for pennies. Out! Out! Get Out!'

Now, four years later, slightly more assured, our confidence bolstered by having a few pounds in our pockets, we tried again. This time we were in luck. At the far end of the dimly lit narrow shop, in a curtained alcove overheated by a large gas fire, a du Maurier cigarette held between pink lips, with an inch of ash waiting to fall on her large silk-covered bosom, sat Marie Gray (spelt like the poet, not the colour, she informed us), Miss Apricot. We became instant friends.

Marie 'managed' Louis Meier. In the 1920s and '30s she commanded a small band of women ('my girls'), to whom she taught the mysteries of hand-colouring old prints. When etchings and engravings fell out of fashion after the stockmarket crash, she moved in on Louis.

Cecil Court, Seven Dials and the area around them had a bad reputation, and Marie decided that Louis, as a bachelor, couldn't look after himself. She could also keep the many young prostitutes from hanging around outside and inside his shop.

Apart from the shop in Cecil Court, Louis also owned the one we first noted in Seven Dials; an extensive warren of cellars under the offices of *The Lady* magazine; a Tudor warehouse, formerly stables, in Drury Lane, and a barn somewhere in Wood Green, all filled to overflowing with goodies.

When we first met Marie, Louis was busily sorting through his innumerable possessions and packing up the best to be sent to Switzerland. Marie was affectionate and enjoyed fussing around him, but he was a true-blue old curmudgeon, a Scrooge shuffling between his properties, his being entirely focused on money. He had none of the joy in life we saw in Mr Davis but he did have a keen eye.

We once bought a piece of a Bassano, animals entering the ark, black and dark with heavy varnish and the grime of centuries covering it. After I cleaned it and it was framed, we hung the painting in the front room at Highbury. Although part of a larger picture, perhaps a third to a half, it was beautiful. Marie and Louis arrived unexpectedly and Louis, on seeing it glowing richly above the mantelpiece, was so angry at letting it slip through his fingers that for a year or so he refused to sell anything to us: we could only buy through Marie, but not if he was around.

We were lucky to find the shop unlocked – it rarely was. About a year before we met, Marie had an encounter there with the diabolist Aleister Crowley. 'The Beast', so Marie told us, had behaved improperly. We never found out what it was he had done, but she ordered him out. As he left he put a curse on the shop. Two days later, when Marie had to go to a sale, she asked one of her 'girls' to sit in for her, and the poor woman was hacked to death with an Arabic knife. Marie called in a priest for a cleansing ritual or exorcism but never again felt comfortable in the shop, and blamed Crowley's curse for causing the murder.

From Marie we bought the Sir Peter Lely portrait of a woman, the Bassano, a big Flemish painting of a court scene which, after I had cleaned it, turned out to be *The Judgement of Solomon*: the babies had bunches of flowers painted over them. Two six-foot canvases in hand-carved gilded frames from the collection of Lord Kitchener (of Khartoum fame) – one, a lovely portrait of a Spanish nobleman, was sold at Sotheby's for a paltry two hundred pounds. The other, dark and gloomy, proved to be a line drawing on a dark mustard ground of King James of Scotland and England, the queer one. (When Elizabeth I died the courtiers cried out, 'The Queen is dead. Long live the Queen,' in reference to James.) He was not a handsome man but Eric and I did our best, painting the picture in glowing colours, and sold it as a decorator's item. Under all the guff there is a rather nice period drawing of the King which I hope one day will resurface and be enjoyed in its original state.

Underneath a pile of nineteenth-century sporting prints in one of the smaller storehouses off Tottenham Court Road was a completely black canvas. What the subject might be was impossible to see, but the back, the canvas, looked interesting. Marie sold it to us for a few pounds and after I cleaned it we possessed (but not for long – Mr Davis seized it) a lovely Roman *Charity* in excellent condition. It depicted the starving old prisoner suckling at the Roman matron's breast, whilst an infant looked on with a beatific smile. The colour was particularly fine. Anthony Blunt, on seeing a photograph, thought it Genoese, possibly an early Van Dyck.

Marie sold us many drawings, in particular a set of fifty Burne-Jones sketches in red chalk that I literally picked up from the floor in Drury Lane. The ground floor of the stables was covered in a thick, decaying carpet of prints, mainly from the 1930s, thrown down to soak up the damp. Seeing something glinting golden amongst the papers, I bent down and unearthed a stash of the remnants of several Mandarin crowns. The silk had rotted but the gold wires holding gold medallions filled with semi-precious stones and kingfisher feathers were, though flattened, intact. I carefully collected a bag of them and Marie gave them to us.

The cellars under *The Lady* often flooded and were a doomsday record of mouldering prints, books and antiques. For one afternoon Eric and I battled to lift objects, rotting and wet, from the floor, but Louis turned up and ordered us out. Part of his 'Swiss' collection was stored here and he guarded it jealously.

Leaning against the outside wall of the stable at Wood Green were a series of pottery casts from the Luca della Robbia *Cantoria*, Museo dell'Opera del Duomo in Florence. Louis wouldn't let us buy them but Marie sold us a broken one which, after I had glued it together, looked very fine.

The back quarter of this building was piled almost to the ceiling with prints. Marie had me ascend a ladder and crawl on my stomach across this huge stack, slither down the far side to turn on a light switch and open a far door from the inside as they, Marie and Louis, had mislaid the key. In my slithering I dislodged many prints, including several Dürer etchings and a portfolio of his woodcuts. Again, Louis wouldn't sell them to us. In spite of this, Eric and I made friends with him – or rather became as friendly as one could with the tetchy old man.

But it was Marie we enjoyed. When we first met, Eric and I had little money but she took us out to eat. Lunch at Simpson's or Fortnum's, tea at the Dorchester, dinner at the Savoy Grill and, for me, much nicer places like the original Bertorelli's, Schmidt's or Madame Maurer's (whose almost life-size blue-and-white model cow filled her window), and Mario and Franco's. At all of the above, including the Savoy Grill and the Dorchester, she was greeted as an old friend, which of course she was, by the owners and staff.

Generous with her money and lavishly affectionate in her praise and enjoyment of fine food and good service, she could also freeze you with an icy stare over her glasses, the brim of her hat lowered. 'I know what Eric's up to,' she told me one day in her apartment, fixing me with that look. Thinking, as she had recently handed Eric several pages of blank antique paper, that she was referring to his forging, I was flustered. But it wasn't fakery but thievery she meant. If we ate well and the service had been excellent, Marie always left a large tip and, according to her, Eric had been stealing them.

'Marie, are you sure? That's an awful thing to accuse someone of,' I replied.

She was always 'missing' something; great searches would be undertaken and eventually she would 'remember' that so-and-so was the last person near the missing articles. A cardboard shoebox filled with Mycenaean beads, five thousand years old; a Roman marble head of a young girl; her leather jewel box containing her collection of art nouveau jewellery; a large Egyptian wall painting; a small leather bag of emeralds: all these and more went missing. Then, of course, they turned up. 'They must have been replaced,' she'd say mysteriously.

But Marie was quite sure about Eric and the tips, and later when I confronted him he admitted it. Her knowledge didn't stop him either. Years later at the Sibilla in Tivoli I saw him pocket the tip she left. We didn't need the money then. I don't know why he bothered. The thrill, the risk of being discovered, just being a naughty boy?

Marie and Louis's flat, like the shop in Cecil Court, was packed tight. Under her bed were hundreds of Japanese prints that she had accumulated over thirty years or more. Her collection of miniatures – shelf upon shelf of miniature objects, Mycenaean, Greek, Roman, Egyptian, Coptic, Aztec, Georgian, doll's-house furniture, Meissen and Chelsea journeyman figurines – a hodge-podge ranging through millennia was extraordinary, the variety quite magical.

The salon, with the kitchen second, formed the centre of her flat. We ate for years at the big pine kitchen table off an eighteenth-century hand-painted service until a dealer offered her two hundred pounds per plate. Knives and forks were all either late eighteenth century or early nineteenth and the glasses a mixture from the seventeenth century onwards.

Her salon was extraordinary. A collection of large Roman glass jars and bottles covered several tables. Shelves were stocked with Greek terracottas and several eighteenth-century fakes that, in their own delicate and stylised way, were as beautiful as the originals. Chinese and Japanese bronzes, cloisonné, two beautiful white porcelain five-foot Chinese figures. Were they European chinoiserie or the genuine article? We never found out. The most amazing object in this apartment of amazing things was tucked into the space made by the bay windows: Tutankhamun's bed, or rather a meticulous replica of the original. Thick with gold leaf, it served as a table for Marie's collection of early Italian prints.

The great love of Marie's life was a woman. I think she was French, and she lived in Egypt. Although the woman was married – unhappily, so Marie informed us – and gave birth to a daughter, Marie's devotion was unwavering. She knew Eric and I were lovers but she never used that word, the generic 'friends' covered all.

'My dear, you mustn't let Eric tell you what to do all the time. It's not wise,' she'd say, giving me a smile, a knowing look, and tap the side of her nose. 'I think Eric is a little jealous of you, my dear,' she told me another time. 'He doesn't approve of you taking attention away from him.'

I had noticed this – Eric did like to be the star of the evening. Listening to the same stories repeated again and again throughout the years was becoming something of a problem for me. I was bored. As much as I tried, there were times when I couldn't hide how weary I was with his one-man performance.

But Marie had her own stories of Frederick Ashton, the young Margot Fonteyn, of Jacob Epstein and Augustus John and how Christine Keeler used Marie's shop for assignations with a Russian spy, one of her lovers. She proudly related how a car had come for her, and of the many hours of questioning she had endured at Scotland Yard.

Because of Marie, Eric and I now could enter expensive restaurants and hotels easily and without embarrassment. My cooking skills improved and extended with exposure to good food and wine. I was learning, trying to be the perfect 'wife', only the image was a little frayed at the edges. I did my best but there was really no way I could fit myself into the role of middle-class domesticity.

At last Eric and I left the Cumberland and moved into a duplex in Packington Street close to Collins's music hall and Islington Green. We could afford to move and the Cumber Ho, for two upwardly mobile young gentlemen, was fast becoming completely impossible. Not only did we have to dissuade our guests from using the lavatory, unless it was a dire emergency (which, thank goodness, it never was, for we were never sure in what state they would find it) but worse – someone was carrying on a rather unpleasant guerrilla war against us. On several occasions when bringing food from the kitchen to the front room I had found deposits of excrement, piles of the stuff, deposited in the centre of the hall floor and, once, smeared on our door. I cleaned the stuff up, opening the front door to clear the smell of shit and pine disinfectant. Whether it was a strike against our 'posh' front room or bigotry or both, we never discovered. But it was time to get out.

Here in Packington Street, after a pause of several weeks during which he finished the translations for the engravings to Lorca's *Gypsy Ballads*, Eric started a series of quite interesting fakes, beginning with a set of red chalk drawings after Goya's *Disasters of War* in the style of a minor French artist and several Gainsborough drawings: landscapes with figures, farm carts and animals, and a preparatory study, black conté on blue paper, for Gainsborough's painting, *The Blue Boy*. We sent a photograph of this drawing to the art critic Ellis Waterhouse, whose splendidly produced tome on Gainsborough we had recently purchased. He authenticated it and we sold it at Sotheby's for the miserly sum (so I thought) of two hundred pounds.

I bought a Romney from Sotheby's at a sale of English drawings. It was a lucky buy that happened in one of those pauses when a previous lot fetches more than was expected and the bidding becomes slightly erratic and hesitant. It was a fierce, vibrant drawing of Medea howling over the dead bodies of her children in a dark sepia pen and wash that had leached through the paper.

From the Holloway Road salesrooms I bought a Jan Brueghel, ruins of a Roman temple or bathhouse by a seashore, a delicate pen-and-wash drawing with touches of blue. Previously sold by Colnaghi's, it was an incredible bargain at seventy pounds. I was obviously the only one attending the sale who knew anything about drawing.

Eric claimed in his autobiography that he made copies of both. He didn't. Also around this time, he wrote that he drew a portrait of a child from a photograph of the painting *Louis Robert* by Corot in the Louvre which, he says, he sold to Colnaghi's although they have no record of the sale. Again, he didn't. I can be certain about this as we lived in a small flat and we shared the upstairs front room as our studio. Even had we worked apart – me restoring the paintings, Eric on his faking – I would have known, for Eric consulted me. Everything he did was passed by me for changes, suggestions and a final yea or nay.

Pannini Galleries was founded shortly after we settled in. We had a catalogue printed and Eric had a metal plate made, covered with prominent collectors' marks. Hundreds of copies of the catalogue were sent out all over the world to museums, galleries and collectors. We had one bite. A man and a woman came round and bought two fakes and one original. One fake was a Mantegna – school of, that is – a small pen-and-ink drawing of Vulcan from the Parnassus painting. The other was a Reynolds wash drawing of a standing woman. The original was of the Romney Medea. It was a big disappointment. The catalogue was supposed to propel us into the world of dealing. It failed. It wasn't a bad catalogue either. A small Samuel Palmer pencil drawing, the Romney, a lovely small eighteenth-century tempera of the Pantheon in Rome, three fakes by Eric, the Mantegna, the Reynolds and a Campagnola landscape. I can't really remember the other drawings.

Eric continued at Watford as head of the Print Department. I went on doggedly restoring paintings. Eric soon became despondent, drinking solidly through the evenings at home. The poet Stephen Spender was supposed to have written a preface to the Lorca translation but it didn't happen – although Spender approved of Eric's verse translation. It was excellent, capturing the mood of the original while transposing the form into English balladry.

Nothing seemed to be working out. In desperation I bullied him into a series of wrestler drawings. As far as he was concerned, there was no point in him trying to create his own work. Nobody wanted it. 'Do them for me,' I insisted, 'just for me, I want your work.' Grudgingly he began as I supplied him with wrestling magazines. I channelled my frustrated creative energy in an attempt to make Eric break out of what he said was a feeling of futility. Of course I wanted to be working on them. I wanted them to be my drawings. I saw the set as a *Dance of Death* series and I urged Eric to have wrestlers naked and use the skeletal figure of death not only as a referee but also as one or both of the combatants. To make it a commentary on contemporary life, the cold war, the bomb, racism, capitalism versus communism.

But they were Eric's drawings and, while he allowed me to push him into creating them, he finally made them his own. They form a remarkable series, powerful and immediate, and the design of every image is brilliant and forceful.

More scattered memories. Janet, Sylvia, David Hockney and I on the Aldermaston March through London and demonstrating outside the American Embassy in Grosvenor Square; being picked up as we sat in non-violent protest, one policeman holding us under our arms, the other by our legs, all very proper. Until they dropped us on the edge of the kerb and walked away with self-satisfied, sadistic grins.

Reading James Baldwin, *Nobody Knows My Name* and *The Fire Next Time*, his electrifying essays, and *Another Country*, shocked, and for the first time I was aware of how widespread, how evil, how all-pervasive bigotry is in our society; realising how cocooned I was, how lucky I had been. I tried to interest Eric in this, but he wanted nothing to do with it. ('What has a black American got to do with me?'; 'Just the kind of book [*Another Country*] I'd expect you to read. It's filth') or with anything that was happening. He inveighed against 'The Young Contemporaries'. The young painters I had been at college with dismayed and upset him and he was bitter at their success.

Squatting in the pouring rain one Saturday night in a railway yard with Celia Hammond, Norman Parkinson's girl of the '60s. She, Sylvia, Terence Donovan (Sylvia's boyfriend), Eric and I had been out to dinner at Sam's in Salmon Lane, then on to the Roman Way, an 'in' pub. Here all the smartly dressed young Mods kept telling Celia: 'Coo, girl, you could make something of yourself if you dressed nice and wore make-up.' They had no idea who she was. Celia, extraordinarily beautiful, glowed even in a pair of old trousers and Terence Donovan's old jean jacket.

Dinners, parties and the Royal College of Art revues. Janet caused a sensation and received a standing ovation when she appeared in black net stockings, high-heeled shoes, elbow-length gloves and a small sequined corset with a fantail of shimmering pheasant feathers. She mimed a strip to 'Let Me Entertain You' from *Gypsy*. David joined in the fun in a similar costume. His make-up (silent screen vamp, a cross between Theda Bara and Joan Crawford, more suited for one of the ugly sisters in *Cinderella* than for a chorine) produced an almost Kabuki-like mask which somehow complemented his high-heeled gangling walk. David enjoyed himself immensely. He didn't think for one moment that he was a 'glamour girl', but instead had a true instinct for the absurd and played to it. Then there were trips up the river to Hampton Court and Kew, getting to know the affluent queens in Islington and Canonbury who made clear their resentment at me being with Eric.

1963. A big New Year's party. I cooked and baked for a couple of days. We bought gallons of booze. Marie and Louis, Barry and Rita Cole and Jessica, their newborn daughter who, in a little carry-cot, delighted Louis. Around midnight it snowed and us chaps created a long ice slide in the middle of the road and ran and slid until our lungs felt on fire and our breath rasped in our throats.

By Easter we'd had enough of the cold so Eric and I spent the holidays at the Hotel Inghilterra in Rome. Janet journeyed with us as far as Florence and then came on down to Rome with Ferrill, an American friend.

Back in London it was still cold and dirty. I was restoring a vast seventeenth-century Spanish painting of Prometheus bound with an eagle chewing on his liver, a German painting of various ghastly martyrdoms and minor nineteenth-century French landscapes – and I was hating it. Eric loathed teaching and Janet, who was supposed to be moving into David's flat, was furious. Behind her back, David had instead invited her very cute boyfriend to move in. I found her in tears on our doorstep and together we confronted David and the boyfriend in Powis Square – an unhappy hour which ended with David and the boyfriend in and Janet out.

My embassy lover in his double bed, looking at his purple blackness and my whiteness in the overhead mirror; me, exhausted by several hours of heavy sex lying almost asleep, his body a dark silhouette against the white sheets: 'Why don't you move in with me? You're not happy.' Time for me to leave. Leave and not return.

Eric staying out all night: 'I was at Peter Greenham's (or Anthony Blunt's) and I drank too much,' he would say. I cared, but there was nothing I could say now. No longer was I the injured and faithful lover.

Lavatory sex. I had sent Eric off with Marie on a trip to Italy the previous summer. She needed an escort and he and I needed a break from each other. On his return he recounted how everyone, yes everyone, thought he was her gigolo. Marie was very amused by it all. Walking back from a late dinner with Louis Meier in Soho while they were away, I stopped off for a pee in an old urinal built against the wall of Lincoln's Inn Fields. It was packed, quite literally packed, and an orgy was in progress. It had never occurred to me to consider public lavatories as a place for sex. Not connecting what had happened to me as a child in the lavatory at Barkingside, I was at twenty-five quite ignorant of such things. I stayed. There was no light but I could feel the flesh of the many bodies I used and who were using me. I didn't return. I could see that that kind of experience could easily become addictive.

Casual lavatory sex with men during the day and one fifteen-year-old schoolboy in his school blazer and peaked cap, whom I met again and again. A stocky young man with a cocky grin in jeans and a short navy-blue workman's jacket. Nothing was said as he fucked me until one day he asked if I'd like to meet his friend. 'Okay,' I replied, and we walked together for a few minutes. Then he turned and said, 'Perhaps it's not such a good idea.' We shook hands and he walked away. Years later I recognised him from a photograph. It was Joe Orton. These were occasional sporadic visits for I hadn't as yet developed a taste for (or the habit of) cruising.

Eric, Janet and I were fed up with the cold, the dirt and the prospect of a life pottering around art schools. The decision to go to Rome was almost unanimous. Eric needed some persuading about the move and of Janet accompanying us. He wasn't happy about that, but I was adamant.

Marie had sold us a large drawing in black chalk on blue paper, a view from the Via Appia Antica across the Roman *campagna* to Frascati, a delicate sweet landscape touched with white chalk highlights. Our first thought was that it was an early Corot but, as there are more fake Corots in existence than genuine ones, we decided to attribute it to Camille Pisarro. Eric gave it a C.P. in Pisarro's hand and it was bought by Joe McCrindle, the editor of *Transatlantic Review*, along with several strange Flemish and Dutch allegorical drawings – more of Eric's handiwork. With the money from these four and Augustus Johns (two sold at Christie's salesrooms, and two in Bond Street), we had about three or four thousand pounds in all.

Shippers came in and we left as soon as they had finished packing our stuff and the flat was empty. The taxi broke down halfway to Victoria Station and the driver, furious that I didn't give him a tip, threw the handful of coins at me shouting, 'You fucking miserly sod.' We arrived just in time for the boat train and settled ourselves into our compartment.

Piazza Paganica, Rome

APART FROM ERIC SUCCUMBING TO FOOD POISONING, THE train journey was uneventful. We stayed at La Sorena, a hotel in Piazza San Silvestro, a dark and gloomy place, for a couple of days while he recovered. Then we went down to Positano. Sheer joy: my first taste of the Mediterranean. It was warm, the sea was warm! I could stay in it for hours. I did – and came down with sunstroke. So, disregarding the *bella figura*, I bought a hat and wore it all day, even when swimming.

For just over two weeks we swam, sunbathed, had afternoon-tea at the Bucco di Bacco on the beach, then showered, dressed, dined, danced (well, Janet and I danced); then, exhausted by the sun, the sea, the food and wine and the sheer beauty of Positano, we retired early. Evening meals on the vine-covered terrace of our small hotel overlooking the sea; watching the moon rise above the mountains as we ate; our occasional siestas, Eric and I naked and sweating in the mid-afternoon heat, gorged on food and wine, our bodies slippery and wet in dazed, sensual sex.

We went back to Rome. Dante appeared, accompanied by a pretty young woman whom he introduced as his fiancée. We wanted an apartment? Great, he had one, a large one, which he was vacating at the end of summer. Why not take it over? Why not indeed? Eric wasn't keen. He imagined further knife attacks in the middle of the night, but Janet and I promised we'd protect him. And so it was settled.

We stayed for a week or so in a tiny place adjacent to the Portico d'Ottavia looking out onto the Teatro di Marcello. We couldn't be more 'in' Rome, surrounded by architecture from the classical period through the millennia to Mussolini's fascist tidying-up, all mixed in as though to welcome us. Gianni reappeared on the scene, looking like a Pekinese. Having gone to Paris to have his perfect nose made *retroussé*, he'd returned from the plastic surgery with a 'pug'. Eric would go off for long afternoons and evenings, making contacts, whatever, and I enjoyed the sheer intoxication of living in Rome.

Dante's apartment was at the top of an old building, a minor palazzo, in what had been the Jewish ghetto. Number 13 Piazza Paganica had ninety-odd marble steps to climb and no elevator, and we felt we were floating above the roof once we got up there. L-shaped, with fourteen rooms in ruinous condition, it was large and wonderful. When Dante and his fiancée left after a few weeks, Eric, Janet and I launched an attack on the decay and neglect. The three large rooms looking onto the courtyard had false ceilings of canvas, covering wooden beams. These we pulled down and began to strip the old wood of centuries of paint and gesso.

At some time in the 1920s two sisters had lived in the apartment. One was reputed to be over six feet, the other a hunched-back dwarf. The apartment had been wired for electricity to accommodate these two disproportionate women, with one set of light switches slightly higher than usual, and a corresponding set about three feet from the floor. The switches were connected by swatches of wire hanging with cobwebs and dirt like ancient Christmas decorations. Going to the fuse box I switched everything off; then, armed with a pair of cutting shears, I marched into the kitchen. Climbing on a stool balanced on the round table, I grabbed a handful of wires and cut. I saw the flash, but that was all. Janet, who was in attendance on the idiot, said I shot backwards off the stool, banged my head on a main beam and sort of crumpled to the floor, luckily not damaged, just shook up. We agreed to call in a professional electrician, an efficient young man who, like us, was also rather eccentric.

Lying in the old-fashioned enamel bath in the tiny red-brick-floored bathroom on a warm summer evening, I reached for a towel. Slowly, so slowly that I didn't at first realise what was happening, the bath tipped over on to its side. I tried to stop its gentle progress as I flowed out with the tidal wave but had no luck. The brick absorbed and carried the deluge through to the apartment below. Count and Contessa Guidi, a charming elderly couple, were restrained but adamant that this sort of thing mustn't happen again. Of course not, we assured them.

A few weeks later, the bath upright again on wooden blocks, I turned on the electric heater – and promptly forgot about it. Hours later, with the small room almost solid with steam, the old pipe connecting the heater with the bath taps burst, and the Guidis were inundated again. This time we offered to pay for the damage but were gently refused. 'Please, please no more,' the Contessa begged us. We again reassured her.

After a general conference we decided to build a bathroom in a large room which had a tiny balcony overlooking the courtyard. Empty except for a lavatory and coal stove that centrally heated the apartment, it seemed ideal. A team of plumbers was called in and proceeded with great energy to rip up the floor and walls and disconnect the lavatory. Lavatory-less for a month or so I peeped in one day and, lo and behold, saw our new lav was perched on its little wooden throne. The old cistern on the wall high above it was still there. Full of joy, I rushed in and made a deposit. But when I yanked on the chain, the disconnected pipe sprayed water all over me. It seemed an unusually long discharge and the water, after soaking me and having no floor to spread across, went straight through to the Guidis.

As I pulled up my wet trousers I heard our doorbell ring and, looking across the well of the courtyard, could see two women hammering on the door. The Contessa and her maid were in tears. I tried my best to comfort them but after only a month or two in Rome my Italian was minimal.

'Has it stopped?' wailed the Contessa.

Seeking to reassure her, and thinking she was asking if it was going to happen again, I replied with what I hoped was a sympathetic smile, 'No, Contessa.'

Her shocked white face surprised me. It was not the happy reaction I expected. I dimly realised perhaps my Italian wasn't as good as I thought it might be. 'It's going to continue?' she shrieked at me.

I paused. Then, with a diffident smile, having translated her question as 'Has it stopped?' I replied. 'Yes, certainly, certainly, Contessa.'

She gave me a wild look and with an animal howl intense for so frail a figure, started pounding on the wall with her tiny fists.

At this point Eric, who had been enjoying the exchange behind our bedroom door, and who later translated it for me, stepped forward and made peace. The Contessa and her maid, a woman who appeared ancient beside her elderly employer, were invited in, seated, and given sherry and biscuits. Thankfully it was the last flood and, after the traumatic beginning, we became good neighbours.

Janet and I were sent up to Florence to collect her American friend Ferrill, who had a generous allowance and plenty of money in the bank. To put it simply, we needed money, and Ferrill had some. Soon after Ferrill's joining Pannini Galleries, our stuff arrived from England and the plumbers went on strike. Thinking us rich foreigners, they demanded double the price on which we had agreed. We fired them from a point of strength, for the new bath and lavatory were now functioning.

The dining-room was panelled in hardboard and Eric copied a series of figures from the Villa of the Mysteries in Pompeii, so it was designated the Pompeian room. I began painting a 'red room' with a baroque pattern, little realising how many fiddly bits there were to complete. On and on we worked: sanding, painting, perfecting, until our apartment was at last as ready as it would ever be. The wooden-beamed ceilings and the two-hundred-year-old doors were stripped and waxed. We had painted twelve rooms white and almost translucent. My 'red room', which I wished I hadn't started, was nearly finished and, after many false starts, our new black-tiled bathroom was working.

We were both worried about money. Ferrill was supporting us and was none too happy about the situation, but I had no idea how tense Eric was about things until one night I found him shaking uncontrollably, hardly able to speak. An attack of nerves. Dressing quickly, I ran into the L'Argo Argentina. It was late, around midnight, but a light shone out from the *farmarcia*. Banging on the glass door, I roused a sleepy chemist and in my execrable Italian explained Eric's symptoms to him. Bless him for he understood my babbling and sold me a bottle of a herbal mixture, a strong nerve tonic and tranquilliser called Neurobiol. The instructions on the label read 'Dose: two teaspoons'. I saw the words 'two' and 'spoon' and, not understanding, gave Eric two *table*spoons of the mixture and then a third for good measure. Within minutes the spasms stopped and he was asleep. I sat on the bed with him for about an hour and, unable to sleep myself, took two tablespoons and went off to bed.

Christmas time came and for a while Janet, Ferrill, Eric and I relaxed and celebrated. It was one of the happiest times at Piazza Paganica. Christmas in Rome is very busy and exciting. Although *Befana*, Twelfth Night – the night the witch gives presents to all the good children and punishes the bad ones – is considered more important, Christmas in Rome is magical. We toured the Nativity scenes. All the churches had one – some very old and quite spectacular with many beautiful figures in panoramic settings.

We bought our Christmas cards from a shop in Via di Cestari, near the Pantheon. Hundreds of years old, it still sells gold- and silver-plated thread by the ounce to be woven into and embroidered onto silk and velvet fabric using patterns that date back thousands of years. It also stocks sumptuous religious regalia, simple outfits for nuns and priests, and large elaborate statues of the holy family and the hierarchy of saints.

We just couldn't resist the fake parchment envelopes lined with a richly patterned Renaissance design with touches of gold everywhere. And although the reproductions of Old Master paintings on the front of the cards were rather crude and fuzzy, the general effect was delightful – very different from the cards sold in England at the time. The selection was vast and we ended up buying far more than we needed.

The four of us decided to have an old-fashioned Christmas and, as Eric and I had done the previous year in London, to invite friends and acquaintances who were on their own. We didn't make a great play of decorating, instead concentrating all our efforts on the food.

After enduring the various disasters and privations during the remodelling of the apartment, we felt close to each other and were determined to have a good time and throw a great party.

Firstly, to the surprise of the locals, we bought an enormous turkey – it barely fitted into the oven – from the window of our local butcher's. They had put it there only as a display, to attract customers, and were curious to know how we were going to cook it. Our descriptions of the stuffing horrified them. The list of ingredients seemed to them to have been concocted by a madman. Raisins, dates, ground pork, chestnuts, breadcrumbs, sage, turkey and chicken livers brought grimaces to their faces. 'What a horrible mess,' they declared. 'This is for eating?' The *stranieri* – the foreigners – were crazy.

Our insanity was confirmed when Eric ordered several kilos of kidney fat or suet. This wasn't the nicely packaged and wrapped processed fat from a supermarket, but instead was fresh from the carcass, with blood and bits of meat adhering to it. 'Gives a good flavour,' Eric said.

'What is the fat to be used for?' we were asked. When we explained Christmas pudding, plum pudding, *Dolce di Natale*, the entire shopful of customers and assistants raised their palms upwards, lifted their eyebrows, looked heavenwards, some even crossing themselves. We were considered definitely crazy, and rather disgusting to boot.

Eric was in charge of the pudding, a classic Christmas pudding full of dark beer, brandy, blanched and chopped almonds, fruit, glacé fruit, flour, butter and kidney fat. The mixture was so thick and heavy that only he could stir it. Janet, Ferrill and I tackled the stuffing for the turkey. Ferrill made a large cream cake, Janet and I a trifle. There were mounds of baked and creamed vegetables, a ham, mince pies and plenty of wine and spirits.

A mixed lot joined us: Ugo Trama, Pope John's favourite bass baritone – with Gianni; the writer Aubrey Menen with his young male secretary, and new, very young companion, Pierino; the novelist Eugene Walters, who was also working as a casting agent for Fellini; George and Ann, two new friends; students from various academies, and other expatriates.

Our Italian guests poked gingerly at the food as though it might attack them. They hovered about the tables making grimaces of distaste and giggling. They were, in the early 1960s, extremely conservative, especially in the area of the kitchen. There was but one Chinese restaurant in Rome in those days, and only foreigners patronised it. Finding the ham and most of the vegetables acceptably traditional, they ate those, but with care and a certain reluctance. The turkey stuffing and the pudding were quite beyond them.

After the food, Janet played her collection of 45s including the Beatles' 'Twist and Shout', and she and I danced for a while. We settled in the red room, sitting in a circle on the carpet, drinking, talking and laughing. One of Ferrill's friends, a very agile young man from the American Academy, showed us some new positions he had been practising for intercourse. He did the splits on the floor and on his head. He even managed, quite effortlessly, to put his legs behind his shoulders and head.

Having run out of cigarettes, we were passing the last one around, far too comfortable to think of going out and buying more. Suddenly Aubrey jumped to his feet, furiously angry, and marched out, forcing his two companions to follow him. He thought we were passing round a joint – he abhorred drugs. Days later, when we explained, he took us out to dinner by way of apologising.

Eugene invited us to spend New Year's Eve at his apartment. We had been primed by him several weeks before to keep all our empty bottles and cans and to bring them with us. This we did, also adding a large bag of streamers to the collection.

Several minutes before midnight the four of us together with Eugene and several other guests, were on his large balcony waiting expectantly. Rome was deserted and still. A lone car below us sped towards Piazza del Jesù in a last-minute effort to escape. On New Year's Eve a wise motorist saw that his vehicle was garaged or parked well outside the city limits, out of danger.

When the church bells rang out at midnight, Rome exploded in a riot of noise and light. Fireworks and rubbish were tossed from rooftops, windows and balconies in an orgy of pagan celebratory destruction. We had plenty of ammunition: pots, pans, crockery, glasses, paper and broken chairs. Another car sped past in a vain attempt to flee disaster, a fast-moving target which we bombarded with glee. All of us were in a frenzy; it was a bacchanalian orgy to end the old year, and, for Janet, Eric and myself, the prospect of a new life, a happy future in our adopted home.

Across the street the french windows of an apartment were thrown open. A group of men appeared carrying a vast brown paper parcel, tied with cord. Its shape suggested an upright piano. They struggled to lift it onto the rail of the balcony and then, with a shout, heaved it into space.

When the 'parcel' hit the street it burst with a dreadful sound, a sound so loud the priests from the sacristy of the Chiesa del Jesù came to see what disaster had befallen the city. It *was* a piano. It lay in a great broken mound with the other rubbish on the pavement. Waving to us, the group closed the windows. Eugene told us Anna Magnani lived in that apartment. This had been her splendid contribution to the night's activities.

Walking home rather drunk in the early morning, we waded through piles of rubbish, ankle deep in some places. Every year the Roman garbage collectors threaten strike action and say they will not clean up the mess. But in a few days it was all gone, the men having yet again performed their yearly Herculean task.

January passed and in early February we had an important guest: Sir

152

Anthony Blunt, KCVO, Keeper of the Queen's pictures and Director of the Courtauld Institute. He was the man responsible for turning the Courtauld into the most important and the most acclaimed centre for the study and teaching of art history in the world. International museums, art institutes, universities and libraries are still staffed by ex-students of his. Through his writings, his teachings and direction, he elevated the profession of art history to a level unknown before. Intimate of the royal family, he was one of the most respected figures in the world of art.

He was also the so-called 'Fourth Man' in the Burgess-Maclean-Philby spy ring that infiltrated the CIA, FBI, MI5 and, through them, most of the Western secret service agencies. Although suspected of involvement because of his friendship with Guy Burgess, there was at this time no proof against him, though that situation was soon to change. We were unaware of Anthony's connection with either Burgess or Maclean until he related how he had been taken away by the police for questioning while giving a lecture, at the Slade school of Art, I think. He told us that he'd gone on a cruise to get away from the fuss and was annoyed to find an ex-student of his on the ship who imposed himself on Anthony, who wanted peace and quiet. It wasn't anything more than an interesting story. And we couldn't imagine this tall, thin, charming man as a spy, lurking in dark corners, passing on secret coded messages to sinister foreign agents. It didn't fit.

I suppose, had I been Eric, I might have fussed as much as he did. Everything had to be 'right and proper', befitting the residence of an international art dealer, English gentleman, artist and would-be scholar, as Eric was trying to be. Of course I was the one Eric fussed and grumbled at. I was the one who had to see that everything ran smoothly. Poor Eric – he had us to contend with, Janet, Ferrill and me. Not that we planned or conspired against his attempts at image-making. Janet remembers even Ferrill 'actually making a real effort to be smart in his little American jacket'. None of us truly realised how much Anthony's visit meant to Eric and how concerned he was. We felt quite simply that if Anthony was to stay with us in our home then we were going to make sure he was welcomed and treated as a friend – whereas Eric seemed to want to treat Anthony as visiting royalty. Anthony would be living with us for a couple of weeks and we knew that, as my stepmother often said, he would 'have to take us as he found us'. This attitude worried Eric.

In spite of our intentions, we were all rather formal on Anthony's arrival, a formality which melted almost immediately after a few drinks. Ferrill insisted on cooking our first meal together and it was a disaster: shrivelled calves liver, hard and leathery with an over-salted roux. I think Ferrill must have been suffering from nerves too. Eric kept banging pieces of liver on his plate and complaining. Anthony was polite, a study in diplomacy. Besides, there was a profusion of cheeses, that gloriously crusty Roman bread, fruit and wine. Within hours we had all relaxed and were enjoying each other's company.

While we were having coffee that first night, Janet left the table to have a bath. She returned, one towel around her body and one around her head, turban-style. Leaning back in his chair and smiling, Anthony was delighted. I think this made him feel totally accepted as a friend and a part of the 'family'. Eric, though, was furious about it for days after and I was his target. At night, in bed, he lectured me on what should and should not be happening.

When Anthony had arrived, with his tiny battered leather suitcase, we had escorted him to our guest bedroom. He described it as a monk's cell. Below a small window set high in the far wall was a long, creaking, cast-iron bed. Its springs groaned and it wobbled when you sat or lay down on it. The towering headboard (a sheet of iron painted and 'combed' to resemble wood) leaned perilously inwards as you slept. It was not the most imposing article to offer a guest, but it was the only bed in the place long enough for him. He was convinced that the bed would collapse and the headboard crush him. I lent him James Thurber's story, *The Night the Bed Fell*, to read, which he enjoyed immensely. He set about casting what he termed an *opera buffo* production. He decided that Eric would play Herman, the strong support. Ferrill could try his hand at Briggs choking on a glass of camphor. Janet and I could take turns as either Mother convinced that Father (played by Anthony) needed rescuing, or old Aunt Melissa Beall with her stock of shoes to throw in all directions at burglars.

'All we lack for a performance is a dog,' he said, 'but I'm sure that could be easily arranged.'

The four of us accompanied Anthony to the British Council, where they almost drooled over him. They wanted him to make an appearance: a cocktail party, a lecture, just an informal talk? He firmly declined but managed to acquire a car from them, a large comfortable sedan. Ferrill drove it. To quote Janet: 'Ferrill was to be the chauffeur. Anthony liked the idea and so did Ferrill.' Anthony was our tour guide for several delightful excursions.

Our first trip was to Anagni, thirty-five miles south-west of Rome, and a nearby Dominican abbey. Anagni is now a small cathedral town but has had a great past. Pope Alexander III signed the Peace of Anagni with Frederick I; Barbarrossa, Emperor of the two Sicilys, and Pope Gregory IX met there to make peace with Frederick II, Barbarrossa's grandson, in 1230.

It was a cold day, with snow on the mountains; an icy but invigorating wind was blowing. As Ferrill parked the car in the piazza I noticed the men of the town hanging around in groups, talking and smoking. I also noticed that many of them had erections showing quite plainly underneath their baggy trousers. Anthony was fascinated. The men of Anagni were robust, stocky farmers and peasants, and several were unusually handsome – definitely Anthony's type. He, Janet, Ferrill and I spent some time checking them out and discussing my theory that this wind, this cold winter/spring wind, creates a sexual itchiness; just as the summer wind – the south wind of Norman Douglas – supposedly causes nervousness and mental disorder. Eric joined in and told me that all I ever thought about was sex. Again we three weren't behaving properly.

After the splendour of the Roman churches we were surprised to find the one at the Dominican abbey so simple. The windows, though, were glazed with rich swirling patterns of thinly sliced agate marble, giving a warm honey-ochre glow to the plain interior. There were several peacocks on the terrace of the main building. 'They make the most awful noise,' said Anthony, 'especially at night.' (It's true; one night back in London, I heard peacocks calling to each other from inside Holland Park, mournful shrieks like lost and sad spirits.)

The monks in their brown-and-cream habits were digging the foundation for a new building and had discovered the remains of a Roman villa. Their finds were stacked haphazardly in untidy heaps in a small room, which they unlocked for us. Unsupervised, we were allowed to inspect and examine the treasure trove.

Among the piles of bricks, pots and broken columns – the detritus of most archaeological digs – was a marble disc, an oscillum, made to hang as a mobile. Perhaps ten to twelve inches in diameter, on one side it had a prancing satyr playing a flute carved in delicate bas-relief. It was exquisite. As I picked it up from the floor and placed it on a table, I remarked that I hoped it would be properly looked after. Anthony suggested I might take it, saying he doubted it would be missed. Looking at the confusion in the room, I could believe it.

Later I asked him if he really wanted me to steal it, to 'rescue' it, or whether it was a test. 'I was interested in what you might do,' he replied. 'Did you not take it because I was there?'

'Partly yes, and partly because I felt I had no right to it,' I answered. 'In fact, until you suggested it, it hadn't occurred to me to steal it. But, when you did, I admit I was sorely tempted.'

'I thought you were,' he said.

I still don't know if this was a test Anthony had set me or whether I passed or failed. It was a peculiar exchange.

When we left the abbey I insisted on buying a bottle of the monks' coffee liqueur. It was foul, tasting of weak chicory, sugar and rubbing alcohol, and was thrown away that same day.

Our apartment overlooked Piazza Mattei (although 'overlook' perhaps isn't quite the right word as the piazza couldn't actually be seen from our windows). It is a tiny space, quite nondescript in appearance, yet it holds in its centre one of the most beautiful of all Renaissance fountains, designed by Giacomo della Porta and executed by Taddeo Landini in 1585. Small and charming, it seems out of place in that shabby quarter. There are four naked ephebe with enigmatic smiles, treading on dolphins, balanced over four rather toad-like basins. The youths are reaching up with one arm to touch four bronze tortoises climbing into the circular basin above them. It seemed a pity that there was no bar or restaurant in the piazza where one could sit and contemplate this delight. The tiny square and the narrow streets leading into it were filled from very early morning until late at night with trucks, cars and Vespas, the noise from the vehicles drowning the play of water falling in elegant arcs from basin to basin.

Opposite our building loomed the Palazzo Costaguti. On its roof, in elegant and contemporary splendour, was the apartment of a wealthy Italian whose valet blew kisses at us. Anthony gained admission to the palazzo. The plain and almost derelict entrance was in one corner of Piazza Mattei. We were greeted by the Principessa herself, a small, plump woman in a black dress and pearls. She seemed nervous and shy but acted as our guide.

The building meandered through the streets and tiny piazzas in a seemingly haphazard way. Like many of the large townhouses in Pompeii and Herculaneum, there were stores and small businesses on the ground floor. The palazzo had tiny corridors opening into little rooms; then suddenly you'd come across a vast stateroom or ballroom, or a wide ornate corridor. Passages were truncated or sealed off. Doorways, which presumably led to private apartments, were plastered over. In one room were frescoes by Gaspard Dughet, Poussin's brother-in-law. These were the reason for our visit. There was also a beautiful harpsichord painted in a similar style. The frescoes were being shaken off the walls by the vibration of the traffic in the surrounding narrow streets. Anthony was concerned about their condition. He asked the Principessa if anything was being done to save them. She said she was in touch with Belle Arte, the ministry responsible for the preservation of works of art in Italy, but nothing was being done; so many other treasures of major importance also needed attention.

There was a feeling of neglect and poverty about the place. The palace gave the impression of several period filmsets, in poor condition, which had been pushed together in storage and then forgotten. The owners were obviously selling or renting bits and pieces of this huge amorphous place, a shabby twin to the summer palace in Lampedusa's *The Leopard*. (It was also similar to the one we visited with a friend in the mountains to the north-east of Rome: the courtyard filled with laughing children, splashing springwater, chickens, potbellied pigs and tiny Tibetan goats – a courtyard alive and noisy. The palace itself, dark and empty because of bitter family disputes, drove us quickly back into the sunshine.) I felt glad to get back into the bustle and noise of Piazza Mattei; I think we all did.

On another outing, Anthony, Eric, Ferrill and I toured the juvenile prison, a vast building with immensely thick walls by the Tiber in the Trastevere quarter. Walking through the entrance, a policeman and a young boy, the latter's hands cuffed behind him, preceded us. The sight shocked me. Anthony said, 'Well, Eric, I'll take that policeman. And you?'

Eric laughed, but made no answer.

The outside of the prison gave the impression of a fortress and I had imagined a dark, dank, medieval interior, but in fact it seemed almost light and airy – not at all a Piranesi *carceri*. The cells were big, arranged around large central halls. All had pin-ups and photos cut from magazines or some kind of mural decoration. These ranged from garish half-naked women and many Madonnas to galleons cresting mountainous waves. Most were quite ordinary but one had such energy and power it captured our attention. The Mother of Christ sat holding her baby in a traditional pose facing the onlooker. They were surrounded by a group of contemporary working-class Italians holding bottles and glasses of wine in a toast to the infant Jesus. A large woman carrying a baby on one arm, with a basket of laundry balanced on her head, was turning away to look down at her son. The group was crudely, amateurishly drawn and painted, but it nevertheless had an amazing intensity and power. The young artist, lying indolently on his bed, accepted our fulsome praise with an almost patronising disdain, a sort of 'of course it's good, I did it' attitude – very Roman. Anthony asked him whether he had studied art or was going to go to art school. Smiling, the boy replied, 'There's no money in it. Why should I bother?'

One evening in the 'salon', Anthony, seated in a gilt armchair, talked about Poussin. We were all very relaxed because he wasn't giving a lecture, but just discussing the artist with us. Even today Janet recalls that Anthony 'was glorious to listen to because it was the most structured and intelligent discussion that I'd ever heard on any painter. And I felt that this is what life ought to be about. I remember receiving part of my education that evening.'

157

That night Anthony involved us passionately in one of the great loves of his life. He spoke of Poussin's admiration of the antique, particularly bas-reliefs. He was scrupulous in his research to make each costume authentic for whatever period he was painting. Anthony explained that Poussin sketched an idea first and then made small wax figurines, draping them afterwards. He made toy theatres in which he would set out the models almost mathematically like pieces on a chessboard. He would light the figures for dramatic effect and draw them again and again until he achieved the design he wanted. Anthony explained how, in spite of this long, tedious and pedantic approach, Poussin's paintings shine with colour, light and movement. It was joy and privilege to listen to him.

We ate breakfast at the large round white table in the kitchen with coffee for Ferrill and tea usually for us. Freshly baked brioche cornetti or crusty bread rolls, with butter and preserves, were our mainstay, but occasionally we indulged in eggs and bacon. The free-range eggs with their dark yolks were delicious, but the thin, fatty Roman bacon was nothing like the thick gammon rashers we were used to in England.

Most mornings after breakfast Anthony set off on research, going through libraries and archives for his students. He carried with him pages of notes and questions from them. These were tasks which he enjoyed and carried out assiduously. Occasionally we would walk with him and listen, enthralled, as he talked about architecture, the history of various buildings, fountains and piazzas, who designed them, who commissioned them, the fights and intrigues, the later alterations and the additions.

One Sunday morning we visited the Palazzo Farnese, now the French Embassy. Begun by Antonio Sangallo, continued after his death by Michelangelo, and completed by Giacomo della Porta, it is the finest Renaissance palace in Rome. Anthony explained how Sangallo had based his design of the entrance and the beautiful stuccoed arched ceiling on Vitruvius. He showed us Michelangelo's rather plain third floor of the courtyard, which sits oddly on Sangallo's elegantly arched first two storeys. The most famous room, now used on state occasions as a dining-room, was painted by Annibale Carracci. The ceiling, with its central panel of Bacchus and Ariadne, is aglow with the most exuberant colour and sensuality. Carracci chose as his theme the loves of the gods and goddesses taken from Ovid's *Metamorphoses* – thanks to the superb Penguin translation, I knew the stories behind each panel. Depressed by the small fee he received after completing this amazing series of paintings, Carracci became an alcoholic and died. We three young artists, Janet, Eric and I, were in total sympathy and expressed our outrage. In all probability, Alessandro Farnese spent more in a year on clothes or food than he paid either Annibale Carracci or his brother Agostino, who assisted him.

Most evenings we ate out, usually at the family-owned trattorias where the food and wine were simple but delicious. One night in Trastevere as we were having coffee, my favourite street-singer came around. The woman, who claimed she was Russian (Eugene insisted she came from Bulgaria), sang and played her balalaika in front of us. Unimpressed, Anthony claimed that with a little practice he could do as well. We concocted a scenario of him as a Roman street-singer, pronouncing Italian with an affected English accent similar to that used by two British scholars from the British School in Rome. (This couple dubbed all the Laurel and Hardy films shown in Italy. Speaking with stilted and clipped upper-class English accents, they produced roars of laughter as they butchered the Italian language.)

For our fantasy Janet decided Anthony should have a black cloak and a large black felt hat to add character. As he spoke French fluently (he had been made a member of the Académie Française, a rare honour for an Englishman), we decided he could expand his repertoire to include some Piaf numbers and a Josephine Baker song, 'J'ai deux amours, ma patrie et Paris'. In fact, we became carried away imagining him as a kind of pied-piper-cum-impresario leading a band of various street performers. These would include the Russian-Bulgarian woman, a blood-spitting consumptive piper from the Ponte Fabricio, a lady who had 'medical accidents' and, of course, several handsome young men. In his hat and cloak we envisioned Anthony conducting and participating in a type of international cabaret through the many piazzas of Rome. A fire-eating, tumbling, dancing, theatre Diaghilev.

He thought the idea had great potential but wondered if he would have the necessary energy or stamina. 'Nevertheless,' he said, 'I shall mark it down as possibility for my retirement.' We gave up on this fantasy as four or five good-looking young Romans came and sat at a table next to us. As we admired them, the conversation changed direction.

I had a fake-fur Russian hat and a pair of thigh-length soft leather boots which Eric liked me to wear in bed. Anthony claimed the hat and spent one entire morning walking about the apartment with it on his head. He looked very funny and revelled in performing for us. A Jacques Tati figure, tall and lanky, he posed in front of our floor-to-ceiling mirror, hands on hips. We, of course, encouraged him. Unlike Edward Fox's portrayal of him in the Alan Bennett play, *A Question of Attribution*, Anthony was not camp or swishy in any way, just very funny. He considered taking the hat back to London to wear at the Courtauld Institute. He assured us that no one, with the possible exception of his secretary, would notice it. He was truly tempted. Janet and I dared him to do it, but at the last moment reality bit and he left it behind.

One afternoon he sat with Eric and me in Piazza Navona talking about the fountains and the tremendous impact Bernini had on Rome. He listened patiently as I attempted to explain my deep attraction to the paintings of Piero della Francesca. His round sculptural forms have for me a monumental stillness that paradoxically vibrates with intense energy and passion. Anthony took my stumbling efforts and, exploring all the side issues, the influences on the painter's work and the period in which he worked, wove all the threads together effortlessly to make a complete whole, a complete thought. 'Thank you,' I said to him when he finished, and added jokingly, 'I couldn't have put it better myself.' He roared with laughter.

He and Eric talked all the time, sometimes arguing but never heatedly. I could see that Anthony was intrigued by Eric's intelligence and was often amused by Eric's narrow outlook – Rembrandt and Hals were still *the masters* – and his passionate efforts to defend his theories. But, although the two shared a love of art, Eric didn't have Anthony's brilliant mind. Nor was Eric, unlike Anthony, open to the wide world of art in all its many aspects. Anthony certainly learned from Eric's knowledge as a painter but I don't think Eric learned from Anthony. Eric thought himself superior, and often said so, dismissing Anthony in private as a 'file clerk who knew all the names, dates and places', but nothing else.

Considering that Janet, Eric, Ferrill and I weren't particularly well educated or well informed, Anthony never patronised us. He never let his superior intellect make us feel small. And, unlike many other homosexuals, although he was attracted sexually to Eric, he never attacked me or showed any of the signs of jealousy I was used to receiving.

From the first moment he entered our apartment it seemed as if we had known him for years. He was easy to talk to and very different from the worried, unhappy man Eric and I stayed with in London a few years later.

He got on especially well with Janet. She told me recently that she thought this was because she had had an affair with Jack Millar, a teacher at Walthamstow, who was sixteen years her senior, so she was used to older men. But I believe there was more to it than that. I could see quite clearly that Anthony was charmed and delighted with Janet. He found pleasure in her personality, her passion for life and her sense of fun and daring. Knowing Anthony then and knowing now about his life, I realise he spent the major part of it hiding. He hid his homosexuality, his very core; he hid his and his friends' spying. Upholding his position as a scholar, he conformed to very stringent establishment rules. It was not a life where a sense of fun gets much of an opportunity to thrive. With Janet, though, while recognising her genuine talent and commitment to painting, his innate sense of fun and naughtiness found a soulmate. In Anticoli once he remarked to me that I must find life very different without her friendship. I agreed with him. On this first visit I believe Anthony was reliving in some way his happy days as a student at Oxford. And he never once mentioned his lover back in London.

When he left, we said goodbye to a friend. Janet suggested he phone the Courtauld and extend his stay – he was the boss, after all. We could see he was tempted, but he decided against it.

Less than two months later, confronted by MI5 in London, he confessed to being a Russian spy. He was granted immunity from prosecution and exposure for co-operating with the American and British secret services. This promise was broken years later by Margaret Thatcher.

Fellini and the First Major Fake

AFTER ANTHONY'S DEPARTURE ERIC, JANET AND I ORGANISED an exhibition, 'From Brueghel to Berman: Drawings of Italy'. There were about forty to fifty drawings in all, including the small Samuel Palmer, the Brueghel, an Edward Lear, fifteen large sepia watercolours of eighteenth-century Rome by Jean Desprez, a couple of Eric's originals and one fake, the Campagnola landscape.

Eugene supervised the reception as the majority of the guests were friends of his, ranging from the Principessa di Monte Luppi and the Principessa di Salaparuta to indigent artists and actors and lesser luminaries of the Italian screen – not the kind of clientèle to buy drawings.

The exhibition was truly interesting and would have been a success if held now, but in the early 1960s there was little interest in Rome for drawings, and we sold nothing. It was a great disappointment and left us just about penniless.

During this period, from our arrival in Rome to the exhibition, Eric had produced very little of his own work and no forgeries at all. With the exception of the Pompeian room, a few tiny nightscapes – which, again, I had forced him into producing – and some charming red-pencil views, Eric had given up. He did his best to squeeze more money from Ferrill but our American friend's hands were tight around his own purse strings.

On one of our trips to the Wallace Collection in London years before, we had drooled over the small Italian bronzes. Some time later, in an antique and junk shop in Islington, we had noticed a small, slightly rubbed bronze statue of Narcissus. 'Haven't we seen it somewhere before?' Eric murmured.

'Yes, but I can't remember where,' I replied. We bought it – for ten pounds we really couldn't go wrong.

Then, in the middle of the night, Eric woke me up. 'The Wallace Collection,' he said. 'It's in the Wallace Collection. We'll go and check tomorrow.'

It seemed identical but whether it was a good copy or not we didn't know. Through a friend we arranged a meeting with Sir John Pope-Hennessy – that is, we bought him lunch – and he authenticated our bronze as Paduan, an original from the same cast as its companion in the Wallace. Our statuette had been slightly rubbed, the rich dark patina lost in several places. With thin washes of burnt umber and black oil paint, I replaced what had vanished; when the paint had dried, I finished it off with several coats of black and ox-blood shoe-polish. We had also purchased a larger figure, a bronze of Neptune that Brian Sewell considered was a maquette for a fountain at Versailles.

Back in Rome, Eric sent Ferrill and me with the two bronzes to Carlo Sestieri in Piazza di Spagna. We had been introduced to Carlo by Tony Clarke, then director of the Minneapolis Institute. Carlo and his brother Marcello were the pre-eminent dealers in fine art in Rome. I cannot recall why Ferrill accompanied me or why Eric refused to attend. I do know he was very upset at having to sell the bronzes and angry with Ferrill for refusing to give us any more money. The Paduan bronze especially was extremely difficult for him to part with. We had also had a scare in London before we left; Mr Davis, who had taken a couple of Eric's fake Augustus Johns to Sotheby's, was informed by the salesroom that they were copies. The resulting fuss had dimmed Eric's enthusiasm for forgery and the recent failed exhibition, like the Pannini Gallery catalogue, had been an attempt to establish ourselves as reputable dealers. So we had no fakes to sell – or, rather, we possessed no important fakes that would bring in enough money to carry on.

Carlo Sestieri bargained fiercely but didn't spot my restoration of the Paduan bronze patina. After a lengthy back-and-forth session, I phoned Eric. 'The best I can do is five and a half thousand pounds. Do I take it?'

Eric grumbled that I should get twice the amount Carlo was offering.

'Okay, *you* come down and bargain with him. *I've* done my best.'

More grumbling from Eric.

'Look, we don't have to sell them today,' I said to him. 'You can bring them back here another time.'

Eric refused. He didn't want to deal with Carlo.

'All right, do I accept or not?' I said finally.

He told me to take the money. Carlo came with us to the bank and I withdrew it in cash, thick piles of Italian lire in large, colourful, beautiful banknotes which, when I got back to Piazza Paganica, I unwrapped and threw in the air. I'd never seen so much money before.

Eric didn't feel like celebrating. The small Paduan bronze had been his prize possession, with the Neptune a close second.

One evening Janet, Eric and I ate out in a little trattoria in Trastevere. Somehow we connected with a group of students from the British Schools and settled in for an evening of drinking. Eric began his storytelling to a rapt audience – with the exception of Janet and myself. We had heard the stories before and Janet decided to return to our apartment. I couldn't let a young, attractive redhead walk through Trastevere at night by herself, so I told Eric I was escorting her home and we left. Walking back later to rejoin Eric, I met him marching grim-faced along the Lungotevere. He punched me in the chest, knocking me against the parapet of the river.

'What the hell's wrong with you?' I shouted at him as he strode away.

No answer. Shaken and completely in the dark as to what was going on, I waited for several minutes before following him. As I climbed the stairs to the apartment I could hear crashes and bangs as furniture was thrown around. Eric had marched through each room overturning chairs, grabbing my books and hurling them at the walls, even throwing a bust of me by a teacher at Walthamstow on the floor – but not, I noticed later, breaking anything of any value.

Furious, I confronted him in the red room. 'If you want to break something, hit me!' I shouted, lashing out at him. 'Go on, hit me, you bugger!'

As his arm went up to strike me, his hand connected with a carved wood candelabra and, wrenching it from the ceiling, he hit me on the top of the head.

Janet intervened. 'You two just stop it and go to bed. We've got a business to run. For heaven's sake, grow up.'

The next morning Eric refused to tell me what had sparked this violent outburst. 'If you don't know, what's the point in telling you?' he sulked.

'But Eric,' I said, 'I have to know so that we can clear it up.'

Adamant, he refused to explain and I was left to turn the episode into a story, to make light of it and pretend it was really nothing much, just an entertainment for our friends.

This time we didn't make up afterwards. There were no excuses, no exchanges of loving words or kisses, no apologies murmured in the dark before we fell asleep. Something had happened, though what it was I didn't find out until years later.

Paul Cooper, grandson of Robert Graves, was tall and good-looking in a Byronic manner. Eric met him at the British Schools and he became a friend. His large apartment, in which he sub-let rooms, had its own private roof, great for sunbathing and parties. Of the many parties and dinners we gave and attended in this *dolce vita* time, two were outstanding, both for different reasons.

Janet, Ferrill and I held one party in Paul's apartment while Eric went on a buying trip to London with some of the money from the sale of the bronzes. I didn't go with him; we were still shaky from the candelabra fight. I think he also wanted to escape from us and Piazza Paganica and to have an adventure, which he did, with a young Asian who owned an antique shop in Camden Passage, Islington.

The party at Paul's was, I thought, a great success. We invited the pretty young manservant from the rooftop apartment on Palazzo Costaguti and he brought several very gay friends with him. Gianni came in sequins, made up as Gina Lollobrigida, with several other boys accompanying him. Stewart Perowne, author and self-styled diplomat, who was staying with us as a guest of Eric's, became drunk with several of Gianni's friends, especially so with a student from the British Schools.

Aubrey Menen arrived with an English hustler in tow, Spanish Ricky, namesake of the young villain in London who had so intrigued Terence Donovan.

Before long, the party had turned into a ribald and bacchanalian rout, with Spanish Ricky performing a strip to start the fun. It became a 'them and us' affair, with Paul's heterosexual friends lined up against our Paganica contingent. Paul's girlfriend Lily, a lovely and talented young woman who later became his wife, found us too much to deal with and retired to bed after noisily causing the schism to widen.

When Eric got back from London and heard about the goings-on at the party, he was furious. It was another black mark against me. He told me to go and apologise to Paul. As I felt I had done nothing wrong, it was difficult to sound genuinely apologetic.

The other party of note, held at Piazza Paganica, seemed on the surface to be a more formal affair, at least for the first hour or so. Janet's mother had arrived for a visit and she adored Eric. At the party she went round telling everyone, 'Oh, I can tell Eric's a real artist. I can see it in his eyes.' Unused to alcohol, she followed the Principessa di Salaparuta around the room, endlessly repeating the same question: 'If you're a princess, where's your tiara?' Then she would giggle to herself. No one minded, the Princess least of all. Ella Deuters became a sort of mascot for the evening, her small plump figure darting around, chatting to everybody, but always returning to La Salaparuta.

Some time before, Eric and Janet had purchased a suite of Edwardian salon furniture, carved wood covered with gold leaf and upholstered in crimson silk, probably looted from a Neapolitan palazzo. The large sofa, two armchairs and eight straight-backed chairs were all riddled with woodworm. I de-loused the suite and, once it was restored, it looked quite wonderfully vulgar in our salon in its dated red-and-gold splendour. Aubrey seated himself at one end of the grand settee and held court, enjoying himself thoroughly.

The food Janet and I had prepared was delicious, the drinks bountiful, the party a success – when suddenly the settee legs under Aubrey broke off, sending him rolling onto the floor. He was not amused, and neither was Eric.

Aubrey's fall was accompanied by a crash of thunder and the heavens opened in a typical Roman cloudburst. A few weeks before the party, a group of workmen had been busy fixing new television aerials for the tenants of our building and had walked about on the terracotta tiles of the roof. The tiles, probably hundreds of years old, cracked under the men's heavy boots. The downpour, without the protection of the old canvas false ceilings, came straight through the roof and inundated us, payment in kind, I suppose for our flooding of the count and countess.

After placing cans of paint under the settee to replace the legs and making sure that Aubrey was unscathed, Janet, Ferrill and I then rushed about, attempting to contain the steady streams of water with plastic buckets, bowls and saucepans, mopping up the overflow with towels. Eric, meanwhile, continued as the nonchalant host, ignoring the escalating chaos as furniture was moved about to avoid the newly formed Niagaras. Our guests huddled in corners.

Oblivious to the disaster, Ella Deuters continued with her partying; when our guests eventually left, she was still singing and dancing. 'Come on boys,' she trilled, 'where's your spirit? The night is young.'

My brother Peter and his new wife Shirley came out for a visit. They must have thought the set-up rather strange and our dinner parties – with guests ranging from Harry Ward Bailey (Christie's representative in Rome), Stewart Perowne and the Monseigneur from the English College to various actors and students, all presided over by Guy, our newly acquired, wonderfully camp French chef, who had moved in and adopted us – quite eccentric.

Eric, Janet, Ferrill and I went back to Positano for a short holiday with Ferrill's mother and aunt. Eric and Janet became rather ill towards the end of our stay – shellfish poisoning, I think – and we left them together in one small hotel room to recover. I didn't get sick but a month or so later, having my first pee in the morning, I was horrified to find it had turned black overnight. I was rushed to the Salvatore Mundi hospital where Janet had been taken a few days before, both of us later diagnosed as suffering from hepatitis. Our recovery was long and slow, and lasted several months.

It was an American woman, a schoolteacher from the Midwest who'd retired to Rome with an inheritance, who unwittingly got me a part in a Fellini film. Janet had sent Fellini a set of photographs which Ferrill had taken of her. She looked beautiful and ethereal but with an undercurrent of passion, too. Eugene, who had been working as a casting agent for the director, told us Fellini had them pinned on his office walls – apparently, he loved photographs. Ferrill had taken several of me and many of this schoolteacher in fancy-dress costumes. It was armed with these that she intended to wow Fellini and get a part in his upcoming film. She needed someone to go with her and hold her hand. She was nervous. I'm not sure why I went, apart from wanting to see *il maestro*. I didn't know her well or even like her, so I suppose it must have been curiosity.

I took some photographs of myself with me, the ones Ferrill had taken. No one ever went to see Fellini without taking along photographs of themselves. It was the golden rule – you couldn't get in to see him when he was casting without a pile of photos. They were the key; even family snapshots would do.

The schoolteacher had a folder with about fifty carefully posed images of herself in various roles. She was Theda Bara as, perhaps Mata Hari or Cleopatra; Gloria Swanson as – definitely – Queen Kelly. Totally mad get-ups with her ordinary, ageing face over made-up and her large vacant eyes lined with black, staring out from under an array of lumpily stuffed stockings writhing awkwardly above her head: this represented her Medusa look. Other photographs showed her with badly made wigs twined with leaves and bunches of wax grapes and 'jewel'-encrusted tiaras and crowns. Altogether it was a wonderful and completely bizarre offering for *il maestro*.

Fellini was seated at a desk piled high with photos. A couple of people stood behind him making comments. The teacher, as she handed over her passport to stardom, gushed about how she'd always admired his work, how she'd always admired him, how she loved his films. Fellini was not impressed. He showed the photographs to a woman behind him, muttered something, turned to the schoolteacher and said, 'Yes, thank you,' as he handed the bundle back to her.

He then turned to me. With a rather tired, world-weary smile, he clicked thumb and forefinger together and stretched out his hand.

I gave him my collection. He spread them out on his desk. Turning to the woman again, he made a few undecipherable comments and then looked at me.

'*Fatto un' riso* – smile,' he commanded.

Rather nervously, I did.

'*Bene, bene!*' Then, 'Thank you – *grazie*,' and we were dismissed. But he kept my photographs.

Although I said I wasn't particularly interested in being in a film – in fact, the idea terrified me – I felt let down. The interview had been so very brief and matter-of-fact. I don't know what I had expected – obviously something more exciting than what had just occurred. Perhaps, secretly, I wanted to be 'discovered' and was disappointed that it hadn't happened.

At least a month later, the phone rang. It was for me. 'Oh, hell,' I thought, 'the Salvatore Mundi collection agency.' I hadn't as yet finished paying the bill. But, no! I was wanted in Fregene for *un piccolo conversazione con il maestro, il maestro Fellini,* to talk about a part in his latest film. I was white and emaciated from hepatitis. I weighed about eight stone. My eyes were circled as though I was wearing make-up and I tired very quickly. But now I felt nervous and excited – besides we needed the money.

A villa had been built on the edge of the pine woods, bordering on wheatfields. Fregene was an upper-middle-class enclave on the coast north-west of Rome. A pretty little villa with an art nouveau flavour, complete with a garden and lawn, it was the set for *Giulietta.* Giulietta's home. Fellini was in the bedroom, sitting on the bed.

'Ah, *buon giorno. Viene, viene.* Come, sit down.' He patted a place on the bed next to him. 'Come, sit.' I sat.

He talked briefly with a secretary, then turned to me, taking my chin in his hand, turning my face toward the attending minions.

'*Un' angelo,*' he said simply.

(It was Pope Gregory who, stopping in ancient Rome's marketplace, said about the captured blond British boys being sold into slavery, 'These are not Angles [the Latin term for us Brits], but angels.')

'*Un vero angelo inglese,*' Fellini continued, '*Bello, bello, un' angelo, ma . . .*' He changed to English. 'You are a little decadent, English?'

I blushed. 'Gosh, no,' I replied. 'Not really.'

He threw back his head and laughed. 'Oh, yes. You look like an angel but *sotto* very decadent. I know.' Again he took my face in his hands, squeezing my lips, pursing them. 'English, English. So proper, so good manners, so decadent. I adore English, so corrupt. Will you be an angel for me? A decadent angel?'

How could I refuse?

At 5 a.m. on the first day of filming, I was collected in a limousine with several other would-bes. I felt awful. Dressed in a big white shirt and black trousers I was made up, and then I was on. There was no script to memorise, but I gathered I was to play Valentina Cortese's lover, a photographer. She was a delight, supportive, friendly and truly helpful. Valentina realised I was nervous, but she was with me all the way, turning what began as an embarrassing ordeal into a game we played together. Of course I rushed back home and told Eric all about her. Because of his frozen response, I never called the number she gave me, never took her up on her offer to get together, have dinner, talk and be silly.

About 7 a.m., the sparkling morning light filtering through the pines, I was on. Just me. Just me alone. Shit. Fellini told me what I was supposed to be doing – taking photos of the arriving guests for Giulietta's party. I was to back down the garden path, snapping away. He turned to a man (the man who was later to steal all my drawings of the cast and the film), took his camera with its telephoto lens – a massive thing – and handed it to me. 'You know how to take a photograph?' he asked me.

'Oh, yes,' I replied, frozen.

'So, take my photo, English.'

Everyone was watching me – the entire cast and production team. I was the only actor 'on stage'. I lifted the heavy camera with its telephoto lens attachment. Lifted it, pointed it at Fellini – and dropped it. Dropped it at his feet. I heard a communal gasp, a sprinkling of '*Madonna*' and '*Gesù, comme stupido*'. Then silence. The whole world stopped. But *il maestro* leaned forward smiling and pinching my cheek between his thumb and forefinger. '*Mia gioia. Perfetto, mia gioia.*'

And from then on, whenever I was needed on camera, a voice would boom out: '*Dov'è mia gioia?* – where is my joy?'

Throughout the next twelve days of filming, the passionate under-currents, behind-the-scenes gossip and plotting – a film in itself – I was 'my joy'. Even when, one glorious evening, Eugene came down to the set and there was a picnic supper and the remaining cast and crew played charades, I was still 'my joy'. I might be a decadent, clumsy English angel, but I was always 'my joy'.

Virtually all of my small contribution to the film ended up on the floor of the editing room. What is left is my face filling the entire screen and some distant views of me dancing on the lawn of Giulietta's house. My limited acting ability wasn't to blame, neither was my inability to remember lines, for no script was proferred – dialogue was completely ad lib. Eugene told me later that Giulietta Massina, irked that her role was overshadowed by the visions that plagued her throughout the film and the large, eccentric supporting cast, sued the company and won a re-editing. Gone were many brilliantly dramatic confrontations between the character of Giulietta and her phantoms. Gone, too, was my part and, more impor-tantly, the terrifying ending when, like spirits from hell emerging from the smoke and flames of a burning hayfield in front of Giulitta's villa, the rays of the early morning sun streaming through the inferno, the visions made a final, desperate attack.

After the film was finished I was offered a couple of parts in films to be shot in Tunisia and Morocco. Stewart ('my father and his father before him were peers of the realm') Perowne put an end to those offers: 'Oh, she'll love it,' he said referring to me, 'they're hung like horses out there.' With a remark like that, I knew there would be the most awful rows with Eric should I ever entertain the idea, so I didn't.

After our candelabra fight Eric's behaviour became progressively erratic. Neither drawing nor painting, he would shut himself up in our bedroom for hours at a time. While Janet and I convalesced he had been kind and very supportive, cooking meals and taking care of us, but once we were up and about again his mood changes were extraordinary – one minute funny and helpful and the next angry or withdrawn. Money, or the lack of it, was partly to blame but I knew there had to be another reason which, try as I might, I could not fathom. Eric refused to communicate. It was during this period that Janet left. Perhaps I could have persuaded her to stay but I was so confused and upset by Eric's behaviour that I did nothing.

Eric and I were so hard-pressed for money that we rented out a room to an English couple and their child substitute, a pet budgerigar. Delighted to find themselves in such a lovely place, they were charmingly obsequious for several days; then, having firmly ensconced themselves, they proceeded to tyrannise us with endless petty disputes. The husband was working on a romantic novel and insisted on complete quiet; any noise that Eric and I made brought his wife, a former nurse, thundering down upon us. The litany of complaining proved neverending.

Ferrill then left the sinking ship and we were rescued by an American family from San Francisco, the Brentanos – a medieval historian, his wife and three children – who wanted the apartment and were prepared to give us substantially more than the rent we were paying.

So Eric and I fled our palatial Piazza Paganica apartment, leaving the awful English couple and their budgerigar to fight it out with the Brentanos. We felt rather guilty about the situation, but Robert and Margaret Brentano dealt with the pettiness and bickering in a far more responsible and practical way than either Eric or I managed. But they also had an Italian housekeeper on their side, a large, formidable woman who spoke no English and never backed down, fighting each battle with an enthusiasm and determination that precluded defeat.

Crossing the Tiber, we settled into a tiny apartment in the gatehouse of the Villa Doria Pamphili. The park in those days was then quite private. The Principessa Doria Pamphili Pogson and her husband, Don Frank Pogson, were generous in giving permission to visit their estate, but you had to apply in advance. No passer-by, no impromptu visitor was allowed entry. Apart from a few wild and unruly Italian shepherds with their much-lamented flocks of sheep that seemed to have hobbled out of the pages of *Cold Comfort Farm*, and the occasional weekend cricket match, we had the whole place almost to ourselves.

The only other person who regularly seemed to 'Pamphili' (Tony Clarke's word for the long walks through the grounds), was the delightfully eccentric and brilliant Babs Johnson. She was working on her guidebook to Rome – the best I've ever read, and one that has never been out of print. She also photographed and wrote the beautiful *Italian Gardens* and *Italian Villas and Palaces*, all under the pseudonym Georgina Masson.

We often saw Babs in hot pursuit of Willy, a large tawny-coloured hound of mixed pedigree and independent nature. Her frequent call, 'Have you seen my little Willy?', was a source of great amusement to us. Babs seemed totally unaware of its phallic connotations.

The estate was an overgrown and neglected series of romantic views by Oudry, Hubert Robert or Fragonard, a beautiful sanctuary where Eric and I walked every day, even in the rain. Marble statues, some truly ancient, were scattered throughout the grounds, lining the paths and peeping coyly from stands of evergreen. Part of what had been a romantically classical garden in the eighteenth century, an elegant semi-circle of marble, rusticated stone and plasterwork, opposite a large decaying fountain, struggled to maintain a semblance of dignity. The delicate bas-reliefs were cracking, being eased from the walls by a tangle of ivy. The fountain itself, its stonework overgrown with moss and lichen, the surface of its deep pool covered in the summer by waterlilies and frogs, was the scene of a dramatic and hilarious rescue.

Babs often took her little Willy for short runs in her car – but in a rather unusual way. She would drive slowly, one hand on the wheel, the other hanging out the window holding on to the dog's leash, as he ran alongside the vehicle, talking to him, encouraging him along, often shouting at him if he pulled away – and pull away he did. Willy was constantly escaping. On a hot afternoon Eric, Babs and I, as well as several shepherds, spent an exhausting hour or so in the fountain dealing with the results of one of his flights.

Chugging serenely past the romantic garden, Willy had noticed one of the many flocks of sheep and, with an excited bound, had freed himself. According to the shepherds, the dog had deliberately herded as many sheep into the fountain as he could before being captured. I think the animals had jumped and scrambled into the water in a state of hysterical fright rather than face Willy. He was a very big dog.

Eric and I arrived on the scene as the first rescue was attempted, with Babs shrieking at the shepherds and the men shouting back, all attempting in vain to pull the sheep out. Trying to lift frightened, water-sodden sheep, even with seven or eight people helping, is not an easy task. Eric and I got into the water with several shepherds and heaved and pushed while Babs and the others pulled. The terrified animals struggled and bleated, kicking against their rescuers, while Willy, locked securely in Babs's car, howled in frustration from the half-open window.

Babs and the shepherds weren't silent either; they had begun to loathe each other. Soaking wet, covered in weeds and mud from the fountain and filth from the sheep, we eventually dragged the beasts onto dry land. Babs drove us home, muttering invectives against the shepherds and their flocks and scolding her now totally indifferent and certainly unrepentant dog, who stared out of the car window with an air of hurt dignity.

The shepherds brought us several kilos of ricotta to thank us for helping them. They uttered dire threats about what they would do should they catch Willy alone one day and what they thought should be done to the *signora inglese*. There was far too much cheese for us to eat, but it was welcomed downstairs by the *portiere* and her husband.

We often watched the cheese being made. In a tree-covered glade by a low tunnel of stone and clay tiles – the shepherds' living quarters – was a large stone trough fed by a spring. Neither the shepherds (especially their hands) nor the sheep were very clean, but they produced wonderful cheese, creamy and soft. The sheep were milked into metal buckets. When these were filled, the milk was left to firm. Then it was scooped into wicker baskets to set and drain. The whole process, from the sheep grazing under pines and cypresses amongst marble statuary, tended by Pinelli-type shepherds living in medieval squalor in an arcadian setting, to the final wicker-imprinted mounds of ricotta, belonged to another age, soon to be lost for ever.

There were grottoes, rusticated and shadowy, formal though overgrown gardens, a small lake fed by a long, elegant cascade from a high-walled pool and, at the far end of the park, standing in a field of tall grass and wild-flowers looking rather lost and lonely, a dolphin and shell fountain. This was by Bernini and had been scooped up from the Piazza Navona by Donna Olympia Pamphili, a much hated ancestor, in the mid-1700s. Pines, cypresses, oaks, clusters of cacti and bamboo – all this we had virtually to ourselves. We picnicked, sunbathed and even swam in the ambassadorial pool of the villa on hot summer nights. It was a vast enchanted garden, solely for our enjoyment.

I tried to encourage Eric to paint it, to capture its magic and decaying grandeur before it disappeared. He completed several canvases, two in the gardens where we rescued the sheep, but his heart wasn't in it. Frustrated and bitter, he told me he was turning out 'hack' views for an audience that didn't exist. Yet we did savour the beauty of the place. How could we not?

The gatehouse was at the apex of the park at the junction of Via San Pancrazio and Via Aurelia Antica. Embedded in the ochre walls on the right-hand side of Via San Pancrazio leading up to the park gates, there are still cannonballs, relics of the battle between Garibaldi and his followers and the French and Papal armies in 1849.

When we set off on our walks, our 'Pamphiling', the gatekeeper's wife was usually on her doorstep and would let us know who had been in and out. We would saunter up the drive to the Arch of the Quattro Venti, a monument commemorating the battle. This had been built on the site of a large villa destroyed during the fighting. The villa, in turn, had been erected on the foundations of an ancient Roman house, parts of which were being excavated during our stay. At the arch, we usually took the right-hand path, which wandered down past a deep, tree-lined valley. Here, before the Second World War, deer were kept, but during the war they had all been killed for food.

Above the valley was a plain square nineteenth-century building divided into apartments and, below this, tucked almost against the Aurelian aqueduct (which formed a short part of the park's boundary wall) were stables. These had been converted into a cavernous and shadowy apartment where Babs lived. She had a small private garden in a little courtyard and a larger one outside, which was constantly being invaded by 'those bloody sheep'. Almost daily, we stopped for a quick chat as she pottered about, pruning, planting and weeding.

Walking past the valley, we could hear the sound of the water pouring through the tunnel of the ancient aqueduct. Here the path turned left, bordering the grounds of the Villa Pamphili itself. We could see only the back and the sides of the villa. Placed at the far end of a large, very formal garden of boxwood parterres, washed in a fading yellow ochre, it is a handsome building. What makes it singular is the frieze encircling it, a continuous sculptural ribbon of white marble Roman sarcophagi, battle scenes, heroes, heroines, gods and goddesses, all frozen in stone. I often became giddy studying them through binoculars.

A statue of Venus opposite a small bubbling rustic fountain marked where we turned right to the place where I found a garden of my own to tend. The flowerbeds at the base of the formal, ornamental gardens of the villa were as wild and neglected as most of the park. Hacking and chopping, I made a valiant attempt at clearing the largest and most prolific weeds. With packets of seeds sent from England, it was only a matter of months before I had a semblance, an Italian semblance, of an English herbaceous border. In spite of a brilliant but brief blaze of colour, it was untidy and ragged, and I'm not sure it was worth the effort.

Rome is a city of gossip. When I was living there, it was a maelstrom of rumour running the gamut from the merely silly or benevolent to the most vicious. The Doria Pamphili Pogsons were the subject of many a story, and Babs was our source. She liked and even grudgingly admired the Principessa – but not Don Frank, whom she found pretentious. As Babs said of herself, 'I'm a snob. I like aristocrats and artists, but I don't have much time for the rest.'

Long before the Second World War, and while recuperating from a severe illness, the old Prince Doria, father of our landlord, had married his Scottish nurse. He was at that time one of the richest and most prestigious Italian princes, with another large palace in Genoa and properties in the south. The Romans considered this marriage scandalous. That he had wedded a foreigner, a commoner without money, was made worse by the fact that he and his wife were anti-fascists. When Italian women were supposedly giving their gold wedding rings to support Mussolini's war effort, the Scots Principessa refused to relinquish hers, a courageous act which fuelled the scandal. Husband and wife were placed under house arrest and ostracised. At the end of the war, Roman society attempted friendship with these two brave people, but were spurned.

During this period, the Pamphilis' daughter ('our' Principessa) met and fell in love with an English officer in the army of occupation, Frank Pogson. She married him, according to Babs, after her father died. The Principessa and Frank then adopted two Italian orphans. On one hand, Babs admired them for this, yet at the same time she was horrified by the Pamphili Pogsons' seeming ignorance of the plots, schemes and general malevolence directed towards them. 'The poor things' – meaning the Principessa, Don Frank and the two children – 'will be involved in lawsuits well into the grave and beyond. The rest of the family will fight to disinherit those children. And of course it's another nail in the coffin of the park's future. Mark my words: the city council, the mayor and the rest of the family are in cahoots to bring them down.' ('Cahoots' was a favourite expression of Babs. Everyone she knew was in cahoots about something.)

At the time of our move from Piazza Paganica to Villa Pamphili, the mayor of Rome and the city council were indeed on the attack, according to Babs. Nearly a third of the far end of the park had been appropriated for the use of the Roman citizenry. The mayor and council were now set on taking the rest. (Eventually they did, but it was after I left Rome.) For whatever reason, although the Pamphili Pogsons still owned large tracts of forest in the south and a lot of other property, their situation seemed desperate. Don Frank often toured the park, encouraging my labours on the herbaceous border, but I met the Principessa there only once.

The tenant of the flat above ours had moved out of the gatehouse, and one day, hearing noises upstairs and knowing the apartment was empty, I went up to investigate. I found the Principessa, notebook in hand, looking like a middle-aged schoolteacher, making a list of the various bits and pieces left in the room. Unlike our apartment, this place had been let furnished. She was checking her list of chipped and cracked china, mismatched cutlery and furniture – jumble-sale items.

The Principessa grumbled about Italy and the impossibility of getting anything done. She seemed entirely at ease in our artistic mess. She admired a view of the park which Eric had painted, and seemed to understand his technique. She commented that it was 'comforting' to know that there were artists still interested in landscape painting. Then she lamented that keeping the park in some semblance of order was prohibitive. Tall and thin, with a genuine warmth, she seemed a charming and intelligent woman.

When she left, I phoned Babs, who rushed up in her battered car. More tea, more gossip. I couldn't comprehend a princess who lived in one of the largest and most splendid Roman palaces making an inventory of a series of oddments that were truly rubbish.

'Well, my dear,' said Babs, 'when Princess Margaret visited, she cooked dinner and washed up afterwards. I was there.'

We were baffled.

Eric and I were still broke. We had a small – very small – amount of money from the extra rent we were charging the Brentanos, but that was all. Eric wasn't faking drawings. It seemed too dangerous to us, and we were both worried we would be caught. We sold a few of our antique prints to Nardecchia, a dealer who had a little shop in Piazza Navona, but these were mere stopgaps. In desperation, we even tried to sell our large book of Pinelli etchings, but the modern binding was against us.

Eric executed a couple of brightly coloured and stylish copies from a set of large sepia pen, ink and wash views of Rome which we had bought from Marie Gray in London. He used modern paper, and we made no attempt to pass them off as fakes.

Nardecchia enthused, but haggled over the price. Then, to our horror, he suggested that he could supply us with 'old paper' so that Eric could then draw antique views on them, which would fetch a far higher price.

Shortly before this, Aubrey Menen and his secretary paid us a visit. A tense situation was developing between young Pierino and the secretary who felt jealous and suspicious that the boy was trying to oust him from his job. We spent a difficult half-hour sitting uncomfortably on a suite of furniture 'looted' from Piazza Paganica. Delicately carved, covered in a pale yellow velvet, it was out of place in our small, ugly apartment in the gatehouse. Aubrey seemed angry with us for living in such a place. He hated the flat and the unending noise of the nearby traffic, and he told us that he expected better from us both.

Still grumbling, he allowed Eric and me to take them both to dinner at the Trattoria Scarpone – the 'big boot' – just a short distance from the gatehouse, in Via San Pancrazio. We found Babs and the Principessa Rospigliosi there eating under the pergolas. With some wine, good food and the Principessa's lively sense of humour, Aubrey's bad mood disappeared. Yet when he said goodnight he told us he wasn't going to visit us again until we had moved back to Piazza Paganica – but of course we couldn't afford to.

Our lack of money was driving us crazy. What were we to do?

Eric borrowed some money from Paul Cooper, giving him as a guarantee for the loan a pencil drawing of Dorelia, which Eric signed 'John', and swore to Paul was an original. Yet fake it was.

I returned from shopping one afternoon to find that Eric had thrown all his drawings, all his *original* drawings, into the bins on the landing. He was sitting almost weeping, tears in his eyes. 'Nobody wants them, so there's no reason to keep them,' he explained.

I put the large drawings back in his portfolio; the smaller ones I collected and mounted on paper. I later had them bound. But this didn't solve our financial crisis. What were we to do?

We had tried to make an honest venture, to establish ourselves as dealers in original Old Masters. With the Pannini Gallery catalogue and the exhibition in Rome, we had put a great deal of energy and hope into this. 'We're more honest than any dealer I know,' Eric once said to me. He loathed and despised them. Their indifference to his own work had really soured him.

Of course Eric and I discussed faking, but an alliance in forgery with Nardecchia seemed unthinkable. It would only have given him a tremendous hold over us. So Eric told the dealer that he couldn't conceive of faking drawings, which was why he had done his copies on modern paper. Nardecchia seemed to accept this.

But we talked endlessly around the subject on our long walks. We both felt it could be a trap of our own making, that we really couldn't invest in it as we had in Pannini Galleries. The fear of being caught was too great. Yet, if we stuck to the original concept, Marie Gray's idea, of drawing on old paper and handing them over unsigned to the dealers and salesrooms, what could anyone do?

Prison and the police were never far from our thoughts during these discussions. We were preoccupied with the 'August Johns'. Eric had signed these and established himself as the seller. Signing a work of art, copying the artist's signature, was forgery. There was no argument about this. It was a criminal act for which we could both be prosecuted. Would someone connect these modern pencil drawings with future Old Master drawings? We didn't think so. But if they did, what would be the repercussions? It was a rhetorical question, for we knew only too well what would happen, and the knowledge scared us.

Finally, as our financial situation worsened, we decided that hopefully no one would make the connection and that living in Italy was ideal for 'finding' treasures. Newly unearthed, or from old collections, art smuggled out of the country was always turning up in international sales. Really, all we had to do was to include a modest number of Eric's forgeries and – *coraggio* – live happily ever after. And, if we were going to live off forgeries, we decided to make them important ones. No more little fish.

After a week or so, having debated all the pros and cons, we were still considering what Eric should attempt. First, the Leonardo book – my school prize – was consulted. We dismissed a Leonardo or even a 'school of' as too risky for a first attempt. Remembering the reception to the Mantegna *Vulcan*, however, we both felt another Mantegna would do nicely.

The paper for the drawing came from the oldest of a number of vellum-bound ecclesiastical books that we had bought as a job lot in the Porta Portese. I gave it several thin coats of rabbit-skin glue so that the ink wouldn't spread. The surface of old paper loses its ability to hold a pen line, and simply absorbs it, rather like blotting paper would.

Eric sat at the window, facing the Via San Pancrazio, in our cramped living-room, dining-room and studio, with several books on drawing in front of him. I hovered in the background, making suggestions and tea, offering criticism and support.

After three or four days of intense effort, Eric produced the powerful and interesting *Lamentation of the Three Marys*. He stamped the Richardson and Reynolds collectors' marks on the drawing, cut the sheet down and gave it to me to 'antique'.

First, the collectors' marks needed blotting off. Then, as Eric had drawn in pencil to block out the design, I erased all his preliminary lines. He had used Pelican waterproof ink, as he had on the first Mantegna. With a razorblade, I carefully scraped away the thick lumps where the pen lines had crossed one another.

Before I poured boiling water over it to deaden the gloss of the modern ink, I wrote, in a shaky imitation of what I thought might pass as a florid Victorian hand, the capitals 'E.H.'. This was to give Eric a way out, should he need one.

'Well, look, Graham signed it with my initials. Ha ha.'

With the drawing finished and ready for presentation, Eric flew off to London and Colnaghi's, and to the beginning, the real beginning, of his career as a master forger.

It is so easy to look back with hindsight, but in comparing Eric's drawing with the reproductions of drawings by Mantegna and Giovanni Bellini (the two masters have much in common), I can see how different Eric's work is. His drawing has much of the uncertain, nervous energy of the mid- to late-twentieth century, and little of the calm, positive energy which radiates through the Italian Renaissance. The folds of the garments in Eric's drawings, for example, are fussy and small in form, lacking the statuesque certainty of the fifteenth century. They seem, at times, to rocket out and away from the figures they should be encompassing. Examine the four saints from the Chatsworth collection attributed to Mantegna and Bellini, how the architectural lines, still with a touch of the Gothic, are worlds away from the amorphous forms of Eric's drawing, which bears a relationship closer to Henry Moore than to either of the above. The right arm of Christ appears as if cut out of another drawing and pasted on, and is proportionally too small for his body. The three heads, though, are full of pathos, particularly the middle one, with a cry of pain as fixed as a Greek tragic mask.

Fussy and overworked as it is, *Lamentation of the Three Marys* remains a drawing which holds the attention. As it was the first major fake, the intensity of effort shows through. It has an internal excitement which one can find in Eric's early work, but which seems to be lacking in his later efforts.

Villa San Filipo, Anticoli Corrado

Going up the further hills from the
Villa San Filipo, through thin cypresses
and thinner paths to Anticoli Corrado
(such trees of death fade in the light
of an autumn sun). Drinking sambucca
in the village square, but remembering
the more mundane: the hot home-made
pasta in the foothill trattoria, dusty
taste, uneven texture; the sound of
lorries heading north; barking of dogs.
And back in the villa, tiles pressing
cold against naked feet; the hillside
garden's brambles tearing at skin, cotton
the absolute impossibility of repetition.

Barry Cole, 'How it was in Italy'

IMAGINE A NARROW FERTILE VALLEY, SCATTERED WITH TREES and small-holdings, winding between high, rounded hills and edging up into wild mountains. A small river flows at their base, shallow and clear, bubbling over a pebble-strewn sandy bed; a trout stream also rich with crayfish.

This was the Aniene valley in the mid-1960s. The Roman poet Horace retired to a forest-ringed farm here and lived and wrote in harmony with his surroundings. His dark forest and its feral inhabitants are long gone although, so the story goes, in the 1940s a postman was eaten by a pack of wolves when delivering letters to the Villa San Filipo. Perched on a low hill overlooking the valley, this L-shaped two-storey building, sheltered by pines and cypresses, edged to the north by a spinney of sweet chestnut, was to be my home for the next few years, and was itself overlooked by the ancient village of Anticoli Corrado.

179

It was a simple old country house. Its plaster walls, beamed ceilings, brick and tiled floors were all virtually unaltered. Two luxurious modern bathrooms covered in agate marble had been added for a visit by Princess Margaret when she also stayed with the Pamphili Pogsons.

Luigi Pirandello also lived here; D.H. Lawrence stayed here, as did Norman Douglas, author of *South Wind* and *Old Calabria*, before he was 'escorted' from the province of Tivoli on account of moral turpitude. He had organised a masturbation race amongst a group of Anticoli boys down by the river. He should have known better, for instead of rewarding every participant he gave prize money only to the first three boys to ejaculate. The losers naturally complained, and news of the affair eventually reached the authorities.

After our sojourn in the Doria Pamphili park, Eric and I returned to Piazza Paganica, the Brentano family having left for America though not before routing, with the assistance of their maid, the ghastly English couple. But the Brentanos wanted to return and settle in Rome and as the Villa San Filipo had been vacant for years, Eric decided to lease it and turn Paganica over to them.

Filled with trepidation, I agreed to move. I had a hunch that I would feel marooned on our little hill, and my hunch proved correct. Eric was intent on setting himself up as the 'guv'nor', the squire of Anticoli. He had at last found his home. He was determined to be seen as a *signore*, an English gentleman, and nothing was to interfere with this. His dream of recognition, of fame and fortune as an artist in his own right, had faded. Bitter and disillusioned, he held fast to one part of his lost hopes: in the villa he would be king of his castle. Here he would hold court and the world would come to him.

For the first time Eric took charge of redecorating while I stayed in Anticoli. I was recovering from jaundice – my liver was still pretty shaky after the hepatitis. He and Renzo, our gardener, had painted the inside of the house. By the time I was better, the interior was finished. I had insisted on white walls, and it looked dazzling. Shelves had been built in a small room off the salon, which I dubbed the library. We had hundreds of books although, as Ellis Waterhouse once told me with glee, a library could only be considered as such if it had over five thousand books. Ellis's own library was well known in art-history circles not only for its size but also for its excellence.

Nemo Piccoli, an ex-patriate American sculptor, architect and naval designer, laid out a central-heating plan which we had installed, and a damp course was dug along the north wall.

The *giardino segreto*, the secret garden, with its foundation and large round pool, walled by tall box hedges and roofed with pine trees, was on a level with the upper floor: the damp from it produced a fine crop of *funghi* in the downstairs rooms. I chose a dark green velvet for the monstrous gilt suite – there were no more collapsing settees – and within a few months we were settled in.

The garden was left to Renzo, who in a matter of weeks cleaned and cleared away the neglect of years. My only complaint was the decimation of a fine stand of black and gold bamboo, which had screened the largest of the pools at the bottom of the garden, containing a dozen koi, big and superbly coloured.

The kitchen garden provided fresh organic vegetables. Bread was baked daily in the village; beef, pork and chicken were local, as was our milk which was delivered warm and frothy by a Sicilian living in the valley and referred to by the Anticolians as 'him, down there'. On Fridays a truck drove around the villages selling fresh fish. A perfect life in a perfect setting.

As well as Nemo and his wife Juanita, we made other friends, in particular Moyra Byrne, an American living nearby with a German painter named Manfred. He and Eric would have extended drinking sessions together. There was also Irina Hale, part Russian, part Anglo-Irish, another painter, who stayed for long periods in Anticoli. These two women became lifelong and precious friends.

I looked on Renzo as an ally rather than a servant. Refusing to address him by the coarse and humiliating *voi* used by the 'upper' classes for their 'inferiors', and realising we were not close enough for me to employ the familiar *tu*, I chose the formal *lei*, out of respect and liking for the man.

Now that we had servants, however, there was little for me to do. Eric, still discouraging me from drawing, suggested I take up embroidery or carpet-making as an outlet for my frustrated creative urges. Although I was still restoring old prints for various Roman dealers, a task I found interesting and rewarding, I needed to draw. So I began a series of illustrations for a play by the Earl of Rochester, a crony of King Charles II, but left them unfinished after being attacked by Eric, and again concentrated my energies towards his work.

I bought a number of prepared zinc plates and persuaded him to turn his wrestler series into etchings which I bit in acid for him and then had printed and bound into books. After Anthony Blunt bought a copy a few others were sold. Tony Clarke purchased one, for the Minneapolis Art Institute, and so did Ellis Waterhouse. We attempted to get an exhibition in Rome but found the only way to do so was to pay for one – and pride decided Eric against this.

With the success of the Mantegna, Eric embarked on a large Pontormo, three French drawings (a mythological scene by Boucher and two

Fragonard landscapes), a Hans Von Kulmbach, a Canaletto, a Benedetto Castiglione (*Young Oriental with his Horse*) and a Francesco del Cossa pageboy. The Pontormo and the Castiglione were sold at Christie's salesroom in London and the Cossa at Sotheby's. Anthony saw the Castiglione at Piazza Paganica and was so impressed that he offered to purchase the drawing.

Eric also produced a series of highly finished capriccios of various Roman ruins, executed in pen and ink and watercolour, using as a basis what remained of our large collection of old engravings and etchings.

The paper came from a couple of Marie Gray's folders which she had put together from late eighteenth- and early nineteenth-century French paper. I soaked the folders in the bath for a day then peeled the large sheets apart, gently sponging off the remaining glue. Elegantly matted and superbly framed, these drawings were sold through several top antique stores in Rome and Milan.

On the same paper as the earlier copies of Goya's disasters, Eric drew an exquisite Renoir in red chalk: a seated woman towelling herself, observed from behind. He added Renoir's signature and I had it matted and framed. Eric showed it to Anthony who, knowing a little about the work of the Impressionists, insisted on taking the drawing with him to England. The verdict form London, strange and laughable, was that the signature was genuine but the drawing a fake. In spite of my protestations, Eric burnt it. He said it was too dangerous to keep.

Here Eric and I had yet another argument. I felt it was a betrayal of trust to ask men who had become our friends – like Anthony, Christopher White and Ellis – to authenticate the fakes. Our initial idea had been simply to pop Eric's forgeries into salesrooms and see what happened without involving anyone else, and letting the drawings speak for themselves. Going straight to Colnaghi's with the Mantegna and using his friendship with Christopher, who was then employed by the firm, was, I thought, a once-only move necessitated by lack of money: putting the drawing through the salesrooms could have taken months and we couldn't afford to wait. But after the sale of the Mantegna, pivotal in Eric's life, I assumed we'd go back to our original plan. But no: Eric was off and running. He didn't care, saying art experts were fools and knew nothing about art, though he did, so serve them right. If their attributions proved wrong, they had only themselves to blame.

Yet he refused to address the kernel of the matter: should we lie to and dupe those who called us friends? For him that wasn't a problem.

Anthony Blunt came to stay with us many times. Although we knew nothing about what he was enduring in London, the ongoing interrogations, it was obvious that here at San Filipo he had found a refuge. Before his first visit Eric told Renzo and Anna (our cook) that a very important guest was due – a friend of the Queen, an English knight, and so on. He wanted no repetition of leathery liver dinners or women in bath towels at the dinner table; everything was to be faultless this time.

When Anthony eventually arrived in his worn tweed jacket and baggy grey flannels, carrying a scuffed suitcase, Renzo was outraged. He felt he had been the victim of a practical joke. Our Don Antonio had nothing of the *bella figura* that mattered to Italians. How could this man be so important when his appearance, to Renzo, was so shabby, so *brutto*?

But this was followed by countless happy days. Every time Anthony came to stay with us, plans were made for long outings to the east of the country, into the mountains, or north as far as the Maremma; explorations of towns and villages to seek out the architecture of Lazio for himself but primarily for his students.

I remember standing on the walls of a cyclopean fort high up on a hillside, a valley spread out far below us in the warm twilight of an Italian summer evening. The valley was silent and empty, a two-lane tarmac road reduced, from our vantage-point, to a mere track; smoke rose in an unbroken column from a clump of trees; nothing else moved.

'It gives me the chills,' I said.

'Yes, the timelessness is uncanny,' Anthony replied.

We stood silent for several minutes, the noise from the village behind us muted. We could smell wood fires lit for the evening meal.

'And now I think it's time for a drink!' said Anthony, bringing us back to the present.

We went in search of a trattoria. But this was a tiny village far from the tourist trail, neglected and impoverished. There was a café but no trattoria and nothing else of interest. Its small dark church had been stripped of everything except a beautiful wooden model of a much grander building; it was worm-eaten but exquisitely made.

We came across another church in a nearby valley, which looked like it had been bombed, probably in the Second World War. The far wall, the altar wall, however, still stood untouched above mounds of rubble. As we sped past I called out for our driver to stop for, attached, floating high near what had been the ceiling, were two large baroque angels, white and serene.

On closer inspection we found that part of the foundation, perhaps of an earlier church, was composed of large blocks of marble decorated in shallow bas-relief. Strange animals and sea monsters, very early – maybe eighth or ninth century – hid behind a fringe of grass and wildflowers, their form and design a replica of those found on old manuscripts.

'Well, Anthony,' I said, 'if I could, I'd steal these.' I was quite un-equivocal about that. 'They should be in a museum – they're gorgeous.'

Anthony agreed and for a while the three of us attempted to formulate a strategy for their removal while our driver, Lelo, sat in the sun and lit another cigarette. His expression of disdainful boredom – a regular feature when the *stranieri*, the foreigners, went poking around these old and uninteresting places – was soon wiped from his face, however.

At the rear of the church under a wide, low arch we came across broad steps leading down to the ancient crypt, but it was impossible to descend for the space was filled to the ceiling with a mass of human bones. Femurs, tibias, humeri, bits and pieces, jawbones, skulls; it was a charnel-house. Without hesitating, I clambered onto the mound of bones and selected a skull in decent condition. I then set about finding a jawbone to match. Successful, I returned from the dark crypt to the sunlight to find Lelo blessing himself in a state of shock. He was horrified by my actions. He didn't want the skull in the car but we were *signori* and there was nothing he could do but cross himself repeatedly and make the horned sign with his fingers against bad luck. The skull was another prop for Eric, for the 'Old Master'.

Renzo, too, was upset when I carried the skull up from the garage to where he stood by the kitchen door – though not so upset as he had been when I had rescued a dozen or more toads, some with male partners clutching their backs, from the bottom of our neighbours' empty swimming-pool. I had truly received the evil-eye treatment that day, and Renzo went so far as to ask if I was a witch.

With Anthony we explored the palazzo above the village and the lake of Bracciano, to see the Bernini busts of a former duke and his wife. The grand salons, with ugly furniture and walls covered with hunting trophies, were dusty and unused. But the Prince's bedroom, monastic in its simplicity with his books and a few personal possessions – pens and paper on a small desk, several pairs of boots lined up against a plain wooden cupboard – spoke of a familiarity of use, as did a small sunlit adjoining terrace. Standing on the top of the highest tower, the lake far below, I recognised a scent from my childhood. Where was it coming from? Peering timidly over the edge, growing out from the ancient stone, I saw bunches of bright saffron-coloured wallflowers – Siberian wallflowers, my father called them. Their colour and scent enthralled me. I had once tried to cover my entire patch of garden at Barkingside with them.

We enjoyed the elegant Renaissance beauty of the Villa Lante at Bagnaia. I remember in particular its charming watercourse, traversing the centre of a stone banqueting table for alfresco dining, then flowing down to where it fed the hidden jets of the splendid Neptune fountain of the formal gardens.

There were so many excursions, every one a delight with Anthony as instructor and guide. But the best of times were spent around the villa with Anthony and Eric sitting in the kitchen keeping me company while I bottled and preserved fruit and vegetables, or in walks up to the village square and dinner at Renzo's with a car for our return: we knew Anthony wouldn't be able to manage the descent on foot.

On one of our first trips up to Anticoli, the local boys (whose insistent propositioning was at times very irritating – I never knew, when exploring the alleys and ruins of lower Anticoli, when one would appear, pull his penis out and wave it at me) greeted us as usual, calling out to me, '*E socio* – partner,' and giving a straight one-arm salute. At this Anthony stopped, his face white, his body shaking at what he supposed was a fascist salutation.

At the local bar I called a couple of the lads to join us. I had told Anthony that the village, if not communist, was certainly socialist – and not the fascist type either – but I could see he wasn't convinced. Over a drink or two, the boys asserted that, no, they definitely weren't fascists and, yes, they were communists, though not like the Russians; they didn't want that kind of régime in Italy. Anthony relaxed and after a few drinks was completely reassured.

In celebration of his sixtieth birthday, we took him to the Sirenusa at Tivoli, the Victorian hotel where marble tablets commemorate the visits of minor European royalty. At the rear of the hotel, standing sentinel above the precipitous ravine, were the ruins of a circular temple; only a few columns remained. Here we drank our coffee and brandy, listening to the roar of the waterfall echoing in the darkness. We gave Anthony a lovely Etruscan black two-handled drinking cup, a cylix, which delighted him.

Occasionally, Anthony's lover, John Gaskin, also came to stay at the villa. A constant tension accompanied his visits and I think we were all glad that they were short, as he used San Filipo as a stopover on his way to and from Greece. Camp, bitter and sarcastic, he was a reminder of the many unpleasant queens of my youth, and I disliked him from the start.

Nothing was good enough for John. I rose early every morning, but was still asleep when Anthony was up and about. I would grind coffee the night before and put it in our pot ready for him to turn on the gas. He ate later with us – that was his preference. But John demanded my appearance first thing in the morning. I laughed. Anthony, while a guest, was also a friend, and the idea of waiting in attendance on him was absurd. Besides, Anthony had made it clear that he liked his early mornings alone, watching the cloak of mist lift slowly from the valley as the sun, reflected through millions of drops of water, rose above the mountains. A perfect time of day. John was furious at my refusal, his anger augmented by jealousy. But he never stayed for long – San Filipo was too quiet for him.

I spent long days with Renzo organising the kitchen garden, spraying, pruning and planting out seedlings. Under a white waterfall of wisteria, we discovered an apple tree bearing bumper crops of the most delicious fruit.

Sunlit days recalling times with my father; happy days, too, with Moyra; long walks through the valley past the sulphur and iron springs and the remains of a Roman villa; being fed by the *contadini* with cheese and ham and fresh baked bread, all washed down with rough local wine. Come, come, they would call out, try some of this. Yes, have another piece, my wife made this too. Sit down, we've all day to talk. Where are you from? Ah, England. Good people, the English.

Sometimes we would got to a trattoria where, from a spring-fed pool, we would choose enormous trout. Grilled fresh, their gutted insides were stuffed with bay leaves, garlic and black pepper. Or we'd detour to a small mill and pick up kilos of fresh wheatgerm; the Italians, having no use for it, fed it to their chickens. Anna made us platefuls of deliciously thick brown fettucine with rich aromatic sauces of chicken livers and hearts.

Other times we'd take slow evening walks up to Anticoli through small-holdings and up steep, rocky donkey tracks under tunnels of old oaks, to have dinner at Renzo's. When the previous occupant of San Filipo had departed, his termination pay to Renzo was enough for him to have a large modern restaurant built, where his wife reigned supreme. She was an incredibly fine cook. Her pork and pork-liver sausages, with whole peppers and thin pieces of lemon and orange peel, were a constant at the villa.

We usually took Emma, our foolish and affectionate boxer dog, with us and left Sara, our tiny Siamese, howling at the edge of the garden. Sara never stepped over the boundaries of the property although she always accompanied us on our daily walks around the pools and terraces. She would sit at the edge of the south terrace by the front door and observe with great disapproval Emma's sallies into a newly discovered game: rural terrorism.

Emma's mother had taught her this on a first visit to San Filipo. The mother, a huge beast, saw the miles of open countryside as her domain and considered anything that moved on it as fair game for attack. Before the arrival of Mama, Emma's roaming took her no further than the village dump where, in joyful excess, she rolled in the most odorous garbage, returning to us happy and contented and never comprehending our yells, her immediate hosing down and exclusion from our company for the rest of the day.

Now, however, there would be a price to pay after each of Emma's predatory escapades. Often only an hour after her return, we would hear someone knocking at the kitchen door (rarely at the front door) and a crestfallen figure would appear, cap in hand, as if Eric and I were despotic and powerful nineteenth-century landowners: 'Scusi, signori, I apologise for disturbing you, I'm sorry but your dog has, today, killed several of my chickens.' We would offer our apologies, followed by a drink at the kitchen table, then restitution for the massacre.

During the winter, when brief flurries of snow transformed the landscape from Italian to Flemish, from Poussin and Claude to Breughel, Eric and I would be the only customers in Renzo's restaurant. We ate with our overcoats on, a charcoal brazier at our feet and Emma, on account of her hairless behind, perched on a chair several feet from the table, drooling with hopeful expectancy. The marble floor was icy and I refused to make her sit on it. The few locals drinking at a table in the far corner thought us crazy, but then they were used to it. For a hundred years or more foreigners had come to Anticoli to enjoy the medieval beauty of the village and to use its handsome inhabitants as models. Besides, we were signori, and therefore not expected to conform.

After our meal we would descend to the villa in the pitch dark, a fiasco (an apt word) or two of wine in our bellies. Usually the journey home was accompanied by many falls and much laughter until, arm in arm, we finally walked through the tunnel of box hedges to be greeted with obvious relief by Sara. Two young men, laughing and clinging together; these were truly happy times.

Neither Emma nor Sara were particularly useful guard dogs, although to be fair Emma was still a puppy the one time we were burgled. It happened shortly after we moved into the villa. The thieves took all our Greek terracottas and several Syrian eighteenth-century forgeries, an Apulian red figure vase, a theatrical scene of a young couple accompanied by several grotesquely masked dwarfs, and a great many of our prints. But the burglars were disturbed by Eric before they could unpack anything else. At each place the thieves stopped to wrap a treasure in our hand-made suits was a small puddle of pee. Eric and I imagined Emma's little round body quivering with excitement at these unexpected guests. How sorry her signori would be at not having been home to welcome them. But even as a fully grown dog, dear Emma was not a guardian of our property. She greeted each and every caller with enthusiasm and joy, dispensing her lopsided toothy grin with largesse.

On a hill opposite San Filipo was a villa belonging to two friends, Joe and Dorothy. Theirs was the swimming-pool from which each year I rescued many dehydrated toads. Emptied during the winter, it was refilled in late spring and Eric and I were given a standing invitation to use it.

At Easter, Anticoli's band would tour the village and outlying houses to play their instruments and collect money. Their arrival at San Filipo was announced by the most discordant noise as they attempted a medley of Verdi. I stood on the terrace and looked down at them as they enthusiastically ripped into Italian opera, tearing it to shreds.

Down the path from Joe and Dorothy's villa came the celebrated American soprano Leontyne Price. Her head covered by a large straw hat, and wearing an ankle-length tent-like dress, she descended on the band. Hands clapping, she called the musicians to order and began conducting them. After a couple of attempts she got the band to play the Easter hymn from *Cavalleria Rusticana*, and sang with them, her glorious voice ringing clear and fine through the early morning. Its sheer beauty united the villagers in what was undoubtedly their finest performance.

Eric and I took a donation and large trays of wine, cheese and ham down to the band when they had finished. We congratulated Leontyne Price whom we had met a couple of years previously at one of Eugene's parties.

Eric was depressed again. The lack of interest shown in his 'Wrestlers' was the last straw, he told me. He was giving up and had decided to produce only Old Master drawings from now on. Although far less passionate than I had been several years previously, I still thought of Eric as a superb artist and tried to interest him in drawing and painting some views of our house and the surrounding countryside. I had little success.

I tried a different approach. Nemo Piccoli, in his studio near the village square, had begun to sculpt using a black wax which softened wonderfully as he held it in his hands. I thought Eric might be interested and on our next foray up to Anticoli we stopped and chatted with him. Eric was dismissive of Nemo as a sculptor and at first was not particularly interested in attempting anything himself. Ignoring his grumbling, however, I bought several kilos of the black wax from the foundry in Rome which Nemo used and after days of intense pressure got him started on a series of heads based on photographs from wrestling magazines I had bought him in London.

It was around this time that we received some bad news. A letter came from Sylvia Ayton informing us that Fin, my old college friend, had died. It appeared that Fin, performing backflips on the cliff-tops at Beachy

Head, had fallen over the edge. It was quite extraordinary and sudden. The shock made me burst out laughing when I read the letter. But Eric took my laughter as a sign of cold-heartedness. Again he withdrew, muttering about my insensitivity, and hardly spoke to me for several days.

Things were definitely not right between us but as Eric refused to communicate, there was little I could do. I was also beginning to realise that there was little I *felt* like doing. There were no big fights; instead, we were in limbo, in a state of unsettled truce, each waiting for the other to make a move so that the battle could commence.

That we needed a break was clear. I didn't mean that we should live apart, just that something had to change so that we were no longer constantly, day and night, in each other's presence. What was to have been my studio at the villa had become a third bedroom. I determined to have a studio in Anticoli, somewhere of my own away from Eric, where I could do – what? That was the big question.

I knew sooner or later Eric would see what I was creating, and that if he disapproved I would be back to square one. Nevertheless, I suggested taking a studio in Anticoli, and the truce broke. All I wanted it for was to have the village boys in for sex, Eric shouted. This was grossly unfair. Before we moved into San Filipo, he and I had once rented a large studio in Anticoli overlooking the castle and the mountains, and one day he invited a group of about six village boys to come in out of the rain. One of them, a Caravaggio lookalike with very bad teeth, told us of a cinema on the outskirts of Rome where older men paid them for sex. In spite of his teeth, the boy was very pretty. Eric described him as a lollipop, and as the boy rolled about on a divan clutching his crotch, we could see he was obviously sexually excited. The other boys joined in, recounting their escapades in various Roman parks and ruins. Eric and I were being propositioned in a very crude manner. I shunted the group out into the rain; there was no way I was going to be escorted out of the province. I told Eric they were nothing more than jail bait. Needless to say, however, I surprised him and his lollipop boy together only a few days later.

All this and much else besides came out as we yelled at each other, a battle royal which ended, as usual, with my capitulation. No studio of my own, no chance to work: what was I doing with my life? It was my thirtieth birthday.

We drove down to Rome and Aubrey Menen took us out to dinner and the three of us ate and drank far too much. The evening was spent laughing and joking together, yet on the journey home the next day I sat in silent misery. My talents, if I possessed any, were untried, unused. And, for the first time, I realised I felt trapped in San Filipo in a relationship that was dying.

Eric, irritated by my silence and convinced I was sulking because he had forgotten to buy me a present, told Lelo to stop the car outside Standa, the Italian equivalent of Woolworth's. He went inside and returned with two cheap blue shirts: my birthday present. Now everything was all right, he informed me, I could cheer up. Happy birthday.

Several days later we were in the dining-room; Emma was stretched out on a rug in front of the fire, Sara lying curled up between Emma's legs: a scene of domestic bliss. While Eric and I drank brandy after our evening meal, I told him what I was feeling and what I thought I needed. I braced myself for another shouting match but this time he was very controlled and icy. He told me he knew what it was all about. I didn't need a studio of my own. I could draw in the garden (I had begun a series of flower drawings); or, if it was absolutely necessary, I might use his studio, which I did when restoring old prints. I had everything I needed here, he said, and I was being selfish, making us both unhappy. But if I felt that what he was providing wasn't enough, he warned, I was free to leave.

I gave up.

Eric put forward what was in effect an ultimatum: stay or leave, but don't rock the boat; do what I tell you and we both will be happy; and he meant it, there was no mistaking his sincerity. So I stayed and gardened and bottled fruit and tried not to rock the boat.

Eric and I took many trips together, sometimes combining business with pleasure, taking drawings to dealers and salesrooms. We spent a fortnight on Stromboli staying with Moyra and Manfred; other times there would be visits to Paris and often, and always on business, to London, where we stayed for part of the time with Anthony in his flat at Portman Square. Sometimes John Gaskin was there, sometimes not. Anthony was more relaxed in his absence and the three of us would eat together in the kitchen or sit drinking in the spacious living-room, our conversation interrupted by much laughter, a rare sound when John was with us.

One visit was particularly memorable on account of a sordidly unpleasant scene that unravelled on our last night.

Our stay had begun well. Eric and I had noticed an overpainted obelisk, a ghost image, in the background of one of the Poussins, *Elijah and Rebecca at the Well*, in the sitting-room. Anthony hadn't noticed it before, nor had anyone else or they would have pointed it out to him. He was thrilled and impressed with our discovery.

There was also a large reproduction of *The Kingdom of Flora* by Poussin hanging on the wall above the kitchen table. Apropos of nothing, Anthony asked me if I knew the characters represented. I did: Ajax in a fit of pique falling on his sword, Echo and Narcissus, Clytie and Apollo and several other figures from Greek mythology. Anthony told me I should become an art historian. I had read a few of the right books – Burckhardt, Pevsner and Gombrich – and he suggested I should study at the Courtauld. I felt honoured and very pleased, but I declined. I couldn't imagine a life spent in minute archival research. I enjoyed hunting down the odd print through Bartsch and Hind and the hours I spent in the British Museum prints and drawings room, but a career in art history didn't appeal.

The last day of our visit began with a sunny, glorious morning, a morning to be treasured in damp, grey England. Eric and John Gaskin went out together to see a dealer in Burlington Arcade. Eric was selling him a bronze of a standing boy (for which I had posed though it bore little resemblance to me).

I spent the morning reading in Anthony's impressive library. He joined me for elevenses: a gin and tonic. I accepted his offer of a sherry. He picked up the bronze head of a wrestler by Eric that we had given him and held it in his hand, caressing it. He liked the sensual forms and the sadness and beauty of the face. The head reminded him of Rodin, he said; it had the same fluid modelling and compact form. The sculpture was very fine, one of Eric's best.

Relaxing with our drinks in the rather worn armchairs, we talked about painting. Anthony was still amazed that Eric and I had found the hidden obelisk in his Poussin. 'We're a very good team,' I said, 'we both have an excellent eye.'

He suggested again that I should become an art historian, but I told him that I couldn't envisage it as a way of life. Besides, one day, one distant day, I hoped to start drawing again.

'Why did you stop?' Anthony enquired.

'Well, having two artists in one household doesn't work. When I start drawing I lose all sense of time – and, besides, Eric doesn't like me drawing, doesn't like my subject matter. He gets upset when I work. We've had many arguments about it.'

'Was that what caused the fight with the wooden chandelier? John dined out on that story for months.'

'No,' I replied. 'I honestly don't know what that was all about. Eric refused to discuss it. Anyhow, one day when we have a little more money, I shall get a studio in the village or in Rome and work there.' It was a dream of mine that I was beginning to realise would probably remain a dream.

Then we got around to the subject of sex. I told him I enjoyed being active and passive, top and bottom, which surprised him.

'Does Eric enjoy that?' he asked.

191

'I think so,' I replied. 'He once compared me fucking him to a mouse on an elephant, which I decided to take as a compliment.'

He laughed. 'I'd like to see that.'

'Do you like watching?' I asked

'Oh, yes.'

'So do I – or rather I would, but I'm never given the chance. Eric is very proper and very jealous.'

I told him about my first love, the young blond soldier, and how I cried for nights, walking through the streets of east London, after he decided to get married and told me our affair was at an end.

'Come with me,' Anthony said. 'I've got something to show you.'

He got up and I followed him out of the room. Rummaging through a cardboard box at the bottom of a cupboard in the corridor, he produced a photograph of a beautiful young man in uniform. Utterly, devastatingly handsome and sensual.

'That's John,' Anthony said, 'when I met him.' Quite brusquely he put the photograph back and shut the cupboard door.

I hadn't recognised John at all. There was no connection between the face of that young, beautiful man and the stooping, shrunken, drink-bloated face of Anthony's John, mincing spitefully about the flat, complaining and bitching.

We went back to the sitting-room and to our discussion of art. Suddenly, without warning, Anthony burst into tears. For a second I froze. Then I took him into my arms and held his tall thin body as it shook with deep, painful sobs.

As abruptly as they began, his tears stopped. 'I do apologise,' he said, or something like that. 'I believe we could do with another drink,' and we went upstairs.

Eric and John returned in a good mood. Eric had sold his bronze and John was pleased with the generous commission Eric had given him for arranging the sale.

After lunch Eric and I went out to visit the Wallace Collection. I related the morning's happenings to him. I was still upset. 'He's probably working too hard,' Eric said. I agreed. Anthony did look tired, really exhausted.

We enjoyed the Watteaus and took a long look at the Paduan Narcissus, lamenting that we had had to part with our cast of it. 'But Eric,' I told him, 'you're sculpting bronzes as fine and better. It's old works for new and that, for us, is a much healthier position to be in.'

I could see, though, that Eric wasn't convinced. He hadn't recovered from selling the beautiful figurine.

John Gaskin prepared a delicious meal that evening, a dinner that began with smoked trout and went on to beef stroganoff. We had several drinks before eating and were fairly well oiled when we sat down in the kitchen. John told us about two rich old ladies who owned a boutique in Mayfair. He gave the impression that he cultivated their friendship solely in the hope of figuring in their wills.

He told us how much he and his friends had enjoyed the wooden candelabra story, and asked me if I had any others. I told him about the time Peter Greenham came to dinner and of the fight Eric and I had had that evening. Eric joined in, giving his version of events. We were relaxed and enjoying the food and a good red wine, when Anthony claimed he had something better. He climbed onto his chair and, after some fumbling, handed down from an overhead cupboard two bottles of Nuits St George. They were the Rothschilds' special reserve and Anthony received a dozen or more bottles every year from the family.

Then, for no apparent reason other than having had too much to drink, John began talking about his youth and our pleasant evening darkened. He told us about his experiences in a prisoner-of-war camp. He had been captured in 1940 as part of the ill-fated British Expeditionary Force, and spent the rest of the war behind barbed wire. John was still a teenager and, to survive, he said, he was forced to become the 'bum boy' of an older man who 'loaned' him out for cigarettes and other luxuries. He insisted vehemently that up until then he had been exclusively heterosexual, that he'd only become 'queer' out of necessity. The man was well endowed and at first sex had been painful. John's voice shook as he spoke of the humiliation he had endured being sent off to satisfy other men and being called a 'brownnoser'; his revulsion, in the beginning, at having to go down on his 'lover' (for want of a better word) and then, with his lover watching and commenting, on other men. These were things he could never forget.

In spite of all this, however, John said he had grown to love and depend on the man. Shouting and banging on the table to emphasise his story, he told us the man had claimed to love him too, and they made plans for a life together after the war. After John was eventually freed, he tracked the man down and, with high hopes, went to see him. He discovered the man was married with children, something he hadn't mentioned; not only did he tell John he never wanted to see him again, but he spat on John, calling him a queer.

By now John was very drunk and angry and I could see how upset Anthony was. Though I imagined he had heard this story before, the compassion Anthony felt for his lover showed in his face. He reached out to hold John's hand but John shook him off. The force of his emotions in recounting his traumatic experiences swept away our happy evening and left us depressed and uncomfortable.

There was a long silence. Anthony refilled our glasses and began talking about Paris, a city he loved, and of an affair he had had there with a young, long-haired French student. The boy was sweet and gentle, and from what he said Anthony had obviously been in love with him.

John interrupted, his bitterness and anger exploding: 'All big eyes and butter wouldn't melt in her mouth. I could see what was going on and I soon put an end to her. I wasn't having any bloody French bitch putting on airs around here!'

He stood unsteadily, glaring down at Anthony, his thick Northern Irish accent distorting his carefully acquired English vowels.

'Giving him ideas, she was, our little Miss French. Making him think he was a man. He tried to bugger me. *Look* at him. Trying it on with *me*. Can you imagine *him* doing *me?*' He stared at Anthony with undisguised hatred. 'Just look at him. I ask you.' He belched and looked sick. 'Oh Christ,' he muttered and lurched out to the bathroom.

The three of us sat in miserable silence. There was nothing we could say.

Anthony rose. 'I'm going to bed,' he said. 'I'll see you in the morning before you leave.' His face was white and strained, but he managed a lopsided smile. 'Sleep well. I know I will.'

It had been an awful day. John's outburst, so unexpected and strident, had shocked us to the core. As we undressed for bed I said something stupid. I realise the alcohol muddled my thinking, but I was upset and felt I should do something to comfort or help Anthony.

'What can I do?' I asked Eric.

'Why do you think you can do anything?'

'I don't know, I feel so helpless,' I replied. 'He's so unhappy and he looks so defenceless. Do you think I should offer to go to bed with him? Would that help, do you think?'

Oh Lord! I knew as soon as the words left my mouth that I couldn't have said anything worse.

Eric turned towards me, shouting: 'Is that all you think about? Sex? You know you're sex mad.'

We went to bed in silence and I lay for hours unable to sleep, thinking of Eric and myself and the two unhappy men at the other end of the flat.

Back at the villa Eric submerged himself in his sculpture. Almost a decade had passed since he had been so involved in his own work. After producing a number of heads, he attempted several groups from his *Lottatori* series but abandoned these as the scale was too small. So he continued with the heads and I posed for days on end as he worked on details such as eyes, nostrils and ears.

Each summer in August, Anticoli would become overcrowded as Roman families left the stuffy heat of the city for the cooler air of the mountains. Eric and I loathed this time of year: teenagers roaring about in their parents' cars, *mangia-dischi* blaring away; all the local restaurants packed, no free tables at the bar; confusion and chaos everywhere as the villagers attempted to deal with and contain their ill-mannered and vulgar relations from town. So when the film director Stanley Kramer turned up with a scouting party and the intention of making a film in the village, *The Secret of Santa Vittoria*, Eric and I rented him San Filipo, though it was the novelist Robert Crichton who eventually stayed there.

I wanted to drive across Italy to the Adriatic, to find a quiet little place where we could try to rebuild our relationship away from everybody. I imagined a house on the edge of a wood by a large sandy beach where Eric and I could perhaps sort out what was right between us and build on it. Instead we went to Positano. Eric insisted. Although a beautiful place, we found it far more crowded than Anticoli could ever be.

Some years ago, when reading Eric's autobiography, I came across the following passage, his description of the Positano trip:

> Graham had for some time been sexually tired of me, and was constantly looking for change – even girls. And at the beginning of this holiday he told me frankly that it would be no holiday for him if he could not have his freedom in the matter. There was nothing I could do but agree, or else live the life of a person sick with jealousy, forever anxious, wondering where and with whom my partner might be and, worse still, knowing that even when Graham was with me he might really be wishing he was elsewhere. Naturally, I warned him that if he had his freedom then I should have mine. Moreover, as I was not happy about sharing my life with somebody intent on sharing theirs with as many takers as they could find, if I were to meet somebody I particularly liked I would cultivate their company. To condense what could be turned into a novel, Graham had his fling, and I turned for solace to a handsome young oriental called Edgar.

I was so angry when I read this that I threw the book at my kitchen wall. I still don't know whether it was sheer hypocrisy or an attempt to ease his conscience that produced this warped view of events. Maybe Eric was just totally and completely unaware of the reality. I can look at it now and smile, but the shock on my initial reading was profound.

Earlier in the year a very good-looking German had turned up at San Filipo and stayed for a few days. He and Eric had met years before while

Eric was walking up the Rhine on his way to Italy for the first time, and they had kept in touch. The German's stay acted as a catalyst for me. Ignoring Eric's protests, I told him I was going to rent a studio in Anticoli, although I had no idea what kind of work I would be doing in it. I also said that I would have affairs on the side if I felt like it, and damn the consequences. If Eric could do it, so could I.

The matter didn't end there. We took it to Positano with us. It was a summer of sun, sea, wine, food, drugs, naked young bodies and sex. We arrived at the vast Edwardian flat we had rented overlooking the beach and almost as soon as the porters had departed we met two Swedish boys whom we shared. We spent several days with them on a small rocky beach, a couple of miles from Positano. The crystal clear sea, wine and grilled fish, the smell of Bain de Soleil and sweat filled these glorious days.

Then Eric met Edgar and a group of other Filipinos who fluttered into our life like a cluster of brightly coloured butterflies and changed it forever. At first we were both intrigued by these beautiful young people in their sarongs, who were unlike anyone we had met before. One night at our regular haunt, the Quicksilver Club (nicknamed the Black Banana in honour of the manager), Eric took off with Edgar and the next morning informed me he was in love. The rest of the holiday was a farce, both of us shouting abuse at each other when we weren't off with different boys. Eric might have been in love with Edgar, but he also slept around.

One day towards the end of our stay Eric disappeared, leaving a note for me: 'Gone to London with Edgar. See you in Anticoli on my return.'

An autumn of sordid quarrelling followed. I couldn't match Eric's motto that 'What's sauce for the goose *isn't* sauce for the gander', or the more wounding 'You were born in the gutter and grew up to prove it', but I did my best as we hammered each other with words.

In despair and frustration I went to London for Christmas and stayed with my old friends Rita and Barry, leaving Eric to celebrate with Edgar in San Filipo. There was more quarrelling when I got back. Eric had decided he wanted to live with Edgar and wanted me to leave, just like that. Pack a couple of suitcases and say goodbye, thanks for the ride. Eric had withdrawn all the money from our joint account and opened a new one for himself, so even if I wanted to leave I couldn't. I was thirty-one years old and penniless. We spent the next few months in an endless round of futile arguing as I tried to get some money out of Eric.

I renewed my friendship with an Englishwoman named Peggy and went to stay with her and her family in their large, ancient apartment near Piazza di Spagna. While I was there the battle between Eric and myself, conducted only by telephone, developed into all-out war. Peggy's husband Hugo tried to mediate but gave up, totally frustrated by Eric's obdurate refusal to part with any money. I wasn't asking for much – just enough to find a place to stay and start my own life.

One morning in the shower I decided I had had enough. Naked and wet, I marched into Peggy's living-room and phoned Eric. 'Listen, you miserly fat bastard' – we had long before descended into name-calling – 'if you don't give me some money, I'm going to Interpol to tell them everything in return for immunity.' I slammed the phone down.

Eric probably held a conference with Edgar, for by the time he called back I was dry and eating breakfast. Total capitulation, of a sort. Yes, he agreed, I should have some money; that was only fair. So we set up a meeting with our lawyers in Parioli. There I signed an agreement not to trouble him and to stay away from San Filipo, and in return Eric would pay me, when he could afford it, between three and four thousand pounds: a meagre sum which worked out at about two hundred pounds for every year of our life together. 'It would have been cheaper to employ a maid,' was one of Eric's oft-repeated statements. Not cheaper, but perhaps less fraught.

Part 2

Freedom

I WALKED DOWN THROUGH PARIOLI AND THE BORGHESE Gardens, thinking, 'I'm free! Oh lord, I'm free at last!' The signing of that rather humiliating document, and my acceptance of the pathetically small amount of money to be dished out grudgingly by Eric whenever he felt like it, finalised our relationship. Set down in black and white, mean-spirited as it was, it meant the struggle had ended and I could begin living my own life.

With Charles, an American friend from New York, and Pietro, a sixteen-year-old Italian I had met while staying at Peggy's, I rented an apartment in Trastevere off Piazza Gioacchino Belli. Large and roomy, it was part of a complex of buildings constructed haphazardly on top of each other over the centuries; after we'd painted the walls white and polished the tiled floor, it was light and airy. I had a six-foot-square mattress and base made which easily accommodated Pietro, his twin brother and me.

I tried hustling on the Spanish Steps. I didn't need the money, but with my new-found liberty I wanted new experiences and a taste of pleasures forbidden in my relationship with Eric. I thought, in my naïveté, that it would be exciting, even glamorous. It wasn't. Perhaps the johns I chose – I could afford to say no – were ordinary with ordinary tastes. The thrill of being selected and paid was soon deadened by the perfunctory sex. I couldn't believe that men would pay for such quick, passionless couplings, but they seemed happy enough with it. The thrill of picking someone up and paying them was sufficient; the sex was only a by-product. After several sessions in grubby hotel rooms and the front seats of cars, I gave up. It wasn't exciting and it certainly wasn't glamorous. There was no passion. These men didn't want any human contact; they needed an object to fulfil a fantasy, and that was all.

One afternoon I struck up a conversation with an elegant and swarthy man who was interested in the volume of de Sade I had bought only minutes before. Finishing the ice-cream I was eating, I went with him to a nearby bar and over coffee he invited me back to his apartment. He told

201

me he was a sadist and I, having no true idea of what that really meant, was intrigued and excited. I think, too, that I entered this encounter weighed down by a bag of collected guilt about my childhood abuse, about my relationship with Eric and anything else I could pull in to make me feel less. In a fuzzy way I probably thought I deserved this.

What I hadn't bargained for was the high – not a sexual one, but a sensual, mental high. Suspended by my wrists, then by my ankles, bitten, beaten and whipped, gagged when my cries and screams grew too loud, this wasn't a beginner's session. I emerged scathed but empowered.

Pietro threw a fit that night when he came to join me in the bath and saw the fine assortment of welts and bruises that covered me both back and front, from my shoulders to my knees. He asked me not to do it again, but I did. I was hooked.

With a very well-paid three-day-a-week stint translating bad Italian into reasonable English, and with the first instalment of Eric's hand-out, I was affluent and life was good. Pietro and I had a very open relationship and we shared a succession of young Italians. He was sixteen, half my age, and some of the boys he brought back for the night were even younger than he was.

It was around this time that Hugo, Peggy's husband, came to see me with a problem. Some months before, they had left Rome for Athens along with their two children and Tonya, their Polish au pair, who was also Peggy's best friend. Now, it seemed, Tonya's visa had expired and Peggy was going crazy at the thought of losing her. The only way of resolving the problem, Hugo suggested on his arrival back in Rome, would be for me to marry Tonya. Then she could obtain an English passport.

After much persuasion, I accepted. At least it would mean a three-week holiday in Athens, all expenses paid. He also asked, when all the details had been arranged, if I would take a small parcel with me. I could carry it as hand luggage, no big deal. Naturally, I said yes.

I left Rome two days after Hugo. Before he left he gave me the parcel. I wondered, as I took it, why he couldn't have taken it to Athens himself, but I didn't really dwell on the matter; it wasn't large or heavy and was no trouble to carry.

On my arrival in Athens I discovered Hugo had booked me into a squalid, dark and smelly downtown hotel. I decided to sleep there for one night only and then move to another hotel, the Carolina, which had been recommended by a friend in Rome.

After dinner I went for a stroll. Athens is not an attractive city, and feeling tired and a little dispirited, I soon retraced my steps to the hotel. As I stopped to light a cigarette, a loud *thump* noise deafened me and I was blown off my feet and hurled against a wall. I didn't fall down but I was badly shaken. So this was what Hugo had meant when he mentioned the 'bit of trouble' that was going on in Greece – random bombings, no less. As police cars screeched in, I retired early.

The following day I settled into the Carolina. My room had a balcony and a view of the Acropolis; it was sheer heaven to stand sipping ouzo on the balcony at night, gazing at its floodlit beauty.

Climbing the hill to the Acropolis the next day, I met a young soldier. Neither of us spoke the other's language, but after an amount of kissing and groping in the bushes I took him back to the Carolina. Not much taller than me, he had a country boy's face, round and open, with dark blue eyes and muddy blond curly hair. Naked, he was glorious: a white muscular body, his hands, forearms and face were darkly tanned; a true ephebus with high pecs, narrow waist and formidable legs. We spent several happy hours together that afternoon and the following one.

Hugo stopped by the hotel to take me to my engagement party in a villa somewhere in the hills to the south of the city. On the way there he confessed that he hadn't been completely honest with me when he'd spoken to me in Rome. It seems I was to marry Tonya not for Peggy's sake but for Hugo's. He was in love with the au pair, and Peggy had run off with the children and a German boatbuilder.

He suggested that I needn't go through with the wedding if I now had reservations but, for the sake of our friendship (his and mine – which up till then had hardly existed) and for the sake of Tonya's freedom, he hoped I would. I reluctantly agreed, and we drove on to the party where I purposely got very drunk. Then Hugo flew back to Rome.

That second afternoon with my soldier was delicious and exhausting – and my last bit of fun in Athens. A friend of Hugo – in fact the woman to whom the parcel I'd been carrying was addressed – turned up at the hotel and collected me, suggesting it would be so much easier if I moved in with her and her family. Flora was the daughter of a Scottish lord. She had married a Greek businessman and had three sons. She swore like a trooper, and so did her three boys, with the result that they were barred from every American and English school in Athens – in fact, any school where English was understood.

I had met Tonya before, when I was staying at Peggy's house in Rome. Now, we made friends with the English consul, and Tonya and I had to pretend we were in love, particularly as her time was running out. Our act was perfection itself. Thrilled to be helping such young and attractive lovers, the consul arranged everything for us – appointments at the Polish Embassy, the Catholic Church (Tonya was a Catholic) and, since the English churches would have nothing to do with us, the American Episcopalian Church, as I was Church of England. Because we didn't share the same religion, it seemed we had to have two marriages. Tonya kept crying and shaking with nerves. Brandy and tranquillisers helped to keep her going.

Once I'd settled into Flora's apartment, I handed her the parcel. Unwrapping it she exploded: 'Hugo's a fucking sneaky bastard giving you this! Why couldn't he have brought it himself?'

'Yes,' I said, 'I thought the same.'

'You realise that if the customs or police had found you with this they'd have imprisoned you? You'd have fucking disappeared.'

It seemed that I had been carting around a desk copier, an early Xerox machine, and to be found with one in these revolutionary times was almost, if not quite, a capital offence. The bit of trouble – understated in such a beautifully English way by Hugo – was a full-blown battle between the army and the rest of Greece.

'This evening I'll take you to the end of our street and you can hear what happens when they get you,' Flora said to me. She took me to a notorious prison and interrogation centre. I heard faint cries and screams that were repeated again and again. We drove away in silence.

One of Flora's friends, a Greek woman whom I had met over dinner with her husband several nights before, took the copier. She was having an affair with a Greek executive of an American oil company. They were both in the underground resistance. I was left with them one afternoon to keep guard in case her husband returned, while in a bedroom at the far end of her apartment she and her lover printed out revolutionary pamphlets.

And her husband did return. A tall, fat man, he handed me a drink and came and sat beside me. 'Whatever you do, keep him occupied,' the woman had warned me. 'He mustn't find out what we're doing.'

Her husband, taking it for granted that because I was queer I'd drop my pants for any man, started in on me. Finding him singularly unattractive in every way, I wouldn't, under different circumstances, have complied, but I had to keep him busy. Lying on my back on his bed, my legs in the air as he pounded and puffed away, I saw his wife peep around the door. She winked and gave me the thumbs-up before disappearing again. Bloody hell.

When he came he rolled off me and lit a cigarette for himself. I wasn't offered one. He also made it clear that while he lay back and got a second wind I was expected to suck him back to erection. Double bloody hell! But he had to be kept occupied. The second time took longer, but it was easier than the first go when he hadn't used any lubrication.

Lying back, lighting himself another cigarette, he ordered me to get him a drink. I got dressed and poured a drink for us both and was taking it back to him when his wife came in through the front door, dressed as though she'd been out, and carrying several packages.

'He's in there,' I gestured to the bedroom.

'Darling, thank you. He's awful, isn't he? Was it ghastly?' she asked me.

'Yes, it bloody well was.'

'Well, darling, I have to live with it.' She gave me a hug and kissed me. 'Darling, you're a hero.'

Big deal, I thought. My bum was very sore. I hadn't intended to do this much for the revolution.

The wedding day arrived. 'Are you going to celebrate your nuptials tonight?' Flora asked, not swearing for once.

'Well, of course. After all I've been through it's the least I could expect,' I replied, half joking. I hadn't given much thought to it.

'I see,' said Flora rather grimly and disappeared.

Tonya looked lovely in a little headband decorated with ivory rosebuds, a short white veil, a creamy white silk knee-length crêpe dress and a small bouquet of roses the same colour as those on her head.

We set off for the Catholic cathedral but not before we'd knocked back several stiffeners and I had passed the tranquillisers round.

The cathedral, empty except for a few old women in black, gave each sound we made a sepulchral echo. On a large red velvet-covered dais in front of the main altar were two spindly gilt chairs. On these we sat, Tonya and I, while the priest performed the ceremony in Greek, translated by a young American novice. Eventually I produced the rings as the American asked, 'Do you, Tonya Padrewski, take Graham Smith to be your lawful wedded wife?'

Pretty high on alcohol and pills, Flora let out a raucous peal of laughter. Like a starting pistol, it was the signal for the rest of the ceremony. Much as Tonya and I tried, we could not help but join in. The older priest, realising something had led the service radically astray, attempted with little success to bring back some degree of gravity to the proceedings, but he was outnumbered. The American tried to intervene, to explain what had happened, but the old man wouldn't be interrupted, and finally the young novice, his shoulders shaking with irrepressible giggles, joined in with us.

One down, one to go. There are a few really steep hills in Athens and the American Presbyterian church is situated on one of them. The car I was in decided, shortly after leaving the cathedral, that it felt left out of the adventures of the day and needed to be included, so it broke down. Flora, swearing mightily, refused to leave the driving seat. As she steered, Tonya and I pushed. It was hot and we were late. After about twenty minutes of false starts during which the car would leap forward with short, spiteful jumps, emitting clouds of greasy exhaust in our faces, it finally came to a complete halt.

'Flora, have you got the bloody brake on?' I shouted.

'Course I bloody haven't!' she screamed back at me.

'Well, it won't budge.'

'Look out, then. I'm putting it into reverse.' And with that the vehicle started cruising backwards downhill for about twenty yards. Then it stopped. More pushing.

It was a glorious autumn day – and would have been enjoyable if we hadn't been pushing a neurotic car up a hill. Machines are, I believe, quite capable of considerable malice, and this vehicle seemed to be enjoying itself.

Soon after we had recovered the ground lost when Flora reversed, the engine started and the car began running smoothly, shooting ahead. Tonya and I sped towards it and got in. No sooner had we sat down than the engine cut out.

I got out, walked into a bar and ordered myself a couple of brandies. The two women joined me. We were onto our third or fourth, supplemented by very sweet thick coffee as an antidote, we said, to the tranquillisers, when we heard the car engine.

'Oh, shit!' cried Flora, 'I've left the bloody thing on.'

We raced out to the car which was beginning a slow backwards descent of the hill, and climbed in. From then on it was plain sailing to the church.

The American priest, irritated by our lateness and shocked by our giggling, shouted at us when we couldn't sing a hymn with him. We just couldn't. The two weeks of visiting officials of both church and state; the playing of a distraught lover; the acres of forms to fill in; and the chaos of Flora's small apartment, filled with her, her husband, their three boys, Tonya, myself and the German boatbuilder, Hugo's and Peggy's two kids who had returned from somewhere after Peggy had fled again, had all taken its toll. With the alcohol and the pills, I was feeling high and carefree. It was my wedding and I would giggle if I wanted to.

Another party in the hills had been planned so I went back to Flora's to change out of my formal wedding suit. I lost track of the time, I think, because when I was finally ready, everyone seemed to have disappeared. I felt I had been rather taken advantage of, conned into coming out here to marry Hugo's paramour, asked to carry a parcel that could have landed me in prison or worse, pulled out of my hotel to live in an overcrowded madhouse and now, after having served Hugo's purpose, discarded.

I sat on the edge of Flora's bed with a bottle of Greek brandy. I felt exhausted and was slowly coming down from the day's high. I picked up the discarded veil and head-dress as I drank and balanced it, lopsided, on my head. Fortified somewhat by the brandy, I picked up a tray of make-up from the floor and, with a rather shaky hand, drew on my face a caricature of a blushing bride – or was it a groom? When I finished, it was definitely a bride with thick black eyebrows, red lipsticked cheeks and vast Bette Davis lips outlined in black. Looking at the ridiculous painted gargoyle staring at me from the wardrobe mirror I felt blissful and truly laid-back. Life was good. Come on, I told myself, you agreed to everything that had happened, even the unwanted sex; just relax.

As I was sliding off the bed to find a more comfortable position on the carpet, Flora burst in. 'Where the bloody hell have you been?' she demanded. 'I was nearly there when I realised you weren't in any of the cars. And I had to drive all the fucking way back here. Come on! We're late!'

I don't remember much about the rest of the day. I know we returned to find Hugo, with a small suitcase, pacing up and down outside. Flora, the bitch, had phoned him in Rome to tell him that I was going to claim my bride, and he had immediately flown out to forestall any possible lechery on my part.

Flora's maid had decorated the guest room with garlands of flowers and covered the nuptial bed with rose petals. But not for me. I was given a couple of blankets and the trampoline in the kids' playroom. By then, quite numb, it was all I needed.

Early next morning, my head throbbing with the giant of all hangovers, I was awakened by the three boys. The eldest, about twelve, came straight to the point, swearing like his mother.

'What the fuck are you doing in here?' he demanded.

'Trying to sleep,' I replied grumpily.

'There's a bloody man in Tonya's bed,' he continued.

'Yes, I know.'

'Why the hell aren't you there?'

'Because I'm not.'

'Didn't you marry her yesterday?'

'Yes.'

'Well, I'm bloody well going to tell my mother.' And, marshalling his two younger siblings, he stalked out.

Life back in Rome went on quite happily until Pietro was told to go and work with his father in Germany. My translating job had collapsed and I was starting to think that perhaps I didn't have a future in Italy. So I returned to London and dumped myself on Barry and Rita in Great Percy Street. Barry had just won an award for one of his books, and no sooner had I arrived in England than I was heading back to Italy as a tour guide and interpreter. The six of us – Barry, Rita and their three girls, Celia, Becky and Jessie and I – had a glorious Christmas in Rome and then went down to Positano for a magical New Year.

Barry and Rita rented a flat halfway down the zigzag road, a lovely old place with a small garden overlooking the sea and a large lemon tree laden with fruit growing on it. The kitchen was built under the road and when it rained Rita and I cooked with plastic sheeting covering us.

The village exploded with light and noise on New Year's Eve. Every building had its own display, but the municipal one on the beach towered over them all. Shattering noise and light.

Returning again to London, I realised I had to do something, but I felt lost and scared. I had allowed Eric to rule my life from when I was sixteen. Now I was a thirty-three-year-old man with no idea of what to do or where to go. So for a time I partied rather than sitting around worrying.

One party I went to was in a dilapidated eighteenth-century building in Drury Lane, behind which was Louis Meier's Tudor warehouse. Lindsay Kemp, the great mime, lay on a bench and was held down while his boyfriend poured hot hydrogen peroxide in his ear to cure, so he said, Lindsay's earache. In the front room, to the enthusiastic cheers and whistles of the rest of the party, David Bowie mimed an exquisitely brilliant and obscene strip. Its comic vulgarity was a direct link from the Attic miming of the classical world, through *commedia dell'arte*, pantomime and music hall to this slim blond young man who, with delicious lewdness, caricatured the art of the burlesque.

I had dinner with Anthony one night. We had chatted several times on the phone and one evening he invited me to eat with him, just cold meat, pickles, cheese and biscuits – a simple meal. He talked about Eric and Edgar. ('The boy carries a handbag with him everywhere,' he told me.) I gathered Edgar wasn't one of Anthony's favourite people. We were relaxing in the kitchen with a superb bottle of wine, when John Gaskin came in. He had been drinking. Rather unsteadily, he began boasting of his affair with a current passion, Peter, a gigolo, going into detailed descriptions of their sexual exploits. He turned on Anthony, sneering and belittling him, a repetition of the night with Eric several years ago. It became too embarrassing and I left before it got completely out of hand. Anthony apologised as he saw me out. Poor man.

In those days I frequented the Speak Easy, a basement club behind Oxford Circus. One afternoon, distraught that I had nothing to wear, I took an old cream silk shirt and carefully painted it with zebra stripes in black and dark brown, on the front, back and sleeves. Wearing it and a pair of very tight silk trousers and white shoes, I sallied forth that evening. It was quite late and I was bopping around when a guy came up and asked me where I had bought my shirt. It had caused quite a lot of very favourable comment.

'Oh, I painted it myself,' I replied.

Pause while we gyrated.

'Do you want to sell it?' he asked.

'Not particularly.'

'I'll give you fifty quid.'

A longer pause. I was in shock. Fifty pounds was a lot of money for a shirt in the early 1970s.

'Okay then,' I managed eventually.

I took off my shirt and he gave me the money. Then he put on my shirt, tied his own around his waist and bounced away across the dance floor.

I saw Anthony Blunt for the last time. I was having a brief affair with a woman who wanted me to go and stay with her in her house in Switzerland. One of her relatives had died and left her some very fine old furniture and some paintings, the most interesting of which was supposedly a Poussin. I thought it might be a Spanish School copy and offered to show a photograph of it to Anthony for her – he was, after all, the foremost expert on Poussin.

We met in his office. The picture, he thought, was possibly by Ribera in the style of Poussin. He asked if he could keep the photograph for the Courtauld files before inviting me upstairs for a drink. He told me I looked 'very flowery'. I suppose I did, in handmade tweed bell-bottoms, courtesy of Rita, an ankle-length granny coat and a big felt hat from Scotts in Bond Street. My hair was down past my shoulder-blades. I was celebrating my freedom, making up for times lost in a truly happy manner.

He asked how I was, how I found life after so long with Eric. I told him I felt free, totally free. He was quiet for some moments. 'In what way?' he asked eventually.

'Oh, free to do and think and be what I want for the first time,' I replied. I was heady with liberation.

His smile made me feel like a small child in front of a parent. 'Freedom is a luxury,' he said. 'Do you think it really exists? I have never felt free, exactly free. Do you truly think you are?'

Of course I wasn't, but I answered, 'Yes!'

He asked me if I had a lover – that is, someone for more than just one night.

'A couple,' I told him. 'One is a draughtsman who was an amateur footballer, and the other is young, rather confused skinhead I am reclaiming from the neo-Nazi party. He is really very sweet, and has had no positive influence in his life at all.' I think Anthony was a bit shocked that I would have anything to do with a 'fascist'. I also told him about the woman: 'I'm having a shot at bisexuality.'

He was really surprised, so I told him about Ruby Miller's advice. Ruby, a dear friend in her eighties, had visited Eric and me several times in Italy. Having dinner with her after the break-up, she told me, 'What you need, my dear, are a couple of months of one-night stands. That's what I did when I left my husband.' This, from an eighty-year-old woman, was advice to be treasured.

'One-night stands, Anthony, I'm playing the field. I've been in love and I don't need it anymore,' I said. Such arrogance and folly.

I asked after John Gaskin, but I can't remember his reply. I think he changed the subject. 'Do you miss Eric?' he asked.

'Not at the moment. Life is just too full.'

He asked what I was doing. I told him I was painting people's walls. In a house near Cheyne Walk, for example, I had painted a dining-room in ultramarine blue, glowing with cascades of pure cadmium yellow and red stripes. In another house, I'd painted huge art deco black, grey, brown and white phallic flowers.

He asked if I was dealing in or restoring Old Masters and if I had reconsidered art history as a profession.

'No,' I answered. 'I've left all that behind.'

We were both formal and a little awkward. For some reason, on this occasion, Eric loomed between us. (I had thought – I don't know why – that Eric and I might one day get back together. But at least at heart I realised that would never happen. And truly, although I still cared about him, I didn't want it to happen.) I asked Anthony how he was himself, how was life? The right side of his upper lip lifted, as it always did when he was annoyed or upset. Then he smiled, got up and walked over to the window. He turned to me. 'Lonely,' he said. 'I feel lonely. It doesn't seem enough.' I wasn't sure what he meant, but didn't ask.

He seemed very tired and frail. He was expecting a visit from a retired policeman, whom he paid for sex.

I refused the offer of another sherry. He accompanied me to the lift and asked me to keep in touch. I didn't. There were too many associations with Eric, and besides, my life had taken to the streets, away from the hallowed halls of Art. Old Master Art. I did write twice, to the Portman Square address, after the disgraceful Thatcher betrayal. Whether he received the letters or not, I don't know. They weren't answered.

One night, dining with a friend in a trendy restaurant off the King's Road, a very attractive red-haired woman, accompanied by a rather sweet ex-public schoolboy, sat down at the table next to ours. As the tables were close together we soon struck up a conversation with them. The woman turned out to be Christine Keeler. Quietly spoken, with a wry sense of humour, she appeared almost faded. Perhaps faded is not quite the right word – shellshocked might be a better description. Her beauty was still there but was screened, as though she was waiting, like an abused child, for something bad to happen.

The four of us wanted to go on for a drink somewhere, but couldn't agree on a bar that we all liked. Eventually I suggested one of my favourites, a drag pub just south of the river called the Vauxhall Tavern. I'd spent many happy evenings there and had had two brief affairs with a couple of the artistes. On one of my first visits I had picked up what I thought was a young blonde girl (I was experimenting, really, going through my bisexual period with steely determination), who turned out to be a black-haired man. The other affair was with a drag queen whom I knew was a man, but I was intrigued nevertheless by his humour and his charm. Months later I was in turn picked up by an Afro-Caribbean transvestite and his girlfriend. Sex with a well-endowed man in full drag including wig, make-up, underwear, stockings and high-heeled shoes was, I found, strangely exciting. For five days I was in masochist heaven: tied up, diapered, fed from a bottle like a baby, beaten and covered from head to toe in rubber, a further excursion and exploration into the world of S&M. All in all, I found the Vauxhall a great pick-up pub, rarely leaving on my own.

Christine and I and the others had a pleasant hour standing at the back of the bar, talking to each other rather than watching the show. A small, ugly man – a dwarf, really – kept pestering me. He had declared his passion for me weeks earlier and wouldn't take no for an answer. Intruding on our conversation, he insisted on buying several rounds for us. His irritating presence soon made us leave, however, and we decided to go on some-where else.

Once outside, I was shocked to find I was foaming at the mouth. I couldn't stem the flow. I wasn't vomiting – it was just pure froth. I got out of the car and lay down, fairly sober – certainly not drunk – but suddenly quite numb and unable to move. The stuff was still flowing. Christine, very solicitous, knelt on the road beside me, holding my hand. Had that awful man in the pub put something in my drink, she wondered. It was a possibility. Nothing else seemed to account for it, as I was totally conscious and able to see, hear and speak clearly.

'I have to go,' she said. 'I'm sorry, but I can't be caught by the police, not again. If it is drugs, I'd never hear the end of it. They'd never leave me alone. You'll be all right. I'm calling an ambulance.' She kissed the top of my head and left.

I spent the night in a hospital corridor on a gurney. My friend came with me and then left. Early next morning I found I could move again and practised walking slowly up and down before I discharged myself. I didn't return to the hospital to find out the results of the analysis of my foam and urine, and never again did I accept free drinks from the little man in the Vauxhall.

My favourite club, the Catacomb, was in a side street near Victoria Station. With its arched brick cellars way below street level, it was everything a queer club should be. It even boasted a restaurant which served reasonable food and cheap wine. I always took a change of clothing with me, as three or four hours of dancing and sex in its hot, damp darkness left me soaked to the skin. Orgies were known to develop in the furthest corners. No age-limit was set and the dancers were hot, wild and horny.

I even took a woman down there with me one night. I was bored with the clubs she went to, such as Annabel's, so I suggested the Catacomb. We had a glorious evening, eating upstairs first of all and then descending to the depths. She sat at the bar, the centre of an adoring crowd who at first thought she must be a drag queen or a transsexual, but then realised she was a real woman, a 'lady' in fact, probably the first one ever to visit.

Through a couple of friends in Chelsea, I met another beautiful red-haired woman, Jeri Scott. She was absolutely gorgeous – small and slim with a little fox face. Over a period of time, hanging out with her in her deco stall in one of the King's Road antique markets and at our local wine bar near Onslow Gardens, we became buddies.

It was at one of her parties, organised in honour of Hugo and Tonya who were staying in London over Christmas, that I met John Taylor, Australian John. We became lovers soon after. A kind man, for some time he literally took care of me. I was totally lost; there appeared to be nothing I could do. I seemed to have no real skills whatsoever, and even if I had discovered some talent, I would have had no idea how to market it. John also had a stall off the King's Road, and he allowed me a pause, a respite, while I gathered what wits I possessed and thought about my future.

It was because of John Taylor that I seriously began hand-painting shirts. When I'd sold my zebra shirt at the Speak Easy, it didn't occur to me that this was a way I could make a living. When my brother Peter asked me what I intended to do, and I replied, off the top of my head, that I was going to get a studio in central London and design fabrics, I was obviously in a state of internal panic. Being the wonderful friend he is, Peter said simply, 'Well, when you need some money to get set up, just ask. It's there for you; just let me know, any time.'

Through John Taylor I met Jimmy Gardiner, who worked for Catherine Buckley, and it was through her boutique that I sold my first shirts and dresses made from my hand-painted fabrics. A few were quite good; many were awful.

I used Clarice Cliff, the wonderfully eccentric English potter, and art deco in general (which John Taylor was selling) as a basis for many of my designs. But my idol, Fortuny, was paramount. I never achieved anything comparable with his marvellous clothes but I tried and, in trying, had a great time and made some money.

From Catherine Buckley I rented a ground-floor studio in Ganton Street, just steps away from Carnaby Street. Close to Liberty's and Jaeger's, it was ideal for many reasons, not the least of which was the steady stream of Scandinavian boys who found me, my studio and the huge carpeted and mirrored cellar below irresistible.

I painted huge parrots and birds of paradise on leather, and some fabric for Bill Gibb; I designed art deco fabrics for Biba and bouquets of flowers for Jean Muir. I was written up in several newspapers, and even made it into the Sunday colour supplements.

Then one evening Eric turned up. He'd call me every time he visited London and we'd have dinner. These evenings were never easy. Eric often suggested we have sex, but I always turned him down very quickly. Still hurt by the break-up, I couldn't relax in his company. This particular evening he suggested meeting me at my studio. He'd heard about my new career from Barry and Rita in whose flat he usually stayed on these visits. I met him outside, having locked the door first. 'I'm not letting you in, Eric,' I told him. 'I know you'll say something awful and I don't want to hear it. Let's just have a drink next door.'

Over our drinks he asked what I was doing. I was probably over-enthusiastic as I told him, as I was truly enjoying myself. Waiting outside the pub for the taxi that was taking us on to dinner, he turned to me. I shall never forget his words. 'You need to find someone rich like you found me,' he said. 'You've never been good at anything and you never will be. This won't last, nothing you do will ever last. Take it from me. I know you.'

The evening went downhill from there. We almost had a fight in the restaurant. First Eric assured me that he knew Janet and I were having an affair in Rome. How else could we both have caught hepatitis? So this had been the cause of the candelabra fight and his terrible moods. He wouldn't listen to any reasonable explanation. He went on to tell me that he knew when Edgar was unfaithful, as he called it. With a self-satisfied grin, he said he didn't mind because he was so happy. I picked up the wine bottle and swung it above my head to hit him, the wine running down my arm. Just then a waiter stepped up behind me, smoothly taking the bottle from my hand and presenting us with the bill.

Alone at home that night I broke down totally. Years of anger, frustration, hope and love combined in a flood of painful tears. Early the next morning I called Eric and told him it would be best if we never saw each other again. It was over at last. I didn't wait for his reply but hung up as soon as I had finished speaking.

Things seemed to break down from there. I couldn't work for a week or so; John Taylor left for Australia; Catherine wanted me to produce designs for clothes I thought quite hideous. I gave up fabric painting, gave up the studio, and went into a kind of tailspin. Obviously, Eric was right, for the whole business went to pot. I let it go.

Marie Gray often dropped in at the studio and we'd go out for tea or dinner together. She always wanted to buy something for her goddaughter, but the clothes I was painting weren't at all to the young woman's taste. On finding out what was happening, she immediately took me to task.

'Eric, my dear, is jealous of you, of your imagination and energy and your talent,' she said. 'If you're going to let that stop you, you're a lesser man than I thought you were.'

She was pretty tough and her strength was exactly what I needed. She offered no sympathy, just told me to go out and get on with it. This was advice I couldn't help but follow. I found myself an agent, a dear woman named Brigitte, and began designing fabrics. And, as it does when we take control, life once again changed completely for me.

John Kenneth Elliker

BEING A HEALTHY, UNATTACHED MAN I CONTINUED MY tomcatting around town, dropping in to pubs, clubs, bars and baths. I wandered as I did when a child, not with any definite intention of scoring (although I often did), but developing and expanding this early habit mostly by listening and watching. I would take a train or bus out of London, not quite as far as the suburbs, which didn't interest me, but well out of the city, as far out as Richmond or Epping. I would then go from pub to pub until I found an interesting place where I'd install myself until closing time, and then go on to a club. Working more or less seven days a week, sometimes far into the night, I needed to get out and explore this new world in which I was discovering myself.

One night I was painting some art deco designs for wallpaper, after several days of frustrated effort, when the drawings suddenly came together. Feeling very pleased with myself, I celebrated in a nearby pub. After many pints, not feeling at all tired, I took a taxi to Putney to cruise the towpath. Even if I didn't meet anyone, I felt at least it was a pleasant night walk, which I had taken many times before, even going as far as Kew. Afterwards I could get an all-night bus back to bed.

The air was warm, very unusual for early March, and I hadn't walked far when I saw a slim young man, looking handsome and very proper in a jacket, shirt and tie, standing by the boat sheds. Proffering a cigarette, a good way to open a conversation, I asked if he lived nearby. He said yes. His voice and manner were rather belligerent and belied his neat appearance. Oh, I thought, a little piece of rough trade, that's nice, and we walked back to his place, introducing ourselves and shaking hands. He told me his name was John.

Just before we reached his flat he told me he had a boyfriend and I would have to leave before 5 a.m. I'd had my fill of this behind-the-back carry-on with Eric, and I nearly turned and went home; but it was late and I was horny. Well, I might have been horny, but I'd also had too much to drink and couldn't get an erection. My frustration turned to laughter and we slept happily in each other's arms. We both left just after five that morning. John worked on the Tube, and I wasn't allowed to sleep in. There was no boyfriend.

A day later he called me and we went out to dinner in a local curry house, Sam Rat's, then home to bed. This time everything functioned, and between sex and cigarettes we talked for hours. By morning I was in love. It was the last thing I wanted and the last thing I thought I needed. Thoroughly enjoying designing, I had just started having my own fabrics printed, a few of which were made into shirts by Michael Anderson, a friend and very fine tailor, and I was already selling them. The designs themselves were being snapped up in America. I was beginning to feel confident again; I didn't need any new emotional ties to get in my way (I was still involved with John Taylor) or to complicate my life, but that's what I got.

John brought out all my feelings of protectiveness. I just wanted to care for him, to shelter him. His tough, streetwise exterior was just a façade behind which hid a sweet and gentle nature. He was illegitimate, and his mother had left him literally on his grandmother's doorstep and disappeared. His grandmother died, dropped dead in front of him, when he was six and from then on he went from one abusive foster family to another.

At fourteen he was put in a remand home for stealing cigarettes. Constantly running away from the rape and bullying he endured in Borstal, he was eventually sent to prison where he remained until he was nineteen. In order to survive he had developed a 'fuck you, don't get in my way' attitude which never worked very well – he was too kindly, too compassionate, too gentle.

What can one write about domestic bliss, the day-to-day making love? We fought terribly at times, huge battles engulfed us, shook us and exhausted us. We both carried a great deal of baggage. Neither of us had dealt with our past traumas, neither of us even realised we could, that there were ways. I tried therapy with a psychologist recommended by a doctor at the Homoeopathic Hospital in London and enrolled at a house of transcendental meditation near Victoria Station, grasping at straws, feeling I was going crazy at times. Why were we fighting? What the fuck was wrong? John drank heavily in the evenings and alcohol didn't make him a happy drunk, like me.

But over it all, in spite of our fights, we were blissfully happy. If I had been swept away by Eric, I was completely lost at sea and drowned with John.

'You're so bloody lucky,' a friend remarked to me one night in The Bricklayer's, our favourite pub.

'Why?' I asked.

'Well, if I had someone, just once in my life, look at me with such love as John looks at you, I think I could die happy.'

And I took it for granted. I loved him, so naturally he loved me. I just took it for granted.

Zarach's gave me another show, Harrod's and Liberty's were selling my wallpaper and fabrics, and Harrod's also covered several armchairs and a large sofa, making up a display of everything I printed. I almost gave up trying to find a pattern-cutter/seamstress when a motherly woman turned up one day with samples of her work and together we turned out a series of shirts and kimonos, that, with help from another friend, we sold in Europe, America and Japan.

We socialised a lot, had people to dinner, made new friends and reconnected with old ones. Paul Cooper and Lily were now married with two children, Simon and Ben, and had settled in Putney, and John and I became honorary baby-sitters.

Before I met him, John had been a hermit, drinking by himself at home every night. Now he blossomed. He let his hair grow long and permed it into an afro which I hennaed for him. He wore jewellery, chains, rings and bracelets and chucked the shirts and ties in favour of a flower-power look.

We filled our home with the kind of furniture that my childhood friends thought odd: heavy solid pieces, beautifully made in fine wood, mainly nineteenth century, the exception being a Georgian mahogany dining-table – just polished slabs of wood, no ornamentation, but beautiful in its simplicity.

John began collecting blue-and-white china: an assortment of tureens, plates, bowls, several early Wedgewood and little coffee demi-tasses.

He remade the garden, formerly just a square of muddy unkempt grass, and it became a sheer joy. We even had a rockery, a huge mound, at the far end against a low brick wall, that covered a pile of debris. John planted it with white flags and peonies, carnations, mint, rosemary, wallflowers, daffodils, narcissus, crocus, and made steps up and over it so that on warm evenings we could sit on top of the wall surrounded by leafy gardens, smoking and drinking wine, the still air making us feel as if we were miles from London.

With a good tar spray an ancient Victoria plum tree blossomed and year after year produced pounds of fruit. I kicked the small Bramley (John said it had never bloomed), threatened it with an axe and it too began producing huge bulging apples. Victoria plums and Bramleys make the best fruit pies ever. Our strawberry patch, started with cuttings from Tiptree farms, grew larger and larger. Each year after a surfeit of strawberry jam and strawberry fool we opened it to the kids next door to plunder. We had vases and jam pots, too, filled with flowers during the spring and summer.

I introduced John to Marie. She took to him immediately, finding him, as I did, charming and gentle and funny. 'You must try to do something about John's accent, my dear. It doesn't help him socially,' she told me once.

'Oh, Marie, I don't want to change anything, I love him so much.'

'Well, my dear, just think about it. People are very snobbish, you know.'

There were no 'missing' treasures after our visits, which was a first. She even offered her retirement cottage to us for long weekends and holidays, which we readily accepted.

One Easter we visited Maldon and I took John on a tour. The place where Eric and I spent our first summer was stripped. All the beautiful willows, every bush, Beeleigh Oak (or elm) were gone, leaving nothing but smooth, cropped grass. The bath was still there and the pipe still producing the same cold, sweet, crystal water which we drank. The great iron railway bridge across the Blackwater had gone, as had the huge lily-filled pond that marked the Maldon end of the canal. Gone too were the eel traps. In fact, the whole area had been developed and improved quite nicely, a good tidy-up that had destroyed all vestiges of a romantic, burgeoning countryside. I felt no pang, no little tug, no sadness.

We had lunch at the Blue Bear, pottered around the little graveyard, but couldn't find George Washington's grandfather's tomb. We browsed the famous chained library and then walked down the hill towards Maldon's paddling pool. We stopped at the boatyard.

The Cuthbertsons' elegant craft was low in the water, unpainted, a derelict hulk gradually rotting and breaking up. John and I talked to a man who explained that Mrs Cuthbertson lived in a tiny cottage, one of a row opposite, and that she often sat at the window staring out at the boat. Her husband had been dead for many years. She refused to allow anyone to touch the boat, but sat in lonely vigil overseeing its decay. Perhaps when it finally broke up and sank she would take it as an omen and die too. The man told us she never answered the door and was rarely seen except at the window. It seemed pointless to attempt a visit, to intrude on her grief.

We went in search of someone to pierce our ears, and ended up in a tattoo parlour. Now that I was there, I thought I might as well have a tattoo and fulfil a long-held desire. Fascinated as a child by the big butterfly on the back of my dad's hand, I had wanted a tattoo for years. So, that day, I had a dragon tattooed around my left nipple. It didn't hurt yet neither was it pleasant. I sat and endured, imagining it as part of an S&M game, a prelude to the real stuff. At last I had fulfilled a childhood dream, one impossible to realise living with Eric. I had it placed on my chest so that I wouldn't be conscious of it all the time. In fact I eventually forgot it was there and found myself genuinely surprised when people commented on it.

When John and I started living together I told him I wanted an open relationship, one that was honest and free from deception, and included having sex with other people openly and happily. He agreed with me but seemed reluctant. I didn't understand his hesitation; it didn't appear to be due to any reservations about sexual sharing, but rather a fear hidden and unnamed that I put down to a natural and charming shyness on his part.

It was only after our first threesome, with an old boyfriend named Paul, that in tears he begged me not to hold it against him, not use the fact that he had enjoyed himself, had allowed another man to have sex with him, and at a later date to give this as an excuse to leave him. He was completely serious. He truly thought that this would happen, that somewhere I was keeping a list of what he imagined were faults on his part, an account that one day I would tally up to find him wanting. I knew that only time would heal this one. My protestations and affirmations and our love would act as a foundation but it would need years of careful building to repair and cover these scars, and I was not that careful. I did my best, but I was scarred myself, I had my own wounds to deal with. But I gave him my word, a solemn vow, that I would never leave him and I meant it.

After a hilarious weekend in Brighton with friends (stoned, jumping into the sea with all our clothes on, touring the pubs, being completely silly and completely happy), we were sitting opposite each other on the train back to London. It could have been the residual effects of the weekend or perhaps the lighting in the carriage, but looking at John's face (he had fallen asleep) I saw it transformed into the skeletal image of a death's head. There was no reason for me to conjure up such a vision or to place John at its centre – he had a sweet, smiling, lovable face, full of life and energy – but this spectre terrified me. All I wanted to do was to get up and run away and never come back. I was reasoning, rationalising to myself that John would be all right – hurt at first, but strong enough to recover from what would have been an abrupt and cruel departure – when the train pulled into a station.

This was my chance. I rose from my seat, looked at his sleeping figure, and my heart truly felt like that it was melting. I sat down next to him and hugged him, waking him up.

'What?' he said, rather grumpily, more than half asleep. Then, 'I'm all right.'

'Yes, darling,' I whispered, 'You're all right, you're my sweetheart.'

'Okay then, I'm asleep.'

I didn't leave. I had no intention of leaving. It was just a momentary and horrific image that caused a presentiment of death, a glimpse into the future, that had panicked me.

Life had severely traumatised John. He was obsessed with the possibility of me abandoning him, a fear which I don't think ever left him. After a year or so his 'Don't ever leave me, I couldn't bear it' refrain changed to 'What will you do when I leave you? You'll never manage on your own'. It celebrated his new-found strength and confidence, but was really just a stab at a bravado he never fully acquired. What John didn't realise was that I was filled with terror every time he mentioned leaving.

Many times, unable to deal with a spate of quarrels which frustrated me and stopped me working, I'd go and stay with friends in Brighton or the West Country. But after only a day or so, I would phone to inquire if he was okay, and couldn't he take a few days off work to come and join me? If this was manipulation, as I've been told it was, then it was unconscious. For the first time in my life, I felt lopsided, incomplete without John by my side. I had at last found my mate, my other half, and with him I felt whole.

'What would you do if I left you, Graham?'

My reply was always, 'Oh, I'll manage,' yet the thought of his leaving was too awful for me to deal with. It was something I refused to entertain.

John was also hung up on the male-female thing. He felt I had to be 'butch' as he was naturally 'femme', that I should always be 'active' and him 'passive' – the pathetic 'who's Maude and who's Claude?' thing. Not that he was camp. In fact, many people thought at first that he was my bit of rough trade. It took some time to ease him out and away from this stereotypical image and to build up his own masculinity. This is difficult enough for a heterosexual man, who learns from an early age not to cry, rarely to communicate except in anger, and above all not to be vulnerable. It's seemingly impossible (but thank goodness can be done) for a homosexual, who has to contend with being called sissy or pansy from an early age, and society's idea of what a faggot, a queer, must be. This almost overwhelmed John. His solitary night-time drinking, broken by occasional forays on the towpath where he was often arrested (he picked up the same plainclothes policeman three times) forced him to be outwardly butch, tough and aggressive, while the real John, sweet and gentle, grew more and more desperate and without hope.

But now, no longer treated like a domestic or hired help, told to stay in the bedroom when guests arrived, used like an inflatable doll with openings at the top and bottom – the way most of his previous affairs had treated him – he discovered he had a voice that people wanted to hear and a personality which won him friends. It was a total and complete joy to see him grow.

At a gallery opening in Beauchamp Place I introduced him to Sara Churchill. Eric and I had met her several times in Rome, once rather drunk when she was escorted by a dancer from the Catherine Dunham dance group. She appeared now as if she'd shrunk and become a little old lady, sitting hunched next to the owner of the gallery. 'This elegant young man has the impertinence to say that he *knew* me [long pause] when I was in Rome,' she said. The 'knew' was underlined in an obvious biblical sense. Then she burst out laughing and grabbed a wine glass next to her on the floor. John immediately began talking to her as if she was an old friend. She invited him to sit down next to her.

'What were you talking about?' I asked John later. I wasn't included in their tête-à-tête.

'Ooh, about love an' sex. I said I liked men and she said she did too.'

'And?' I pressed him to continue.

'Well, that's about it.'

'But you were talking for about an hour.'

'Yeah, I know.'

'Well, what else? That can't have been the extent of your conversation.'

'She said she liked Italy an' I said I liked France an' I told her about Chiarone, Irina an' Cioppolo an' our walk to Puccini's Tower.'

And that was that. At times John would just shut down. Unlike Eric's refusal to communicate, John's was due to a lack of practice at sober conversation. He could be gloriously verbose after several drinks, but without an alcoholic oiling he often seized up. Yet this time, even after a few glasses, that was about all I could squeeze out of him. But it was a pleasure to see him at ease, taking his rightful place in the world.

John and I spent several long summer holidays in Chiarone, in Italy. These were halcyon days of pleasure, of sun and sand and warm sea, more perfect than the summers at Maldon, for there was no friction, suspicion or jealous tantrums. You won't find Chiarone on a general map of Italy, for it consisted only of a railway station and a small modern hotel and bar built by the fratelli Veleni – the poison brothers – rumoured to have funded their hotel by judicious Etruscan tomb-robbing. A single-track railway ran parallel to the coastline, down which twice a day the Paris and Rome express thundered, cutting through mile after mile of farmland, drained and almost free of mosquitoes and malaria. The Maremma, formerly a place of swamps, fevers, brigands and pirate raids, now produced tomatoes, courgettes and aubergines. The canals and drainage ditches sparkled with the iridescent flash of kingfishers, and little tortoises ambled about around apparently indifferent to the change in the landscape.

My old friend Irina had married Spartaco, a Roman painter, and they divided the year between Chiarone and their *trulli*, one of the almost neolithic 'beehive' houses of the Mediterranean, near Brindisi. At Chiarone, Spartaco, who once worked for the railways, had been allotted a railway house, a solid building of eight small rooms divided by a central stone staircase with a lavatory at its summit. It had electricity but no running water or bath; instead we used about thirty to fifty yards of garden hose which, full of water and left in the sun for several hours, produced an almost scalding shower under a large black fig tree.

Long hot Indian summers. John and I arrived in September after the Italian holidays were at an end – not that there were any crowds to avoid in this vast, flat landscape backed by a distant blue fringe of hills and mountains to the east, and fronted by a coastline of high sandy dunes and wide beaches, stretching for miles and miles in either direction to the west.

On our first trip we stopped in Florence. We spent the day walking and walking. John wouldn't stop even for lunch. We ate little ham rolls and roast chicken washed down with red wine as we walked around the Boboli Gardens. He was so excited he wanted to see everything. Undeterred by the traditional afternoon closing, we toured the castle, the Ponte Vecchio, round and round and up and down until the museums opened again.

Next morning, woken at five thirty to a shadowy, still world, we took our breakfast in the kitchen, hot milky coffee and crusty rolls warm and fresh from the baker. The train journey to Chiarone meandered from town to village to town in a seemingly haphazard manner, loading and unloading masses of parcels, crates and bundles at every stop. We alighted at Pisa for a couple of hours, taking a quick tour of the city, the cathedral, the Pisano pulpit and climbing the leaning tower. John delighted in teasing me by standing on the very edge – there was no guard rail – and leaning outwards, laughing, while I, with my back to the tower's wall, gingerly eased myself around.

The train meandered on until late afternoon when we finally arrived in Chiarone.

There was absolutely nothing to do except enjoy ourselves: long, easy days on the beach; picnics of bread, cheese, ham, wine, grapes and figs, simple and delicious, eaten on a mass of towels in an effort, always futile, to keep the sand out.

A couple of miles away was Puccini's Tower, built as a look-out for raiding pirates centuries before and then requisitioned by the composer. We attempted several times to reach the tower, ploughing through gorse and bramble, surprising the inmates of this virtually impenetrable scrub. Two small owls regarded us from the branch of a stunted, windblown tree with the same long stare of disapproval that Marie Gray so often employed. A small fox with something furry in its mouth trotted off, stopping only to give a backward glance at us interlopers. We saw many snakes as well as countless birds, including herons. We never managed to reach the tower, the closest we came was at least a mile away. We knew there was easier access by a one-lane country road, but this didn't appeal to our romantic adventuring.

We feasted on rigatoni, amatriciana and wild boar with polenta. Evenings walks around the battlements of a small village, the ramparts filled with tiny toads. Sounds and smells of village life floating in the warm, dusky air. Shopping for the basics at Orbetello, a walled seaside town with an impressive old gateway: butter, bread, olive oil, coffee, meat, fish and a gallon or so of red wine, white wine and brandy. We would then load the supplies into Spartaco's truck (which they called 'The Bus') packing it carefully away from the small, elegant goat who always travelled with us.

Irina and Spartaco wanted the animal to breed, so we drove around to several farms. The little creature was on heat and rather skittish, which didn't help our efforts. Quite rightly, she refused to have anything to do with the several large and extremely willing billy goats we came across. They were pedigree animals, with snow-white coats but blazing eyes that were, to say the least, devilish. Backed into a corner and bleating in fear, the little she-goat, dwarfed by these rampant suitors, was terrified.

'This is torture. I'm getting her out of there right now,' said John. He walked into the pen and, with a swipe at the nearest billy goat – they were the size of ponies – led the animal out. 'If you can't do better than that,' he said to Irina, 'best not do anything at all.'

The owner of the white behemoths suggested a farm in the hills which might suit us better and gave us directions. It was a long and pleasant drive, and a successful ending to the day's search.

This farmer bred tiny Tibetan goats and our 'lady' took an immediate liking to their advances. The only problem was that they were very short: imagine a Pekinese attempting a German Shepherd. The farmer knew exactly what to do. He led her into a small wooden pen which fitted her exactly and prevented her from moving. Then, giving her a mixture of grain and hay to chew on, pulled a low ramp up behind her. A little Tibetan goat walked up it and did his duty. We left her there for several days to make certain it 'took'.

We made several perfect trips to Vulci. On approaching the site of the Etruscan town, there was nothing but empty, shorn wheat fields stretching away to the mountains. Then we spotted a small dark hump in the far distance which, as we got closer, resolved itself into the remains of a castle with a low, squat tower. The utter silence of the countryside surrounded us as we got out of the 'bus'. Suddenly a bird gave voice, a clear, sharp trilling reveille; and, like a wake-up call, a distant tractor started, then a soft buzzing from a bees' nest in the Etruscan humped bridge and, as a background, the sound of water from the bottom of a ravine nearby.

The first time we visited, there were only five of us, Irina, Spartaco, John and me and the guardian. There was not much to see inside. The *castello* was gutted but, from the top of the stumpy tower, the view was remarkable. Looking down at the bridge and across the ravine we could see where the shadow of an ancient road disappeared under the fields and around and beyond its fading, low rolling mounds, definitely the work of men. Was this all that remained of the Etruscan city, or were the mounds underground tombs cut into the tufa three or four thousand years ago?

There had been rain in the mountains the day before, so the stream was full and clear. We picnicked, then John and I paddled and wrestled and fooled about. Irina took pictures of us while Spartaco smoked his pipe and read his newspaper.

Back at Chiarone Irina cooked snails, collected from the large garden, in butter, oil and garlic and, encouraged by our praise, made snail stew. For me, though, it was as revolting as it sounds. The snails, grey and slimy, like elongated pieces of rubbery snot, were completely beyond me. John delighted in my faint heart and even fainter stomach, laughing at the meal of bread, olives and cheese I substituted for what I termed an unholy mess. He ate it all. He wanted to experience it all, even snail stew; and though I hate being teased, I was proud of him.

The next day he had terrible stomach pains. It was the first time I had seen him sick. Vomiting and diarrhoea had kept him awake during the night.

I rushed to Orbetello for medicine, but by the time I had returned, he was sitting under a mulberry tree in the afternoon sun, drinking red wine and smoking, looking perfectly healthy. 'I don't know what all the fuss was about. You always make such a fuss,' he said.

'Only over you,' I replied.

An embarrassed silence.

'Well, I'm all right,' he said at last. 'I'm not going to die, you know.'

I pulled him to me and hugged him, kissing his neck and head.

'Oh, don't go all soppy.'

I was near to tears, tears of relief.

'Okay, okay,' he said, returning my hug, a kiss on my lips and snuggling into my arms. 'But you do make a fuss.'

Splitting purple-black figs, hundreds of them, on wooden trays and boards and leaving them to dry in the sun. Half a dozen fennel seeds, a few tissue-thin peelings of lemon and orange skin, a peeled almond: fold and finish in a lukewarm oven for several hours. A small cottage industry that filled easy, placid days, providing a bounteous harvest for Christmas feasting. Our only excitement was battling an occasional foray of sleepy wasps intent on having a last meal before their winter hibernation. Filling brown paper bags with tiny, bullet-hard sloes from the stunted, thorny bushes that lined the stone walls of the garden. Pricking them with a needle, the juice staining our fingers, and putting them into gallons of rough brandy to leave for a month or so until the liquor was transformed. Sloe brandy. We sipped it throughout the next several months.

Almost every evening we would walk several miles to a small bar at Selva Nera, the Black Wood, across the flat landscape, illuminated by cinema-scope sunsets of extraordinary beauty and variation. We were just two minute dots on a straight single-track road, dwarfed by the emptiness and quiet. Selva Nera was no more than two or three buildings at a crossroads. When *la signora* wasn't in attendance behind the bar, the half a dozen local farmers and workers questioned us with the totally open, frank curiosity of the Italian.

'*Allora, chi è il marito?* – who is the husband?'

'We both are,' I replied.

'But it's difficult to both do it at the same time, no?'

'We take turns.'

'*Ahh, capito.*'

Drinking Ramazotti until the shadows blended into total darkness. Walking back under a houri's veil of stars. Giggling, laughing, arm in arm, exchanging slightly drunken kisses, the vast silence and space provoking bursts of lopsided singing: 'Some day when I'm awfully old, And the world is cold, I will feel a glow just thinking of you, And the way you look tonight.' My song, our song, sung more often as a soft lullaby when, at home in Putney, I held John in my arms as he drifted off to sleep, a big ginger cat lying across us. 'You're so soppy,' he would murmur as he snuggled closer to me, his head heavy on my chest.

Mauro, a local farmer, a clumsy cross between a young Marlon Brando and Raf Vallone, would join us on the beach for sandy grapplings, bringing flagons of wine and homegrown pot.

We found a compliant doctor who, for a small sum, declared John was suffering from flu and viral infections, whatever, and filled in a long form which allowed John's two-week holiday to be stretched to four or five or six weeks' vacation, without pay.

Getting through the British Customs was a cinch. Our gallons of sloe brandy, seed and cuttings were laid under weeks of dirty socks and under-wear specially put aside for this purpose. After opening our cases the inspectors, taking one look, one sniff, closed the lids and waved us through and we were back in London.

John and I took part in all the Rock Against Racism and anti-fascist protests we could attend. There was a big rally at Victoria Park in Hackney, that John and I went to. I wept, I couldn't help it, surrounded by so much love. Queers, dykes, straights, old, young, mums, dads, kids and babies coming together to unite against hate, bigotry and ignorance.

'I wish you wouldn't,' said John.

'I truly wish I wouldn't, too,' I replied.

'Well, every time you start, you start me off as well.'

John had at last managed to stop me from getting into fights. Did I imagine I was some kind of skinny Sir Galahad charging in to right wrongs? Sort of. My interference was quite stupid and a little pathetic. I've never been a street-fighter, never really a fighter at all. When I was a child my brother Peter did try to teach me to box. He was a champion flyweight boxer. After several attempts he gave up, realising I just didn't have what it took. But if I saw somebody being victimised, I'd sail in and quite often get the shit knocked out of me.

One evening, when still in the early stages of our relationship, we'd gone out drinking to an Irish pub in Finchley with a group of friends. John was still in his 'fuck you' period and, after several pints, was acting up. I can't remember what he was doing, but I do know his behaviour was not covert. By closing time, he had incensed not only the people behind the bar, but a group of regulars as well. John left ahead of me with a friend. As I turned the corner to catch up with him, I saw what I thought was John's inert body slumped on the ground as a young tough from the pub put the boot in. I grabbed the attacker and swung him round, pushing him against the wall. It was the last aggressive move I made. Slamming his forehead into my face, he stunned me. Then he grabbed my hair and swung me from side to side, kicking my body and face. Before I totally lost consciousness, as I was being hurled against the wall of the pub, I saw John twenty yards or so down the road. Oh shit, I thought, and then blacked out. Through a loud buzzing inside my head, I could hear John screaming out my name, and I realised he was holding me. The massacre was over and my 'opponent' fled. 'Oh God, oh God, Graham, don't die,' John was wailing. Feeling no pain, I assured him that dying was the last thing I had in mind.

The police arrived. My attacker, according to his friends, of course, had never been in the pub that night. The boy on the ground, whom I had thought was John, and I were taken to an emergency clinic, patched up and quickly released.

One broken nose, two broken teeth, a cracked rib, split lip and two black eyes: I looked incredible. Black, blue, orange and yellow bruises gave my face a kind of harlequin swollen sensuality. It reminded me of Eric's bronze head of a boxer he and I had given Anthony.

I got punched a few times outside the Colherne in west London, and another time on Hampstead Heath, intervening in a queer-bashing, but with no real damage done, and I did at least stop several very one-sided attacks.

All this came to an end one evening on a double-decker bus going into town. The bus stopped at a junction and we saw five or six men jump out of a truck and begin smashing the windows of a car. At first we both thought that a film was being made – it happened so quickly and the action seemed almost choreographed. Only when an Indian man and woman were dragged from the car and I saw blood spurting from the man's head did I leap to my feet and head for the stairs.

John pushed in front of me. 'Don't!' he yelled.

'Get out of my way! They're killing those people!'

'Yeah, and if they kill you, what am I supposed to do?'

We were screaming and shouting at each other as I tried to push past him.

'I'm not letting you go down there,' he said, shoving me backwards into an empty seat.

That brought me to my senses. 'Okay, okay, I'm just going to phone. I promise I won't get involved.'

'You promise? Swear on it.'

'I swear I won't get involved.'

He let me up and I ran from the bus, yelling, 'I've called the police, they're coming,' as I rushed into a phone booth. As I dialled, the attackers got into their truck and drove off; the man and woman got into their car and followed them.

I gave the police the licence number of both vehicles and John and I went on with our evening. But he had taught me that there were ways of dealing with violence other than rushing in and getting punched, and that I should stop and think and not always be such a fool.

We had dinner one night at Manzi's, near Leicester Square, then took a taxi to the Vauxhall, intending to drown an excellent dinner and a bottle of good Chablis with several pints of bitter. The main bar, the saloon, was so completely packed that we had difficulty opening the doors, so we went around to the public bar which, except for one other man, was empty.

As we sat down with our beer, wondering whether we should drink up and go on to Putney, the man came over and started talking to us. He said he had noticed what I was wearing, black leather jacket, jeans and boots, and was attracted by them.

He introduced himself as Pier Pasolini – I had thought as he walked over to us that his face was familiar. We talked about drag and the attraction we all felt for a butch guy in drag, especially a bearded one. John and I had spent a riotous Christmas in Wales with Paul Vaughan-Philips, and participated in an orgy with several rugby players dressed in full drag, make-up, stockings and high heels, part of a team collecting for charity. We discussed boys in the Elizabethan theatre, and how a theatrical touring company must at times have resembled a travelling male brothel. I suggested an all-male film of *The Revenger's Tragedy*, with young boys playing the female roles and plenty of burgeoning codpieces making the play a reflection of the passions and deceits ongoing in the company. And so we digressed to S&M games, leather and the thrill of bondage. He asked us if we knew of a leather or S&M club in London. We didn't, but I phoned a friend, David, who would know, and on his instructions the three of us took a taxi to Stepney.

Several years previously I had discovered David and his top-floor flat near Mile End station. On the roof of the house was a small, windowless hut, the inside walls of which were covered in black plastic. I spent many weekends strapped down, hung up, getting well and truly worked over, and in the evenings joining in an orgy with sometimes twenty or more other men. Inside the darkened hut, hot like a sauna, the air was damp with the odours of male sex, sweat and poppers, and echoed with the hard sounds of slapping and punching wet flesh, groans and sighs which went on until the early hours of the morning.

David was the host, the top, and kept open house. He had since moved to a ground-floor flat, a very small place. And it was here that we found a leather orgy just as it was coming to an end.

The centrepiece was a young man, a true Tom of Finland hunk, with straight blond hair halfway down his back, strapped in a sling, in the final stages of being fisted as three or four other men used and abused the rest of him. While the three of us undressed we watched the top man's arm and hand slide slowly out from between the buttocks of the blond hunk. Did we want a turn in the swing? Occasionally John liked me fisting him but his innate shyness prevented him from ever being the centre of any action, and he had told me he still felt embarrassed about having sex with other men while I watched.

We declined the offer and John and I teamed up with a rather nice man who wanted his bottom spanked. Pasolini, by then, was on his hands and knees, wrists and ankles cuffed and a dog-collar around his neck, the leash held by a man in a black leather cap and boots. He stood in front of the kneeling figure and flicked with a thin whip at Pasolini's naked back.

John, the submissive man and I moved into the next room onto a mattress on the floor. As we played we could hear the sounds of heavy blows and muffled cries, like background music to our far more restrained game, coming from the men in the other room. John wanted to leave. Although the ambience at David's was always warm and friendly, never threatening, John was always a little scared when we were there.

John and I spent a disastrous holiday with the Cole family in Rome. Worried by money losses and a block I was experiencing with my work (although my fabrics and wallpapers at Liberty's and Harrod's were still selling), upset by John's constant sneaking off with Barry for yet another drink, I behaved disgracefully and everyone had to endure my tantrums.

I called Eric to ask if I could bring John and the Coles for a visit to the villa. Eric replied that if I did he would have me thrown off his property; more fuel to my pathetic little displays.

After the holiday was over I treated John very badly. Not taking responsibility for my problems or my behaviour, I blamed him, making him miserable. I even threatened to leave, which was very cruel and heartless of me, and reduced him to hysterical pleas and promises of behaving better. The pleas and promises should have come from me.

I caused a rift in my friendship with Rita that, widened by my guilt and my refusal to admit how badly I had behaved, ended with a break of many years.

I was overworking, trying to keep up with John's partying, and worried about the future. My agent, who sold every design I produced, would return from America loaded with printed samples of my work from the previous season, but never with my name on the border, which depressed me further. A shipment of clothes – silk shirts and kimonos printed with my designs – bound for a distributor in New Jersey had vanished in transit, and in spite of phone calls, letters and tracers they never turned up. A parcel of my fabric designs had disappeared several years earlier but I had made pencil copies and was able to repaint them all. These latest clothes had cost me a great deal of money and I hadn't insured them. I went completely bonkers trying to locate them.

Peggy had decided to move to America and was going on holiday to California first of all to look around. 'For God's sake, take Graham with you, he's driving me crazy,' John told her. So we went to Santa Barbara for a month and then I took a Greyhound bus to visit Moyra in Austin. I had long dreamed of crossing America in a Greyhound bus. It was an incredible journey: a day-long wait in the Los Angeles terminal surrounded by hookers, hustlers, pimps and pushers; travelling across the desert to Phoenix with two young gay Latinos, with wine and sex on the back seat; real cowboys getting on and off with saddles, ten-gallon hats and spurs; and finally the surprising greenness of Texas, and my stay with Moyra.

I returned to London from Austin full of energy. Straight away, I tackled some huge wall panels: rather aggressive birds skulking in art deco swamps, a combination of cranes and storks which I called 'crorks'. I printed a couple of these and the fabric sold moderately well in England and very well in America, particularly in Florida.

A cold, wet, typical English summer stretched miserably into an even colder autumn.

> *In August the sun is hot*
> *Is it shining? No, it's not.*
> *In September fogs and mists*
> *Bring the wheezes to your chest.*

California had seemed so warm and so clean. I had been totally over-whelmed by the lavatories in fast-food restaurants. Unlike their English equivalents, they were clean, spotless and smelled not of stale urine and filthy floor mops but of strawberry and cinnamon deodorisers. This, in fact, reflected my whole Californian experience. The fast-food restaurants themselves were a universe away from England, and everything was touched with a kind of Hollywood glamour. Even downtown Los Angeles, on the brink of collapse and the dread redevelopment, was clean and tidy. Of course, I didn't see Watts or South Central LA. Mine was a typical tourist's view, and I was impressed.

Around the end of September, cold and fed up, my suntan a faint shadow of its former glory, I decided to return to America. Within a few days Peggy and I were back once more at the same '50s motel, drinking coffee and making plans to find an apartment. America. America.

230

Laguna Beach and
San Diego, California

PERHAPS THE BIGGEST MISCONCEPTION I HAD WAS THAT America was just another England, only larger and more affluent. I was so wrong. The people might speak English, and Americans, on the whole, like people anywhere, are kind and helpful. Yet they have an energy, even in laid-back California, which at times is quite formidable.

There is also a wildness in America, the remnants of the frontier spirit, and an obsessiveness that is totally un-English, with a thread of paranoia lurking below the surface of everyday life, just waiting to burst out in explosions of moral and religious indignation. And unlike the England I had left behind, cosy old England, America was a very violent country.

After paying a deposit on an apartment with a huge deck overlooking Cahuenga and the Hollywood Hills, Peggy and I were dissuaded by the manager of the complex from moving in. Our block had been attacked while we were waiting at the beach in Ventura County for the apartment to be repainted. Several men in masks had shot up the place and the manager thought we were too nice and not tough enough to survive in LA. He was probably right.

While Peggy visited friends that afternoon I explored a little of Los Angeles. Standing in awe on the corner of Sunset and La Brea looking up at the Hollywood sign, following the bronzed stars in the pavement, I found myself behind a crowd of onlookers blocking the sidewalk. I crossed the road to see what they were looking at – I thought perhaps a film was being made. Half a dozen police cars were angled around a beat-up, dilapidated motel, and I noticed a number of policemen holding guns and rifles squatting behind them. I looked but I couldn't see any cameras or film equipment. Then, suddenly, the police began firing into the motel and the crowd screamed, running for cover. I left, not waiting to see if it was a film or not.

231

Talking to Peggy that evening, we decided to follow the manager's advice and go down to a place called Laguna. 'It is an artist's colony and I think you'll find life easier down there,' he told us. So next day we drove south along the coast.

Laguna Beach, notorious in the 1960s for hippies and LSD was still, a decade later, an island of forbidden pleasures, of cocaine, booze and boys, despite being in the right-wing, self-righteous wasteland of Orange County.

Larry Kramer says the most beautiful boys in America come from Laguna Beach and I wouldn't have argued with him as Peggy and I sat in the restaurant of the Boom Boom Room having breakfast on our first morning there. Gay nirvana – or so it seemed, sixteen years ago. In fact, the entire West Coast from San Francisco to Laguna appeared to be a Mardi Gras celebration of queer sexuality.

The previous night, excited and unable to sleep, I had walked along the bluffs of Heisler Park and found myself in an open-air orgy. After some fumbling and feeling about, I paired off with Bud, a marine, who told me that America was 'the best Goddamned country in the world'. After some good sex in the bushes, he suggested we have a drink downtown, saying meet me at the Wrinkle Room opposite the Boom Boom, as he didn't want any of his marine buddies seeing him walking through town with a 'queer' (his word). Bud was so open and friendly that I accepted, and he spent the night with me.

Eventually John arrived in America, first for a holiday to look around and to find out whether or not he wanted to move for good, and then, a month later, to stay. Being a homemaker, a moon child, the thought of leaving his first real home, his nest, terrified him. I had flown off to California and left him to pack and oversee the dispersal of our belongings, refusing to acknowledge how traumatic this was for him. It was only later that I found out that each object, each piece of furniture we had bought together held a memory for John, and that getting rid of them – each piece cherished, polished and dusted over the years – seemed to him a farewell to those memories, those times.

Southland memories. Our first Christmas together in America spent in Arie and Craig's apartment overlooking the beach. Sunbathing and cooking vast amounts of English, American and Russian food. Arie's Russian grandmother, deaf and almost blind, speaking only her native tongue. Evenings sitting on the rocks below the house, warm sea mist damply blanketing us, smoking pot and drinking wine. Arie had found us an apartment and we had become fast friends, sharing meals and wandering in and out of each other's houses and lives, much as John and I had done with our friends in Putney.

Part of a letter written to a friend in England. 'Well, John and I have settled into our apartment. Five hundred dollars a month and a bargain here. The place is small but has a big bay-window in the sitting-room that looks out onto a view filled with magnolia, jacaranda, hibiscus, palms and birds-of-paradise plants. Subtropical greenery in a semi-desert. Laguna is very beautiful. The little town is cupped against the sea, hemmed in by huge hills, all ranch land, with a two-lane canyon road twisting out to the east, and Coast Highway running alongside the beach like a freeway.

'When we're not working, and not being naughty (there's so much flesh here, young and available), we take long walks from beach to beach, climbing rocks and wading through incoming tides, examining the rockpools full of anemones, scuttling hermit crabs, some in minuscule shells, so tiny all that is visible is the stirring of the fine sand as they scurry along, and shoals of darting baby fish waiting for high tide and freedom. Occasionally there are seals and, in the spring, whales offshore, lots of pelicans and cormorants who sit with their heads on one side, sizing us up. The sunsets are beyond description – huge and flashy; Cecil B. DeMille couldn't come close. They are due to Mount Saint Helens' eruption. We are brown and healthy and life is quite wonderful.'

John learned to drive. He just got in a car and within two days was driving as though born to it. Another mark up for his self-confidence. He drove aggressively and brilliantly.

One New Year's party at someone's house high in the hills above Laguna, the host had told us not to worry, to 'party, man', as we could sleep over. Then he changed his mind, so John, full of champagne cocktails and pot, drove back down the precipitous zigzag road and along Coast Highway. He drove at thirty-five miles an hour as if he had been sober, very sober. I suggested walking – it would have taken an hour – but John, angry at the broken promise, laughed scornfully and I couldn't let him go alone. I really needn't have worried. The roads were empty and John triumphant. I too learned to drive, with John as my instructor, but at dinner one evening it was decided by Arie and several other friends that in the best interests of myself and the rest of humanity I should give it up. Although John teased me, I could tell that he was more than happy to be in charge and to have a skill I couldn't master.

We started a general do-it-all, cleaning, painting and maintenance business. At first Arie, being a realtor, put a lot of work our way but we soon made our own contacts and worked five or six days a week, up to twelve hours a day. Neither of us had done anything like this before, and the sheer physical activity, although at times exhausting, was exhilarating for us both. We cleaned, painted houses and maintained the grounds of apartments and offices.

We spent much of our time in the open air, and I can't recall ever feeling stronger or more healthy. I had given up 'art', given up fabrics,

233

agreeing in part with Eric that I was hopeless. The thought of sitting indoors hour after hour, day in, day out, designing wallpapers and fabrics that ended up with someone else's signature on them, seemed, in this sun-drenched piece of heaven on earth, totally ridiculous. Besides, I enjoyed being with John, working beside him all day.

We still fought sometimes, great battles that blazed up and died quickly. Despite these brief conflagrations, however, we were happy. We'd have been even happier without them, of course, but they had become a part, unwanted and upsetting, of our being together, and neither of us knew how to break the cycle.

When there was no weekend work to keep us in Laguna, John drove us up to Los Angeles. We had bought a Toyota pickup truck with a white camper's shell. The interior was lined with foam padding and covered with black fake fur. With its darkened windows and four large speakers for our tape deck, it was ideal for cruising and making out. We often slept in it, sometimes with one or two companions, strays we had picked up, and in the morning drove down to Santa Monica to shower and shave in cold water on the beach. We also stayed at the Château Marmont several times. It was (still is) my favourite hotel, real old Hollywood, real style, not lavishly pretentious like the Beverly Wilshire or the Beverly Hills, but old-fashioned and solid.

From late afternoon right into the night, Santa Monica Boulevard was lined, hip to jutting hip, with a smorgasbord of young men and boys, all available, some for a small price, all very willing and with a friendly openness that is quite essentially American. Every race, every size, every taste was catered for: blatant, unrestricted sex.

The baths, too, were quite extraordinary. Unlike Porchester Baths or the Mile End Road in London, these American baths contained swimming-pools, hot tubs, saunas and gyms, pool rooms, small cinemas and rooms with a single bed and a large mirror in which the occupants could have complete privacy, should they wish; sometimes the doors were left open so anyone could view the ongoing coupling, or tripling, or whatever. And men of all ages, naked and erect, or with a small white towel around their hips.

John and I were like little children at some hedonistic, extravagant and sumptuous birthday party, not knowing which delicious dessert to taste first or which parcel to unwrap. There were drugs too: from poppers to coke, uppers and downers, acid and speed. The ubiquitous pot, along with beer, was passed freely around: 'Have a joint, man, have a beer.'

Unlike our sampling of the men, our drug-taking – in comparison to those around us – was circumspect. I hadn't touched acid since several bad trips in Positano, for example. Yet spending the entire weekend in the

234

baths – leaving only to eat dinner and then returning quickly – I felt I needed some kind of stimulant to keep up with John, who appeared tireless.

Drugs were everywhere. The handyman-maintenance man for our complex would arrive to mend a leaky tap and then spend several working days working on it. Part of his equipment, a small round mirror and a single-edge razor blade, were used far more than any tools. Before he began work he'd cut a few lines and every hour or so, through the day, he'd cut a few more. When he was arrested, the police found he had nearly a kilo of coke in his apartment, and a couple of million dollars stashed around Laguna in plastic bags and suitcases. About to retire, he'd attempted one last big deal – a deal organised by undercover police.

At times our apartment resembled a home for indigent waifs, for runaway kids or, in many instances, kids thrown out by their parents. The parents were usually middle class, obsessed with their careers and lifestyle, their children no longer cute kittens and cuddly puppies but desperate adolescents who needed time and patience which the moms and dads wouldn't, couldn't, give. Laguna seemed to be adopting the fascist overtones of Orange County. The local newspaper referred to transients and the rag-tag mob of leftover hippies living in the canyon as 'dirt bags', and kids who couldn't shape up and cut it without help and assistance were thrown away like disposable toys.

The girls and boys who stayed with us were never a problem. No alcohol or drugs were allowed in the apartment, not only for their safety but for ours also. The state's puritanical laws set the drinking age at twenty-one and there were heavy fines or imprisonment for any adult supplying drink to anyone under this age.

Peggy's son Tarquin, now in his late teens, was nearly six foot tall, blond and muscular. He was one of the world's beautiful boys, really too beautiful and too charming. In Laguna he was in his element. Women passing him would stop to touch his hair, pause to smile, to introduce themselves and give him their cards. 'Call me sometime soon,' they'd say, caught in a snare of adoration.

Nicknamed 'Donkey Dick' by a later lover, a woman fifteen years older, Peggy, John and I had no idea he was the local stud, no idea that women were giving him money, feeding him coke and letting him use their Mercedes and BMWs.

Tarquin was 'bridesmaid' at a friend's wedding. The bride, six feet tall with vast creamy white breasts and a deep husky voice, had a year or so before undergone a sex change. The groom, a hairy, muscular marine of Sicilian descent, was substantially shorter. His bride-to-be towered over him as they stood side by side before the officiating priest. The groom was the only one present who didn't know his new wife used to be a man. Tarquin, to his great confusion, caught the bride's garter.

Tarquin had always been special to John and me. It wasn't his beauty or the remarkable charm which he often used to scam his way through life. He had an underlying goodness, a compassion, and a natural generosity that touched us both.

One evening we got a call from Peggy. Tarquin had gone to LA, she said, and had been living with a rich older woman in San Marino. She had thrown him out and he had stolen about seventeen thousand dollars in cash from her, and nearly a third of a kilo of cocaine. During a crazy three-week high of partying in luxury suites in five-star hotels, hookers and stretch limousines, the coke and the money vanished. Tarquin and his buddy Simon, who had helped him steal the money and drugs, were both totally wasted when Peggy found them. Simon ran off while Peggy and Tarquin hid out with John and me.

When Tarquin sobered up, he applied a blatant spot of blackmail to his ex-lover, telephoning her and informing her that there was a plastic bag hidden somewhere in her house with her fingerprints on it, full of cocaine. Turning the screw, he told her that unless the hitmen she had hired to find him were called off, he would phone the police and the FBI, and so the drama fizzled out.

The only thing Tarquin learned from his experience was that living on the edge was stimulating and fun. He has continued a fast, high life in Los Angeles ever since.

Eventually, I started drawing again. It's an inborn itch that, unscratched, builds up to an overwhelming irritation which screams for attention.

The first was a series of strange, bound, well-bandaged men, mostly balanced on one leg, blindfolded and impotent – not too distant relatives of the screaming men which I drew at the RCA. I bundled them together under the generic title 'Succubi'. They were shown at a local gallery and upset people, being a bit strong for Laguna. I then produced many clown drawings, all about three feet high, in dark sepia gouache on thick creamy-white handmade paper. These were far more successfully shown, and they sold well. These strange clowns, with fabulously patterned art deco costumes, resulted in my first book, aptly titled *Fools, Clowns and Jesters*, which I wrote and illustrated under the pseudonym Paul Cline. This netted me a job with a publishing company, Green Tiger Press, in San Diego.

I had adopted my pseudonym on arrival in Laguna. There were several reasons why I wanted to change my name, the main one being anonymity from the press in London. An associate had given my phone number to the art journalist Geraldine Norman, and I reluctantly agreed to be interviewed by her. When we met, however, I pretended to be ignorant of Eric's forgery, though I'm sure she only half believed me. I liked Geraldine and wrote to her once from California but then decided I didn't need the Hebborn–Blunt stuff to complicate or interrupt my new life.

John began calling me Paul straight away; others took longer – Peggy couldn't manage it at all. Arie was furious when she found out, telling me that Graham Smith was an unusual name in California, and that half the orthodontists and podiatrists in LA were called Cline. Grudgingly, she eventually accepted my new identity.

There are a couple of drawings and a couple of paintings in *Fools, Clowns and Jesters* that make me wince. A colleague, Patricia McCambridge, added to my text and helped me organise it. I had a general idea of the book's appearance that materialised into reality under the knowledge skills of the Green Tiger design team. All in all, in spite of the wince, I'm still quite pleased with it.

When the book was published I moved to San Diego, and for the first time in my life I had a job, a full-time job, working for someone else from nine to five, five or six days a week. I was an in-house artist, designer and general layabout.

John followed me down to San Diego. We lived together for a year or so in an early Californian house called Edgemont, a spacious four-bedroom building tucked away in a tree-sheltered garden with falcons nesting in a hole in the roof. Only a mile or so away from downtown and the railway station, we shared it with another man, Jerry, a Green Tiger employee, and the company's library of old and rare children's books.

Green Tiger Press, then a small independent publisher of illustrated books with an employee list of eccentrics, was a home from home to me. During the years I worked there, designing and making displays and eventually illustrating a book in-house, *The Angel Who Forgot*, I made several friends – Judythe Sieck, a calligrapher and designer who was responsible for the elegant look of *Fools*, Joe Cahn and several others, including Sybil Hayes, now Bansal. Sybil, John and I spent many happy days together. Sybil and John were like two naughty children egging each other on to be even naughtier.

After a couple of unsatisfactory jobs, first at Green Tiger then for a fine art gallery, John landed a position with an Orange County firm of realtors. He was put in charge of all their properties in San Diego County, listing, photographing and overseeing their maintenance. The job included a luxury apartment in a large complex with swimming-pool, jacuzzi, tennis courts, sauna, the lot – the California dream.

We bought a new truck, a Nissan Hard Body. 'Yeah, I've got a hard body now,' he'd grin.

His work meant he had to drive all over the county, from the coast, up over the mountains to the desert. It was perfect for him. I had never seen him look so confident, so self-assured.

> *Piece from a discarded journal:*
> *San Diego 1986–87. John lying in my arms. I enjoy these times after passion when we literally melt into each other. Then I usually drift off to sleep and John gets up and does something. He is very organised, but on rare occasions we fall asleep together and wake together, nuzzling, and affectionate. Then a cup of tea, very English, and a shower. We are becoming American – English men rarely if ever shower after sex, and in fact showers are not common there. But we shower often, sometimes twice a day. We pull funny faces and dance about in front of the wall-to-ceiling, wall-to-wall mirrors in the master bedroom and the rest of the evening is sheer joy. The master bedroom has a large balcony, not quite big enough to be called a deck. Sitting there watching the lights of Mission Valley and the fireworks of Sea World, we hold hands. When a large blue heron pays a visit to the eucalyptus across the driveway, our clasp tightens, fingers locked together, and we smile at each other. These days are long and peaceful. John is not drinking and I feel the joy that has been missing from our lives filling them again.*

I had virtually given up alcohol; my liver just didn't approve. But John still attacked the bottle, going out two or three nights a week on a tour of the gay bars. His energy was a constant source of amazement to me, as was his total lack of hangovers. I often felt inadequate in comparison, and was at times quite cross when, after a night out, he'd be bouncy and just too bright the next morning when I'd want peace, quiet, mugs of tea and several Tylenol to help me through thunderous headaches.

'You can't hold your drink! You wanna be a man like me!' he'd laugh.

'Oh, go away and tidy up something,' I'd mutter in reply.

Then he'd come over to where I sat huddled and awful, put his arms around me, and kiss the top of my head. 'All be better soon,' he'd say, and brew me yet another cup of tea.

When he went out on his night's adventures alone, I always said a prayer for him. 'Please God let him be safe,' it ran, and I'd lie awake worrying. One night the prayer went unsaid, and as John drove slowly up Broadway, the main street through Downtown San Diego, a policeman dealing with a collapsed drunk stepped back into the street and into the path of John's oncoming truck.

He was dragged from the vehicle, smacked about by the police, breathalysed and put in jail for the night where he was beaten up by a couple of bigots. He tried calling me at Edgemont to come down and get him released but I didn't hear the phone.

He was making the tea the next morning when I came downstairs. He was subdued, sorry for himself. Strangely, I didn't feel guilty. There was no reason I should, of course, but feeling guilty about, well, everything, has always been a constant with me. I knew this was a watershed, for from that night on John never drove when he'd been drinking and he cut back his alcohol intake by nearly a hundred per cent. After that, when we went out for dinner or to a bar we used taxis, and we started entertaining at Edgemont more.

The large, gloomy house was ideal for dinners and parties. Even in summer we lit a fire in the brick fireplace and with the windows and doors open, our parties would spread out into the candlelit garden.

When John moved into his glamorous new apartment I spent the weekends with him and quite often a few nights during the week. We stopped entertaining at Edgemont – his place was far more attractive.

On Fridays after work I'd stop and buy a large bunch of flowers, then take him out for dinner. These were good times. We both enjoyed our work and just being together. We both realised that living apart helped us, gave us a breathing space, even though I spent many nights during the week with him. And John and I got married. A simple ceremony with a few friends. We were both slightly self-conscious and shy. Years before, we had exchanged rings, and this was for us a ceremony of factual and social binding, a public avowal of love. My third marriage, and one I would not have missed. In some intangible way it brought us even closer.

There was a new-age bookshop near John's apartment, one of those places filled with self-help, self-improvement books and tapes, crystals and an air of smug, bogus spirituality. Even now I have a strong aversion to going into a such shops, although I concede that they are great sources for teaching and learning. Perhaps when they open a few places in the ghettoes and barrios and start helping people there rather than just the affluent middle class they mainly cater to, my attitude towards them will become more tolerant.

John loved the bookshop; he kept dragging me along with him on his frequent visits. He had already given me Shirley McLaine's book, *Out on a Limb*, and although I found much in it that made me curl my lip, the honesty and enthusiasm with which she related her story was strangely moving.

One weekend while John was browsing and I was fretting to get out and go to the beach, he noticed a poster advertising a psychic evening and became really enthusiastic about attending. Would I go with him?

'No way,' I replied and walked towards the door, a not very subtle hint.

Then I stopped and considered. John seemed so keen – why should I spoil his fun?

'Okay,' I said, 'I'll go with you, Sunshine.'

The psychic was a plump, ordinary-looking man in his thirties, conventional in dress and behaviour. I had expected something different, something exotic and tacky – a turban, a glass ball, perhaps. I wasn't prepared for such ordinariness.

That evening my scepticism took a shaking, however. The psychic told us many very personal things that we hadn't discussed with anyone else. Good guesswork, sharp intuition? Maybe. Yet he constantly called John a 'naughty boy', a phrase I used only in private. There were many other coincidental things that, strung together, showed the man was either a superb con artist or else, as he claimed, he was channelling information from somewhere out there, through spirit guides.

John asked him if we had known each other before, in past lives. The man burst out laughing: 'Oh many, many times. How else could you stand each other unless you'd played this game over and over again? You both don't just love each other, you're completely and passionately involved.'

And on that, he couldn't have been more right.

For some time I had noticed that there was something wrong with John. He appeared thinner, his colour was just not right, he ate less and he grew quickly tired. 'Oh, stop fussing. You always make such a bloody fuss,' he said whenever I tried to talk to him about it. He would get really angry with me. So I watched from a distance, not daring to say anything.

Pains developed somewhere in his diaphragm that caught and twisted his insides, leaving him gasping and shaking, his lips white, his face drawn. 'I just need something to eat, a snack. You told me I got funny when I didn't eat.'

'Yes, I did, but we're going to the doctor's,' I insisted. 'This is not going to continue.'

Grumbling and scared, he underwent a long examination by the local gay doctor. Exhaustion was the diagnosis; rest and vitamins the prescription.

The pains continued; we were both scared now. I insisted he have an X-ray. We made an appointment and then sat waiting for two hours.

'That's it, I'm going, I'm not hanging about any fucking longer,' said

John eventually.

'Oh, yes you are,' I replied.

Both of us were rigid with tension.

The X-rays showed that John possessed only one kidney – but nothing else abnormal. All those years of drinking with no hangovers and only one kidney working overtime!

'Did you have it cut out?' the doctor asked him.

'Are you a fucking moron or what? Can you see any scars? Jesus Christ!' shouted John.

And so it went on, John angry and scared, me with a terrible sense of foreboding. We saw a couple of other doctors. One of them suggested a shrink, another that it might be withdrawal symptoms from years of alcohol bingeing.

We went back to our gay doctor and had a series of tests. John had AIDS. It was something neither of us had considered. We'd heard vague rumours in Laguna, in the very early 1980s, about men, gay men, dying in New York of some strange new virus. It didn't mean anything much – it certainly couldn't affect us here, several thousand miles away. Even as the years went by, as the Reagan administration lied and cheated their way through his presidency and the vague rumours became facts, we still felt safe from the plague, cocooned and tucked away in San Diego.

The doctor's voice was quiet. This must, by now, have been routine, the handing out of yet another death sentence. I could see John shrinking, his strength crumbling away as the doctor told us. No tears – they weren't allowed – just a numbing, a deadening of feeling. If he was going to be brave, how could I let him down? If he wasn't going to weep then neither would I.

One afternoon John collapsed in terrible pain.

'I'm okay,' he said, face bleached and drawn. 'Don't fuss, I'll be fine.'

Back to the hospital. More tests. John looked so tiny, a lonely little boy in the hospital bed.

'I've got no one to talk to. I wish Murphy was here.' Murphy was a horny English cocker spaniel we were taking care of. I went out and came back with a big, soft toy cocker.

John held him tight. 'Thanks, love. You're a sweetheart.'

He looked so vulnerable. I wouldn't allow myself to cry in front of him, but as I walked back to the elevator they came unbidden and unwanted, streaming down my face.

Yet more tests, more inconclusive results. John was in isolation and the nursing staff all wore latex gloves. 'It makes me feel so dirty,' he said.

The pains continued, worsening.

'They want to cut me open.'

241

'Why? What did they say?' I asked.

'They just want to have a look.'

I phoned the doctor from the hospital and returned to John. 'The doctors think it's some kind of growth.' Neither of us said the word cancer, neither of us dared.

'Just don't make a fuss, okay?' said John.

The tears shed in the hospital elevator were a one-off. I wouldn't indulge myself again. To John, tears were a sign of weakness. In remand homes and foster homes, tears exposed his vulnerability and he had learned to hide them. So would I. No more tears. I had become numb when my mother died; I could do it now for John. No big deal. But inside I was going crazy.

I waited while they operated on him and sat in a basement room with him as he regained consciousness.

'Oh, God, please don't die, John, please don't die,' I howled silently to myself.

As he came to, a sweet, motherly attendant held his hand and made him cough.

He looked at me from under drugged, heavy eyelids. 'See, I told you,' he managed. 'I'm okay.'

And I didn't cry. I knew that if I let go now I wouldn't be able to stop. The cancer the surgeon had cut out was malignant. It had grown through his intestinal wall and attached itself to his pancreas. He would need radiation therapy but that was in the future. We did have a future; for now, there was rest and healing.

No one came round to visit. Word had gotten out about John's AIDS. We were alone, but just how alone I wasn't to find out until later. There was an *I Love Lucy* marathon on television and John laughed. I wrote Lucille Ball a thank-you letter, so happy was I to see John laugh again.

'Oh shit, that hurt,' he said as he attempted to control his laughter. He had been cut open from his sternum to well past his navel and the scar was horrendous. But he started to grow strong again.

Through January and February we took almost daily trips out to the beach to Del Mar, La Jolla, Ocean Beach and Coronado, and walked. John put on weight and began smiling again. Life was great, there was hope.

Then the radiation therapy began. He resisted the idea at first but his surgeon and I persuaded him. The growth had been pretty virulent and the doctor was anxious. In cases like John's there were always little pieces left after surgery and they had to be burnt out. All the weight John had put on dropped off. The treatment was centred around his stomach and, apart from the pain and discomfort he felt, his appetite disappeared. I ordered cases of canned liquid food, a meal in a can, all the proteins, vitamins and so on that a body needs, and he doggedly sipped his way through them.

As the weeks went by he grew thinner and became discouraged. We both listened to hours of new-age tapes and meditated together. The process of spiritual body healing didn't seem to be working for John, yet as he grew physically weaker his inner strength developed. Skeletal, he lay in bed, too weak to move, his lovely hazel eyes shining out from a drawn, fleshless face. 'I'm okay, love. Don't fuss, I'm okay, truly,' he said, trying to reassure me.

The surgeon assured us that the effects of the radiation were only temporary and we clung to this. It would pass, he said, and John would start eating again.

Most of the day he'd lie in bed without the energy to do more than go to the bathroom, shower and return to bed. Small lesions appeared on his legs. Back to the doctor. Karposi syndrome. More drugs.

Then, for a short period, he did get stronger. Took short walks to a nearby park and sat sunning himself in the garden. He even drove us to the beach several times.

I had heard about a place called Commonweal, north of San Francisco, a centre for spiritual growth and rejuvenation. Only the terminally ill were accepted. The selection process was stiff as there were few places available. John wrote to them, saying he wanted help finding his song and singing it before he died. He was accepted.

'Do you think you're strong enough to go, sweetheart? Would you like me to fly up with you?' I asked.

'No, I'll be fine. You've got a lot of work to do.'

We agreed I shouldn't call him; this was to be his time. He didn't need me fussing. I met him at the airport on his return. Thin and tired, he radiated joy. We hugged each other, laughing and crying and kissing, a public display of affection that was rare for John.

His two weeks had been glorious, he told me. There were wild flowers, pine forests, spring sunshine and rain, and people he'd come to know and love – compassionate people, caring and wholly sensible. He'd spent comfortable, relaxed hours walking, meditating and coming together with them.

On one of his last days there, they had each been given a project to work on. John chose a sand tray. He said he didn't know what he was doing until he finished – it just flowed from him – but when it was complete, he understood. He had mapped out his life's journey and in the centre he'd set a clear, bright blue stone, representing himself, standing in front of Buddha. At peace, he'd come back to me to die. I phoned Peggy later that night, and she told me that was what John wanted and needed to do now.

It wasn't long before John started finding it difficult to swallow and had to give up on the canned liquid. In a panic, I phoned the doctor and San

Diego hospice. Whoever founded and organised the modern hospice movement deserves a Nobel prize. They provided a raised hospital bed and showed me how to bathe John and give him alcohol rubs to prevent bed sores; the lesions on his legs appeared dormant, thank God. They also brought a stand and, with tubes up his nose going into his stomach, I was able to feed him from a bag.

I had myself tested for AIDS and was clear. I couldn't believe it so I took another test. It too was negative.

One day I kissed John on the lips. 'Don't.' he said, 'you might get it.'

'I really don't care,' I said, and I meant it. 'If I have to go without kissing you, just to stay healthy, then fuck it. Kissing you is something I truly don't want to live without.'

The tube feeding didn't last long. 'I don't want them,' he said. 'Take them out.' His eyes looked at me calmly from a hollowed-out face.

'But you can't swallow. How are you going to eat?'

'Just take them out, please.' He was too weak to do it for himself.

'Please, darling, for me, no.'

'Take them out. I can't bear them any longer.'

A couple of days later he said, 'I want to go now. Help me.'

I didn't argue. 'I'm coming with you.'

'No, don't, you've got things to do. I'll be all right,' his constant assurance. And it was then that I broke down. I hadn't cried in front of him. I had tried to be efficient and strong and not to let my darling see any emotion other than love, but this was too much. 'I can't bear it,' I sobbed, 'I can't bear the thought of losing you, that you might get tired of waiting for me and move on.' And much, much more. All my fears of losing love surfaced in one hysterical outburst.

John looked shocked. I'd been so calm, so practical, trying to be there whenever he needed me. The pain I saw on his face was like a slap to mine.

'We're going together,' I said. 'You're my joy, my life, it's no big deal.'

It didn't work out. There were over a hundred codeine and morphine pills in the house, which I thought would be enough. They weren't. I crushed them into a powder and mixed them with warm milk and, holding John, helped him to sip his cupful. Then I drank mine and lay next to him holding his hand, waiting.

I had phoned Moyra beforehand to let her know what we were doing. I felt she had the right to know from me and not second-hand from a stranger. I assured her that I wasn't mad, that everything was fine, that I just couldn't bear the thought of life without John. Moyra was in Washington DC. She phoned Joe Cahn after I spoke to her and forced him to come and see us. Poor Joe sat while I vomited into a plastic bucket. John was in a coma. Then Joe left. I told him it was okay.

During the night two policemen came round after another call from Moyra. I told them everything was fine and they left.

In the morning a woman from the hospice arrived and John and I, both groggy, were carted off to hospital. They wanted to pump John's stomach. This was the last thing he needed, and I refused to let them. John, now awake, backed me up. Then we were separated. He was taken upstairs. Succumbing to what drugs were left in my system I was wheelchaired down to the loony bin in the basement where I slept through the night.

The next morning I was handed a couple of pills, which I pretended to swallow, and directed to the table where I was supposed to do craftwork – good, calming therapy for a suicidal lunatic. I was still faintly woozy, but when the headman started on his rounds, I affected total clarity and was released. As I walked through the steel doors there was Moyra, who had flown in to be with us, walking towards me.

John was in an upstairs room, needle in both arms connected to plastic bags and tubes going up his nose, this time for oxygen. I went over to his bed and kissed him. 'I love you, Sunshine.'

I sat while a young doctor told us John had pneumonia and must stay in hospital to get the round-the-clock treatment he needed. I had promised John – in fact, I had sworn an oath – that I wouldn't let him die in hospital. I looked at him and he mouthed the word 'home'. I asked him if I could have the day and the night to clean up and organise things with Moyra. 'No, darling, I'm not abandoning you,' I told him. 'I'll be here first thing tomorrow morning,' and I was.

Sybil wrote us long letters from China where she was teaching and dear John Taylor phoned from Australia. He knew how prohibitive health costs were in America and offered us his savings if it would help.

People came now. People we'd invited to our dinners, our parties, yet who, for the last few months, hadn't been there for us. Hadn't offered to cook a meal, or shop, or do the laundry, or just sit with John while I took a walk, now paraded past my sweetheart. Peggy came down and stayed, then she and Moyra left.

A last phone call from the friends he made at Commonweal. He couldn't speak to them, just listened as I held the receiver to his ear.

Then he tried to speak to me. It was urgent. I knew from his expression. I tried translating to him, trying to decipher his soft, painful croaking. Did he need changing? No. Some water? No. Just a barely discernible shake of the head. He kept trying to tell me. Then, 'You want me to take out the oxygen tubes?' A definite nod of assent. Yes.

I didn't cry. Where I got the strength I don't know. I gently eased the tubes out and held him, looking into his lovely face, and he died, his eyes fixed on mine. 1 June 1987, 6 p.m.

And Now

THERE WAS NO FUNERAL; JOHN AND I HAD AGREED YEARS before that neither of us wanted to stand around being brave whilst the other was buried or burnt. We both consigned ourselves to the University of California, San Diego School of Medicine. I watched, frozen in shock, as John's body, wrapped in a plastic sheet, was wheeled out to a funeral van and driven away.

Peggy arrived later that evening and more or less tucked me under her arm and drove me to San Clemente, to the house she shared with her lover, William. I stayed with them on and off for seven months, spending three or four days a week at their house.

I spent that time working, illustrating a children's book and several series of greetings cards, but as an automaton. And when I finished, shuffling around, so I was told, like an old man, a local doctor told me, 'You're dying of a broken heart.' A strange thing for a doctor to say. I went to her as my appetite had vanished and the constant stream of tears running down my face was more than a public embarrassment. 'Still,' she continued, 'that's your choice, your life.' It was and is.

Peggy, studying a new-age massage technique in Laguna Beach, put her knowledge to work on me. While I was in San Clemente, she spent several hours a day realigning my body, mind and spirit. Her patience and caring were monumental, and the therapy certainly kept me sane. It also opened me to an awareness of life and spirituality that, dormant for fifty years, now blossomed.

At first I had tried to rationalise these new experiences; now I just accept them. The day after John died I lay on Peggy's table as she manipulated my spine. I had a vision – I suppose that is what you would call it – a small, glowing, golden ball appeared. My eyes were shut but it remained there, floating above me as I opened them in surprise. Then it sank into my chest. The sensation I felt was what love is: impermeable, never changing and in each and every one of us.

As the globe disappeared into my body Peggy spoke, although the sessions were silent as a rule. 'Oh,' she said, 'you're covered in a bright gold aura.'

Well, I wasn't then and I still am not a great 'aura' fan. I don't see them floating around and I'm suspicious of those who do. But this time as I wept I also laughed. Peggy's words seemed so right. I *did* feel surrounded by the most deliciously warm, protective cocoon. I also felt I really was going crazy as I would weep and laugh as the same time. But I came to realise that while I was grieving I was also celebrating the fact that I had loved so much and so well, and that I was able to feel this joy in loving John as well as so much pain in his leaving.

I fell into rebirthing – certainly I didn't plan it. Rick, a man I hardly knew, called to tell me he'd managed to wangle me a freebie, a weekend of male genital-heart massage – no sex, more an exploration of a tantric coming-together, a by-product of AIDS and the Californian passion to explore new ways of healing and of dealing with life. There would be around twenty men up in the mountains at a secluded private house, with a swimming-pool hidden by oak trees. All I had to do was to telephone one of the participants to arrange transportation. I didn't bother; it was the last thing I wanted to do. Rick called again on the Friday before the event. He had gone to a great deal of trouble, he explained, to get me a place and he thought the least I could have done was to call him and let him know what my plans were. I immediately felt guilty and arranged transport for myself, and off I went.

The setting was ideal, wild oak-covered hills near the Mexican border. Most of the men were in their mid-twenties and we were all naked, the rule for the next two days. The premise was to have half the men lying on their backs on tables, their eyes closed. The others were to go around and, with one hand, massage their heart chakra and the other their genitals, taking care, whilst vigorously kneading various penises and scrotums, not to bring them to orgasm. They could approach it, however, but not climax.

I think I was the only one that weekend not erect. In other circumstances I would have been enjoying myself but as it was I concentrated on giving each man the best I could offer before moving on. When it came to my turn to be massaged I felt nothing and wondered what the hell I was doing there. But I had noticed, as I moved from table to table, that with several of the men there was an almost electric charge coming from them when I made contact with their bodies. The reaction of one man in particular truly surprised me. When I touched him I felt a strong current shoot through my hands, up my arms and into my chest. As I started to massage him, his body spasmed not in ejaculation but in joy which flowed up into me. I couldn't help laughing in sheer happiness.

He opened his eyes, then closed them: 'I thought it was you,' he said.

His name was Valn Dayne. At the end of the weekend I asked him what he and his friends did or had that made them so different from the rest of the group.

'We're rebirthers,' he replied. 'Why don't you come to our next gathering?' He handed me a pamphlet advertising the meeting with directions on how to get there.

I did just about everything I could not to attend. I caught a bus going in the opposite direction and, when I discovered my mistake, nearly took a taxi home. When I eventually got the right bus, I got off about a mile from my destination. It was a Sunday morning with a Santa Anna, a desert wind, blowing. I was fed up and hot carrying a pillow and a blanket, grumbling my way along the deserted sidewalk, and when I arrived at the community hall Valn had rented, all I wanted was a cup of tea and a smoke. But I had got there in spite of myself.

The day's session began with a touchy-feely greeting where we went around and hugged everybody, telling them we loved them. I'm not opposed to indiscriminate hugging, but I felt it was a bit much telling total strangers first thing in the morning that I loved them, that I cared in any way other than a general, rather fuzzy, benign hail-and-well-met wish for their welfare. I just don't deal well with large groups of people.

Fifteen minutes or so of shuffling around and muttering about a universal love and brother/sisterhood was followed by a three-hour lecture from Valn. Obviously, though I can't recall anything that was said, it interested me enough to stay. Then there was a break, and for me and a few others, including Valn, a chance for a much-needed cigarette. After the break we danced for half an hour or so. I like dancing so this wasn't too bad.

Then came the general rebirthing. We lay in a circle, our heads pointing to the middle, and Valn guided us into breathing through our mouths, one deep breath followed by a shorter, relaxed exhale – not hyperventilating, but filling the body with oxygen. It was, so Valn told us, a way of connecting body, mind and spirit. I found it soothing and relaxing. Breathing like this set up a rhythm of its own: I didn't need to control it or see if I was doing it properly, it just flowed. Then Valn quickened the beat, the same deep intake and a shorter exhale but faster, and I left my body. I was totally unprepared, still being snotty in my English way, making nasty, sarcastic asides to myself about the smelly carpet on which we were lying, about the gullibility of my companions and myself in paying money for this charade, how I could be at the beach . . . Then suddenly I was shooting up out of the building. Higher and higher I went, into a complete and utter velvety blackness. I didn't lose consciousness. I was aware of my surroundings, but at the same time I was not there. I was floating, floating and surrounded by the most brilliant lights. 'Welcome,' they said. Actually, it was more like, 'Hi, there,' and 'What took you so long? We've been waiting for you?' I have to admit that it was the most beautiful and transcendent experience of my life. The lights passed around and through me, enlarging and amplifying the sensations I had experienced my first time on Peggy's table.

For over half an hour after rebirthing ended I lay on my blanket, my body spasming in sheer joyous ecstasy, coming down from a life-altering experience. My first reaction when eventually I could get up and walk was that I wouldn't be doing this again. Too dangerous, I thought, and it could become addictive.

House-sitting in Laguna, walking along the sand feeling sorry for myself on a grey, drizzly morning, the surf crashing down, ripping the sand away and rolling the pebbles noisily over each other. I spotted a young man seated on a rock softly playing 'Just the Way You Look Tonight' on a saxophone. I walked closer, crying as I usually was in those days. Then I turned and looked up at the sky: 'I'm doing my best,' I said.

'No, you're fucking not!'

It was like a punch in my solar plexus, knocking me back against the sandy cliffs. Where the voice came from I have no idea. It wasn't in my head – no inner voice speaking to me. It definitely came from outside. It sounded a great deal like John to me.

And so I went back to rebirthing for three years, including an intensive eight-month course, rebirthing at least three times a week. I chose as my guide a Native American Indian named Carol. Over the three years, beginning with a return to the womb and re-experiencing my birth trauma and entire life, the self-pity in which I wallowed slipped away, to be taken over by a new-found strength and courage. I learned to celebrate myself and, if not accept John's death, at least come to terms with it. Not to stumble through life confused, wondering why this or that was happening to me, but to see it all as a chance to learn and grow. I'm still not convinced that there is a great plan for us all, but this new game certainly beats the old one and I feel open now to new ideas and experiences without judging them.

Waking up one morning I found John sitting at the end of my bed. This, I've since learned, is a common occurrence, finding one's recently dead partner appearing. Wishful thinking, perhaps? I thought I was dreaming and kept saying to myself, 'Please don't wake up.' So many good dreams end too soon by premature awakening.

'Are you okay, sweetheart?' I asked. That question was, still is, uppermost in my mind.

John gave me his shy little grin and familiar hunching of his shoulders. 'I'm fine and you're still fussing.'

I wanted to ask him so many questions, and all I came up with seems so ridiculous, even now. 'Would you like a cup of tea, love?'

John grinned his cocky, happy grin. 'Yeah, a small one, thanks.' This had been a long-standing joke between us. I would ask if he wanted a cup of tea. John would reply, 'A small one.' I'd make the usual large mug and he'd say, 'I wanted a small one,' and I'd tell him to drink only half.

He leaned forward, 'Everything's all right. Don't worry, I'm fine, you're fine. No more fuss, okay?'

I reached out to hug him and he was gone. I sat wanting him back so much it hurt.

With tremendous support and encouragement from my brother Peter, in 1990 I set up my own company, Medlicott Press, using my mother's old Cornish maiden name, publishing children's books which were distributed by Simon & Schuster. Three years later I began drawing my own personal drawings that had caused so much friction between Eric and me. Most of the Laguna Beach drawings, with the rest of my work, I destroyed soon after John's death. I don't regret their going; it was an Augean cleansing that left me free to go forward. But several of the Laguna drawings escaped: I left them with Moyra in Washington DC. She returned them to me, after exacting a promise from me for their safe-keeping. These three or four were the basis for my first exhibition in San Diego at the Rita Dean gallery. I knew there was little chance of selling them – they're too confrontational, not the sort of stuff anyone might hang in their sitting-room. But having avoided them for so long, it was time.

The theme of the show was violence. It is endemic and not only in America, and although gay- and lesbian-bashing is on the rise – the shaky heterosexual male ego is much reinforced after a successful attack on us – it is violence against women that was my first concern. Four million women in America are attacked by men every year. These are the recorded figures; how many more attacks go unrecorded? I used S&M as a metaphor. Its strictly consensual, organised and contained sexual playing, with rules and standards of behaviour, is diametrically opposed to the random violence often encouraged and condoned by the fundamentalist Christian Reich.

The exhibition was well received and gave me the energy to work on a second, but here I came to big block. The drawings were still concerned with violence, but I decided to add the companion figure of death. The first picture contained several figures: a bound and kneeling man performing cunnilingus on a seated woman; a standing male figure in bra and panties holding down a woman, hooded and bound; just behind them is a standing woman, her head bowed in pain, and walking out of the picture is a laughing and happy baby. Over them all hovered a grimacing, skeletal death and here I came to a halt. I worked the whole thing out roughly in pencil but couldn't continue. It was a monumental block. Drawing death frightened me. It was easy when I was young – youth is impervious to death; then it was a romantic and artistic symbol. But now, having experienced John's dying, I froze. The impasse continued for several days until one evening, my will fortified by a few glasses of red wine, I sat down and resolved the whole issue, working in a frenzy through to the early hours of the morning. I broke through the barrier. As yet I cannot call death a friend, as does Stevie Smith, but I now feel a great deal more comfortable with its presence. I certainly don't welcome it, but it no longer frightens me.

I draw on paper covered with a wash of blue watercolour: drawings on blue paper, the *Screaming Queen* drawings, for I am angry and anger, when its source is defined and responsibility for it is taken, is a good energy to use as a starter fuel.

Fear and ignorance form the basis and cause for all bigotry. When in my teens and first introduced to my sisters, the queens, they were unlike anything I experienced in the narrow world of Barkingside or Forest Gate, and the newness and strangeness caused automatic rejection and perhaps, too, a little feeling of superiority on my part. Now, much later in life, feeling secure in myself, I celebrate our queens. I don't have their brilliant, razor-sharp wit or their ability to fence verbally, parry and score with deadly precision. It's an art form I've never managed to acquire. I pay homage to the sublime courage of the queens, their theatrical bravura, their blatant stance against conformity and repression. Never forget Stonewall: the queens fought back, making it a flashpoint in our struggle for tolerance and respect.

I'm angry not only over the hate and spite spewed out at lesbians and gays but at intolerance everywhere. I'm angry at the rise of the neo-Nazis, the Aryan brotherhood, the right-wing religious fundamentalists and the so-called Christian Coalition here in America. All these sick and perverted people who are so busy attempting to deny us lesbian and gays, black, Asian, Hispanic, women, men and free-thinkers, our right to exist freely in society.

So I feel empowered when I draw myself as a screaming queen, in drag, my genitals exposed so that no one is under the illusion that this is a drawing of a woman, though I know many women who feel like screaming, too.

But I'm not so angry that I am blinded to how beautiful this world is and how truly marvellous is the thread of humanity that binds us all no matter how, at times, we strive to break it.

I've always been gay. Being gay isn't a choice. My mother's naming me Betty was an intuitive knowing, an understanding of who she was carrying in her womb. If anything, the rape and sexual abuse enacted on me as a child would have been, if our sexuality were a matter of choice, paramount in a decision to be heterosexual. No heterosexual boy would have, after four years, come to enjoy the sex as I did, though the threats and guilt trips were another matter entirely. No one, child or adult, deserves to live with such fear – to live with fear at all.

But in spite of those years of abuse I haven't grown up to be a child abuser as so many do, and for that I am extremely grateful. Perhaps my father's influence had a lot to do with this. As a teenager I underestimated him. He gave me unconditional love, or as near to it as we can get, much the same as I have from my brother Peter. They are alike in so many ways. My dad might not have understood my sexuality (although he served in the navy for many years, so it wouldn't have been unknown to him), but I am quite certain he would not have withdrawn his love as I feared he would all those years ago. And his love for me kept me sane as a child and gave me a rock-solid basis on which to grow as a caring, fairly reasonable, if somewhat eccentric, man.

Eric is dead. I woke up one morning to a message from Rita on my machine, asking me to call her. I knew immediately he was dead – murdered, according to the Roman coroner, by a blow to the back of his head, a blow which could not have been caused by a drunken fall, which was the first explanation several newspapers put forward. The theory now is that his latest book about the techniques and secrets of forgery upset a few people in high places. The *Daily Telegraph*, among many other newspapers, reports that the Milanese art mafia might have been involved. At the moment the case remains open.

Eric was buried in his beloved Anticoli with a large crowd of friends and journalists and his two sisters in attendance. Many years before when I suggested both of us should make wills he was horrified. 'I'd feel I was signing my death warrant,' Eric said. He never made a will and his family – whom he disliked, so he told me – will probably inherit. His new love, as happens so often in gay and lesbian relationships, will be left out in the cold. If our relationships were accepted by law, which by any decent human standard they must be, especially so in these years of the plague, then Eric's young man, Danny, would have been able to leave Canada, live with Eric and have legal status as his partner. At Eric's funeral Danny, in tears, was ignored by Eric's family and seemingly everyone else. His rightful position as chief mourner was subverted by the two sisters and Edgar. Edgar left Eric several years before, suing him for palimony. 'A hundred thousand pounds,' Eric had informed me in the baby voice he assumed when feeling sorry for himself.

After twenty-odd years of silence he phoned one day in 1991 to tell me he was writing his autobiography and ask if I would clear it.

'Not without seeing a copy first,' I replied.

'Oh, well,' he said in his baby voice, 'it's very heavy and expensive to send.'

Over the next few years we had several similar conversations – funny, sad and quite surreal.

'A hundred thousand, that's more than I got,' a sudden sharp, fleeting thought about unfairness that left me when I realised how little I expected and wanted from him.

'Oh, no, money was worth a great deal more in those days,' Eric countered, adding, 'I'm giving Edgar the villa.' (Not San Filipo but one he had built quite near our old home.) This last conversation occurred when, on his American book-signing tour, he called me from Los Angeles. Edgar got the villa but not the deeds of ownership, which I thought was a very Hebbornish move.

Over the past years I've become quite the hermit. I go for days without speaking to anyone, so great is the wealth of pleasure and peace I find in being by myself. May Sarton's *Journal of Solitude* parallels my own empty days – not, for the uninitiated, lazy days, but time spent ingesting and digesting, watching the sunlight move through the trees that surround my small, scruffy apartment (Sinkhole, San Diego, I call it with affection), and gently planning new ventures. Oh, I do go out occasionally, up to Los Angeles, to party and see friends, Alison and Theo, Bruce, Rick and Tarquin. And in San Diego there's Ruth and just across the canyon, Max, a ten-year-old aspiring writer. I even played a small role, a character part, in a Bruce LaBruce–Rick Castro film, *Hustler White* – an affected English actor of 'a certain age', as Marie Gray would say, who gets strung up in an S&M playroom as Exhibit A. I did say a character part.

Acting and helping on the set was truly enjoyable, and Tony Ward, the romantic lead (and as far as I know, completely heterosexual), is one of the sweetest and most genuine men around. I became totally enamoured of him and another model/porn star, Ryan Block. I ended up, though, with a John Kennedy lookalike, who had an American eagle tattooed across his chest and a tractor across his stomach, but that is quite another story which

253

is developing into my next book, a kind of '90s *Prater Violet*, the Isherwood account of film-making in the early 1930s. Christopher Isherwood's book is a novel whereas mine will be a factual recounting of the film, the hustlers involved and various other characters in the sexual underground. I'm also making notes for a book on Mexico even though my Spanish is very limited, and another one revisiting the many places in Italy where I was with John and Eric – a kind of sentimental journey of then and now.

I need my 'empty days' to plan and think about them. I'm happy, still enjoying new experiences, new passions. I fell in love with a gorgeous young man, a 'naughty boy', like John. Well, he did come up first, kiss me on the lips and say he loved me. Anyway, I'm safe. The young man, Jay, is so much in love with his woman, Marcie, that there's no chance of involvement, just the sheer pleasure of loving. I gave them our wedding rings, John's and mine, at first with the condition that they use them when they married. Realising that putting a condition on a gift isn't really what giving is about, I apologised. 'Do what you want with them.' Passing on those two gold bands made me feel I had really done something right for once.

I miss my John, John Kenneth Elliker. I don't believe in the 'if only' or 'I wish' syndrome, but I do miss his tender smile and his cheeky grin. I miss his goodnight notes to me left on my pillow for morning. I miss holding his hand. I miss the good strong feel of him. He was the only lover who called out my name in orgasm, called out loudly, holding me, loving me.

And if I'm crying now, it's okay, truly okay. I'm all right for I'm also smiling. I've had the best and I'm still having it good, as we say out here, real good. And I have high hopes not only for myself but for us all. I can't as yet see the human race living in a state of beatific love, yet I truly feel we will evolve to a state of tolerance and respect for each other. The alternative is beneath consideration.

The sun is shining as I write, three hundred days of sunshine here in San Diego. It's the beginning of May and I already have what is for me a tan – at least my white bits show up against the rest of my body. The garden, overgrown and neglected except for regular watering, is a riotous mess of plumbago, palm, jasmine, fig, bougainvillea, honeysuckle, peach, bottlebrush and apricot. Sometimes tomatoes and basil are attempted. There is a small pool and a large birdbath. With the visiting mocking and humming birds, jays, doves, orioles, possums and skunks, it's a little inner-city wilderness. From one window of my apartment I can see Tijuana across the border in Mexico, then the Pacific Ocean. A large palm hides most of the mountains from my view, but leaves enough to see them blue, fronting a scarlet sunrise. Time to call Marcie and Jay, I haven't seen them for so long, to drive up to our favourite hot springs for the day to celebrate friendship and being together, their youth and my old bones. To celebrate living and loving, life itself, and why not?

San Diego, Los Angeles,
Little Yeldham, Tijuana